D0076957

BLACK ATHLETES
IN THE UNITED STATES

BLACK ATHLETES
IN THE UNITED STATES

A Bibliography of Books, Articles, Autobiographies,
and Biographies on Black Professional Athletes
in the United States, 1800-1981

Compiled by
Lenwood G. Davis
and Belinda S. Daniels

Foreword by
James E. Newton

GP
GREENWOOD PRESS
Westport, Connecticut • London, England

Library of Congress Cataloging in Publication Data

Davis, Lenwood G.
  Black athletes in the United States.

  Includes index.
  1. Afro-American athletes—Bibliography. I. Daniels,
Belinda S. II. Title.
Z7515.U5D38   [GV697.A1]   016.796'08996073   81-6334
ISBN 0-313-22976-7 (lib. bdg.)   AACR2

Library of Congress Catalog Card Number: 81-6334
ISBN: 0-313-22976-7

First published in 1981

Greenwood Press
A division of Congressional Information Service, Inc.
88 Post Road West, Westport, Connecticut 06881

Printed in the United States of America

10 9 8 7 6 5 4 3 2 1

To
Freddie and Armentine Pickett
and
Mack and Trussie Daniels

Contents

Foreword

Americans throughout history have shown a love for competition. This competitive nature is, perhaps, best manifested by all national groups in the sports arena. The role played by Black Americans constitutes several important chapters in the history of sports, including the arousal of heightened pride and the documentation of despair. Black athletes, as formidable foes in major sports, have become quite commonplace, adding luster to life on and off the field. Margaret Just Butcher, in her classic *The Negro in American Culture* (1973), justified excluding Black athletes from her study by commenting that, "The Negro's contributions to the American world of sports are too numerous and too comprehensive," and, "there have been extensive writings on the subject." Thus, Butcher's observations are in order if one only perceives the Black athlete primarily as a contributor to so-called "popular culture." This, of course, is a historic error, since American culture in its broadest sense includes sports as a major ingredient in the aesthetic and cultural development of the nation.

This current volume by Lenwood G. Davis and Belinda S. Daniels portrays almost two centuries of Black athletes and their feats on and off the field. Needless to say, the activities of Black athletes in American society have done much to open doors that were previously closed. Denied recognition on a national level in years past because of the "color line," Black athletes surged forth with renewed energy, not only to overcome prejudice and discrimination, but ultimately to become catalysts in paving the way for new intergroup relations and promoting racial harmony. Generally the first to integrate and gain acceptance in previously all White social and academic functions, the Black athlete has become a genuine folk hero for all Americans—Black and White. In come cases these folk heroes became bigger than life itself. To many, Jack Johnson and Joe Louis are legendary heroes who transcend both race and color. Such perceptions by the populace have allowed Black athletes to walk somewhat freely among all people in recent times, while harboring less of the race tensions and anxieties than the total group. It is no wonder, therefore that many Black athletes are viewed as hero images by Black youths, who not only idolize them, but hope that their own skills will be converted into fame and fortune.

A keen observer and chronicler of the Black athlete, A. S. "Doc" Young, writing in his *Negro Firsts in Sports* (1963), noted that, ". . . the most marvelous gift of sports is its faculty for making heroes of underdogs, of lifting the downtrodden up to solid ground. The most valuable capital anyone brings to sports are strength and stamina, speed and agility, desire and instinct for the game, and a sense of rhythm or timing."

Many observers would conclude that the role of the Black athlete has been multifaceted and that his or her presence on American soil has been one of national consequence. They are heroes, ambassadors, achievers, image-makers, superstars, youth workers, promoters of the race cause and of American idealization, and they remain the greatest source of pride for the Black community. A. S. "Doc" Young makes a most definitive statement on the subject:

> The Negro's background of toil and sweat and battling with life for mere survival fits him aptly for the game, whatever it be, in which he has a chance to compete on even terms. Although he was low man on the economic totem pole, this has enabled the Negro player to step in as the virtual savior of baseball, the guardian of the nation's reputation in more than one Olympiad, the proof to the world that democracy can work . . . the door-breaker to progress for his fellow Americans of color in varied walks of life not directly connected in any way with sports.

While the versatile feats of Black athletes are well known, actual compilations and reference sources for scholarly documentation outside the familiar sports pages of national daily newspapers and magazines are scant if one is searching for credible reference information on Black athletes. Few bibliographic surveys have focused on the Black athlete, therefore, it is most fortunate that this volume is devoted to an area of high interest to a broad audience. While the volume focuses on six major sports—baseball, basketball, boxing, football, golf, and tennis—its seems quite clear that many of the minor sports have not yet felt the fullest impact of Black athletic presence due to a variety of social and cultural factors.

In the materials presented here are many reference works, books, articles, and dissertations that will bring into broader focus an array of sources that provides us with a nucleus of materials for researching the role of Black athletes in major sports.

Lenwood G. Davis, a noted Black historian and Renaissance bibliographer, has coupled his talents with the capable collaboration of Belinda S. Daniels, Reference Librarian, to produce a much-needed work and bibliographical tool. It is hoped that this work will provide the impetus for future works to include Black athletic development in minor sports. There is no doubt that this volume will gain added importance as the role of the Black athlete in American society is more thoroughly analyzed and researched.

James E. Newton
Director, Black American Studies
University of Delaware
Newark, Delaware

Introduction

Athletes in America are looked upon with admiration and respect by both young and old alike. Many people see them not only as heroes but superheroes. Others see them as all-Americans who reached the epitome of physical fitness. Most of the history of the athlete in the United States is related to the premise that one can attain financial security through excellence in sports. Black athletes, perhaps more than any other group in America, have used sports as an avenue to economic independence and social mobility.

Black youngsters strive to be like the leading Black sports figures in society. They are told that if they excel in sports they may become another Muhammed Ali, O. J. Simpson, Tony Dorsett, Jim Brown, Billy Sims, Earl Campbell, Jessie Owens, Hank Aaron, Julius Erving, Arthur Ashe, Reggie Jackson, or Kareem Abdul-Jabbar.

Black athletes have used their names and prestige to enter into other professions. Many such as Jim Brown, Sugar Ray Leonard, O. J. Simpson, Fred Williamson, Ken Norton, Muhammad Ali, Earl Campbell, Rosey Grier, Gale Sayers, and Woody Strode are making movies, television programs and commercials, or giving other endorsements.

Both Black and White youngsters identify with Black athletes. Many White kids see Black athletes not as Black men, but as men who have the ability to perform incredible feats in the sports arena.

Black athletes, moreover, have larger followings than Black entertainers because historically sports have been relatively free of drug users. Far more frequently entertainers have been associated with the use of drugs. In sports the human body must be in excellent condition to perform to the expectations of spectators. Athletes must train long and hard hours, weeks, months, and sometimes years to reach excellence in their chosen fields.

This bibliography is the first major work to deal with Black professional

athletes in the United States. Since it would be impossible to include all
Black professional athletes in this country, we specifically limited this work
to selected professional Black athletes. Our primary purpose is to list
references about (1) the first Black athletes in the major sports—baseball,
basketball, boxing, football, golf, and tennis; (2) the major and best-known
athletes in these sports; (3) those Black athletes that have significant
autobiographical and biographical materials; and (4) those Black athletes
that are currently in the news.

While some Black athletes may be well known, a limited amount of
autobiographical or biographical materials are available on them. Hence, a
limited amount of references were devoted to them.

It is not clear who the first Black professional athlete was in the
United States. The first Black known to have become a professional and
to earn a living as a boxer was Bill Richmond. He was born in New York on
Staten Island on August 5, 1763. In 1777, at age fourteen, he was taken to
England by Lord Percy. Richmond started his early life as a cabinetmaker,
and if it had not been for Lord Camelford he might have continued in that
trade. However, Lord Camelford noticed his physique and introduced him
to boxing. Although Richmond fought many men of different weights, he
was generally considered a heavyweight. He weighed between 168 and
175 pounds and by current standards he would be considered a light
heavyweight.

Richmond started fighting professionally just before 1800 and ended his
boxing career in 1818. His record includes twelve wins and two losses in
major bouts. Richmond is perhaps best known for his match with Tom
Cribb on October 8, 1805. After fighting for more than an hour and a half,
Cribb won the match. Although Richmond officially retired at age fifty-four,
he fought one final match against Jack Carter on November 12, 1818.
Richmond won the bout in three rounds, when he kayoed Carter.
Richmond died in London on December 29, 1829 at age sixty-six.

Another early Black professional athlete, Tom Molineaux (sometimes
spelled Molyneux), was also a boxer. He was born a slave in the
Washington, D.C. area in 1784 and lived on a plantation in Virginia.
Molineaux is alleged to have gained his freedom in a plantation bout.
He subsequently left the state and settled in New York, where he stayed
until about 1809. The pugilist later traveled to London and continued to
box. He immediately won eight fights, and because of his success
earned a match with Tom Cribb, the British champion. The two bare-knuckle
fighters fought for forty rounds, and finally Molineaux could not answer
the bell. He also lost to Cribb in the eleventh round when he fought him
again in 1811. His last bout was in 1815 when he was thirty-one. He
died three years later at age thirty-four in Scotland.

There were a number of professional Black boxers between 1818 and
1908. George Dixon, born in Halifax, Nova Scotia on July 19, 1870, won

both the Featherweight and Bantamweight titles in 1890 and was champion between 1890 and 1899. Dixon published his autobiography in 1893, one of the earliest Black boxers to do so. He was called "Little Chocolate" because he weighed 122 pounds. The pugilist lost his Featherweight title on January 9, 1900 to Terry McGovern, who knocked him out in the eighth round. Nine years later he died in New York at age thirty-nine.

Joe Gan was born in Philadelphia on November 25, 1874. He won the Lightweight championship in 1901 by defeating Frank Ernie in the first round, holding the title until 1908. One of Gan's best known bouts was in 1906 against Battling Nelson. They fought for forty-two rounds and Gans was awarded the match, but two years later lost the title bout to Nelson. He died in Baltimore on August 10, 1910 at age thirty-three.

One of the most colorful of all Black professional boxers was Jack Johnson. He was born on March 31, 1878 in Galveston, Texas. He became the first Black to win the Heavyweight title when he knocked out Tommy Burns in Sydney, Australia in the fourteenth round on December 26, 1908. Johnson fought 102 bouts and lost only 5, retaining the title until 1915. Because he was a Black man, Whites had great hopes that a White boxer would defeat him, and subsequently the phrase "The Great White Hope" was coined. Whites saw "The Great White Hope" in Jim Jeffries. He had retired as undefeated Heavyweight champion in 1904, but in 1910 at age thirty-five, Jeffries challenged Johnson. Black champion Johnson defeated Jeffries in the fifteenth round of the fight and "The Great White Hope" was no more. Jack Johnson was defeated by Jesse Willard in the twenty-sixth round of a title match at Havana, Cuba on April 5, 1915 when he was thirty-seven years old. He also fought exhibitions when he was in his fifties and early sixties. He died in an automobile accident in Raleigh, North Carolina on June 10, 1946 at the age of sixty-eight.

After Johnson lost the Heavyweight title in 1915 it was held by Whites for more than two decades until Joe Louis won it in 1937. Louis was born on May 13, 1914 in Chambers County, Alabama. He fought James J. Braddock for the Heavyweight championship on June 22, 1937 and won the fight in the eighth round. Joe Louis held the title for twelve years, and in 1949 announced his retirement from boxing after successfully defending his title twenty-five times. In 1950 Louis returned to the ring and was defeated by Ezzard Charles, who held the title from 1949 to 1951. Joe Louis continued to fight even after that defeat, but his boxing career ended at age thirty-seven on October 26, 1951 when he was knocked out by Rocky Marciano at Madison Square Garden in New York City. The "Brown Bomber," as he was called, still remains one of the most popular boxers of all time. Joe Louis died on April 12, 1981.

Another popular boxer is Muhammad Ali. He was born Cassius Clay in Louisville, Kentucky on January 18, 1942. After winning the Olympic gold medal in Rome in 1960, he turned professional. He had fought as a light heavyweight in the Olympics, but because he had put on weight he decided to fight in heavyweight matches. He became Heavyweight champion of the world on February 25, 1964 when he defeated Sonny Liston. He defeated Liston again on May 25, 1965 in Lewiston, Maine, knocking him out in the first round. Ali refused induction into the army in 1967 on the grounds that he was a religious leader and therefore exempted from the armed services. A Houston jury, however, did not see him as a legitimate conscientious objector, and sentenced him to five years in a federal prison. In 1971 the United States Supreme Court reversed the ruling of the lower court. In the meantime, the New York Athletic Commission and the World Boxing Commission (WBA) revoked Ali's title, while other boxing officials banned him from the ring. In 1971 Ali lost his title to Joe Frazier.

A year later Ali defended his title against two-time Heavyweight champion Floyd Patterson in Madison Square Garden in New York City. Ali won the bout in the seventh round. Joe Frazier, however, was recognized by the WBA as the Heavyweight champion between 1970 and 1973. Frazier was kayoed by George Foreman in January, 1973. Foreman was defeated by Ali in October, 1974 in Kinshara, Zaire (Africa), and Ali regained the title, holding it until he was defeated by Leon Spinks in 1974. The World Boxing Council (WBC) recognized Ken Norton as champion after he defeated Ali. Norton subsequently lost his title to Larry Holmes, who was then recognized by the WBC as the Heavyweight champion. Holmes defeated Ali in 1980 in a title bout, but the WBA recognized Mike Weaver as the Heavyweight champion. As of August 1980 the Middleweight division is the only division with a universally recognized title holder.

Although we focused primarily on Heavyweight champions, there were outstanding Black champions in other weight divisions. These are listed in Appendix D. One of these Black champions was Henry Armstrong. Born Henry Jackson on December 12, 1912 in Columbus, Mississippi, Armstrong was the only boxer of any race to hold three boxing titles simultaneously. In a ten month period between October 29, 1937 and August 17, 1938, he held the Featherweight, Welterweight, and Lightweight championships. Ironically, he lost the titles almost as quickly as he had gained them. In late 1938 he abandoned his Featherweight title. He lost the Lightweight title on August 22, 1939 to Lou Ambers, the former Lightweight champion. One year later, on October 4, 1940, he lost the Welterweight title to Fritzie Zivic, who only held it for one year.

Although Armstrong lost his titles he continued to box. In 1942 he started his comeback efforts and won thirteen out of fourteen matches, but at age thirty he was past his prime. He continued to box until he was thirty-three. He enrolled in theology school in 1949, and in 1951 was ordained a Baptist minister. It can be said that of all the champions, both Black and White, none were more versatile than Henry Armstrong.

Currently the most popular fighter is Sugar Ray Leonard. In 1980 he defeated Roberto Duran of Panama for the Welterweight title. This title was recognized by the WBC. Thomas Hearns, however, was recognized by the WBA as the Welterweight champion.

Of the major professional team sports, football was the first to use Black players. Although the Los Angeles Rams signed Kenny Washington and Woody Strode in 1946, and the Cleveland Browns signed Bill Willis on August 6, 1946 and Marion Motley three days later, there were Black professional football players before that era. In the old professional league, Fritz Pollard was player and coach of the Akron (Ohio) Indians between 1919 and 1922. His team won the 1920 "worlds" professional football championship. Paul Robeson also joined the Indians and played with them in 1921. Various Black players such as Mayo Williams, Dick Hudson, Fred Slater, and Joe Lillard played with professional teams from 1921 through 1933. Ironically, there was no Black professional football players between 1933 and 1946.

Kenny Washington, Woody Strode, Bill Willis, and Marion Motley were the first Black professional players of the modern era. Washington played between 1946 and 1948, then went on to make films. Strode played a few years and also became an actor and made numerous films. He was also active as a professional wrestler. Willis also played only a few years. Motley was fullback for the Browns from 1946 to 1953, and after retiring from football, served as a part-time scout for the Washington Redskins, was a mailman, and worked in public relations. At one time it was reported that at the height of his football career he earned $12,000 a year, a considerable sum for that time.

There were a number of popular football players in the 1950s and 1960s. One such player was Jim Brown. He signed a contract in 1957 to play for the Cleveland Browns of the National Football League. In 1962 he was voted Most Valuable Player in the Pro Bowl Game. In 1963, he established a league record of 1,863 yards in 291 attempts. Brown is one of the few players ever to rush for more than 1,000 yards in one season. Three times he gained more than 200 yards in a single game. He holds the NFL lifetime rushing record, and in nine years with the Browns rushed for 12,512 yards and averaged 5.2 yards per carry in over 700 attempts, also scoring 126 touchdowns. He retired from football in 1966 and became a Hollywood film star.

Gale Sayers was another popular football star of the 1960s. He signed with the Chicago Bears of the National Football League in 1965. Sayers led the NFL in rushing in 1966 and 1969, and gained 100 or more yards rushing in twenty games. He holds nine NFL records and sixteen Bears team records. Sayers was Most Valuable Player in the Pro

Bowl three times, and All-League running back five times. Although he played in only sixty-eight games, he holds the NFL records for six touchdowns in one game and twenty-six in one season. Sayers retired from football in 1972 at age twenty-nine after missing the last two seasons because of a knee injury and repeated surgery.

Perhaps the most popular football player in modern times is Orenthal James Simpson, better known as O. J. Simpson. He signed with the Buffalo Bills in 1969 and played for them until 1978, when he was traded to the San Francisco 49ers. He played for that team only one year before retiring from professional football. During his career he broke many records: most yards gained in a single season with 1,250; most yards gained rushing in a single game with 250; named to the American Football League All-Star team in 1970; named to the Pro Bowl team, 1972, 1973, 1974, 1975, and 1976; and named National Football League Player of the Decade. Since his retirement from professional football, Simpson has devoted full time to making motion pictures, television appearances and commercials, and sports commentating for ABC television.

Other outstanding Black professional football players in the 1980s include Tony Dorsett of the Dallas Cowboys, Earl Campbell of the Houston Oilers, Walter Payton of the Chicago Bears, and Billy Sims of the Detroit Lions.

Baseball was the next professional team sport to drop its color line. Many people know that Jackie Robinson was the first Black to play major league baseball, and the story does not need to be repeated here. The only point to be made is that Blacks in the major leagues have come a long way since Branch Rickey decided to bring Jackie Robinson into the Brooklyn Dodgers organization on October 23, 1945. It was two years later, however, before Robinson played his first major league game on April 15, 1947 against the Boston Braves. When Robinson retired in 1956, he left an impressive record behind: first Black to sign to play in modern organized baseball; National League leader in stolen bases (twenty-nine), 1947, and (thirty-seven), 1949; Rookie of the Year (1947); Most Valuable Player, National League, (1949); as well as other accomplishments too numerous to mention.

Other outstanding Black players during the early years of modern baseball include Don Newcombe and Roy Campanella of the Brooklyn Dodgers, and Larry Doby of the Cleveland Indians, who in 1947 was the first Black to play in the American League. Newcombe was the 1949 Rookie of the Year. Campanella was named National League Most Valuable Player for 1951, 1953, and 1955. Doby led the American League in hitting percentage (.541) in 1952, held the record for most consecutive errorless games by an American League outfielder (164) in 1954, and hit three home runs in a game on August 2, 1950.

There were also a number of other Black baseball players that started playing in the major leagues in the late 1940s and early 1950s: Sam Jethro of the Boston Braves; Luke Easter and Harry Simpson of the Cleveland Indians; Joe Black and Dan Bankhead of the Brooklyn Dodgers; and Monte Irvin and Hank Thompson of the New York Giants.

One of the most popular players in the National League was Willie Mays, the "Say-Hey Kid," as he was called. He was born in 1931 in Fairfield, Alabama. In 1951 he signed with the New York Giants and was named National League Rookie of the Year for that year. In 1954 he was named Most Valuable Player in the National League, and again in 1965. Mays led the National League in home runs four times: 1955 (51), 1962 (49), 1964 (47), and 1965 (52). Willie Mays was one of the few players in professional baseball to hit over 650 home runs and to amass over 3,000 hits during his career. He retired from baseball in 1973.

Another popular player was Henry Aaron, the man who broke Babe Ruth's home run record. "Hammering Hank," as he was called, was born February 5, 1934 in Mobile, Alabama. He signed with the Milwaukee Braves in 1954. In 1957 he was voted Most Valuable Player in the National League, leading the league with 118 runs, 44 home runs, and 132 runs batted in. Aaron was a member of the National League All-Star team for 17 consecutive years between 1955 and 1972, more than any other player. He holds the league's record (18) for most consecutive seasons with 20 or more home runs. Aaron also holds the record for the most seasons (15) with 300 or more total bases. He averaged 150 games over a nineteen year period, and holds the record for most times at bat with 12,364. He also holds the record for total bases in a career with 6,856. In addition, Hammering Hank holds the record for the most runs scored in a season, with 755. This record is the high point of his career. He is now an executive with the Atlanta Braves baseball organization.

Other outstanding players in the past two decades include Elston Howard of the New York Yankees, who won the American League Most Valuable Player award in 1962, becoming the first Black American League winner, and Ernie Banks of the Chicago Cubs, who won the National League Most Valuable Player award for both 1958 and 1959, the first National League player to receive this award for two consecutive years. Banks hit more home runs (248) in the 1955 and 1960 seasons than any other major league player. Maury Wills played for the Brooklyn Dodgers between 1959 and 1967, stole 104 bases in 1962, and was named the National League Most Valuable Player that year. He broke Ty Cobb's record of 96 stolen bases in a season, leading the league in that category for six straight years. Richie Allen was named Rookie of the Year in 1964 after knocking in 29 home runs, batting in 91 runs, and ending with a batting average of .318 for the Philadelphia Phillies. Bob Gibson started pitching for the St. Louis Cardinals in 1961. He pitched in the 1967 World Series and won three games, and also was designated Most Outstanding Player of that Series. A year later he was voted National League Most Valuable

Player, leading his team to first place in the National League. He also won the Cy Young Award the same year as the league's top hurling ace. Frank Robinson joined the Cincinnati Redlegs in 1956, and led them to the pennant in 1961. He hit .323, drove in 136 runs, hit 39 home runs, and was voted National League Most Valuable Player. He helped the Baltimore Orioles win the pennants in 1966, 1969, 1970, and 1971, and the World Series in 1966 and 1970. In 1972 Robinson was voted American League Most Valuable Player, thus becoming the first and only player in baseball history to have won that award in both the National and American Leagues. In 1974 Robinson became the first Black to manage a major league baseball team. Willie McCovey of the San Francisco Giants won the 1969 National League Most Valuable Player award with 45 home runs and a batting average of .320. In 1971 Vida Blue won both the American League Most Valuable Player and Cy Young awards.

Basketball was the last major professional team sport to sign Black players to its ranks. It was not until April 1950 that Charles (Chuck) Cooper was signed by Haskell Cohen to play for the Boston Celtics. He became the first Black professional player in the National Basketball Association (NBA). During the 1950-1951 season, Cooper played in 66 games and scored 615 points for an average of 9.3 per game. The New York Knickerbockers also signed Nat "Sweetwater" Clifton to play for them in the summer of 1950, and he also played during the 1950-1951 season. The Knicks obtained Clifton from the Harlem Globetrotters.

Other Black players in the 1950s include Ray Felix who played for the Baltimore Bullets in 1954 before he was traded to the New York Knicks. He played in New York for six years, averaging 12 points per game, and was a leading rebounder. Felix was named 1954 Rookie of the Year. Maurice Stokes signed with the Rochester Royals for the 1955–1956 season and was voted Rookie of the Year in the NBA. He averaged 16.8 points per game and was the league's second leading rebounder. Stokes's career was cut short in 1958 when he was stricken with encephalitis. He died of a heart attack in 1970. John T. Moore signed for the 1955-1956 season with the Philadelphia Warriors, who became the world's champions for that season. Bill Russell signed with the Boston Celtics for the 1956-1957 season, and was the league's fourth top rebounder, averaging 19.6 per game. In the 1957-1958 season Russell won the Most Valuable Player award in a vote of the players. That season he led the NBA in rebounding, averaging 22.7 per game. He was voted Most Valuable Player five times. In 1966 Russell became the first Black coach in the NBA when he became player-coach of the Boston Celtics. Willie Naulls joined the New York Knicks in 1957, and was the first Black in the NBA to be named captain of his team. Naulls played between 1957 and 1966, averaging 15.8 points in 716 games. The Boston Celtics signed Sam Jones in 1957, and K. C. Jones, who is no relation to Sam Jones, in 1958. Hall Greer joined the Syracuse Nationals of the NBA in 1958. During the 1958-1959 season Elgin Baylor joined the Minneapolis Lakers, averaging 24.9 points per game and making the All-NBA team. Only two other players, Alex Groza and Bob Pettit, had previously made that team in their first season. In the 1958 All-Star game, Baylor was named co-winner with Bob Pettit of the Most Valuable Player award. In the 1959-1960 season Wilt Chamberlain joined the NBA after touring a year with the Harlem Globetrotters. He signed with the Philadelphia Warriors, becoming the year's top rebounder with 26.9, and top scorer with 37.6 points per game. He was Rookie and Most Valuable Player of the Year, and headed the All-NBA team. He was named the league's Most Valuable Player four times. Chamberlain set many other records: scored 4,029 points in 80 games for an average of 50.4 points per game; scored 100 points on 36 field goals and 28 foul shots in one game; led the league in scoring for seven straight years; led the league in rebounding five times; and set an NBA rebounding record of 55 for a single game. He was the first player to amass 30,000 points.

The 1960s saw a number of Blacks take honors and awards in the National Basketball Association. Oscar Robinson was Rookie of the Year for 1960-1961. Other Black Rookies of the Year for the 1960s included Walt Bellamy, 1961-1962; Willis Reed, 1964-1965; Dave Bing, 1966-1967; Earl Monroe, 1967-1968; and Wes Unseld, 1968-1969.

The 1970s also saw Blacks receiving Rookie of the Year honors: Lew Alcindor (Kareem Abdul-Jabbar), 1969-1970; Sidney Wicks, 1971-1972; Bob McAdoo, 1972-1973; Keith Wilkes, 1974-1975; Alvin Adams, 1975-1976; Adrian Dantley, 1976-1977; Walter Davis, 1977-1978; and Phil Ford, 1978-1979.

Blacks were also named Most Valuable Players for most years between 1957 and 1979; Bill Russell, 1957-1958; Wilt Chamberlain, 1959-1960; Bill Russell, 1960-1961, 1961-1962, and 1962-1963; Oscar Robertson, 1963-1964; Bill Russell, 1964-1965; Wilt Chamberlain, 1965-1966, 1966-1967, and 1967-1968; Wes Unseld, 1968-1969; Willis Reed, 1969-1970; Kareem Abdul-Jabbar, 1970-1971, 1971-1972, and 1973-1974; Bob McAdoo, 1974-1975; Kareem Abdul-Jabbar, 1975-1976 and 1976-1977; and Moses Malone, 1978-1979.

There were also Black Rookies of the Year in professional basketball's American Basketball Association (ABA) in the 1960s and 1970s: Mel Daniels, 1968; Spencer Haywood, 1970; Charles Scott, 1971, Co-Rookie of the Year; Artis Gilmore, 1972; Marvin Barnes, 1975; and David Thompson, 1976.

Between the 1960s and 1970s Blacks dominated the Most Valuable Player award in the ABA: Connie Hawkins, 1968; Mel Daniels, 1969; Spencer Haywood, 1970; Mel Daniels, 1971; Artis Gilmore, 1972; Julius Erving, 1974 and Co-MVP in 1975 with Black player George McGinnis; and Julius Erving, 1976.

It should be noted that prior to the 1976-1977 season the four American Basketball Association teams were absorbed by the National Basketball Association, thereby terminating the ABA. Hence, all the ABA players became NBA players and are among the more exciting players in the NBA.

Golf was one of the last sports in which Blacks became professionals. It is only during modern times that the Professional Golfers Association (PGA) dropped its White-only clause. Blacks found it difficult to find playing sites or to become members of the prestigious golf clubs that had good grounds and facilities. Many of the earlier Black professional golfers got their starts as caddies for White golfers. One such caddy was Charlie Sifford, who started as a caddy on a public golf course in Charlotte, North Carolina. Sifford usually practiced on the course during the off-season. He soon moved to Philadelphia and started teaching golf to Black entertainers such as Billy Eckstine. In 1952, at age twenty-eight, he began playing the professional tour. He did not win his first professional tournament until 1957, when he won the Long Beach (California) Open. Sifford also finished second in the Pomona (California) Open, that year. In 1961 he became the first Black to play in a major PGA tournament in the South in Greensboro, North Carolina. Charlie Sifford won the Greater Hartford Open in 1967, and his earnings for the year were over $57,000. He was the first Black professional golfer in the United States to win a major tournament.

Another outstanding Black golfer is Lee Elder. He was born in Dallas, Texas, moving to Los Angeles and finally to Washington, D.C. in the early 1960s. Because Blacks were not allowed to play on private golf club courses, he practiced mostly on public courses. In 1968 he played in the American Classics in Akron, Ohio and won $12,750, barely defeated by Jack Nicklaus. Elder finished the year with $31,000. In April 1975 Lee Elder qualified for the Masters Tournament in Augusta, Georgia and became the first Black to play in that prestigious tournament.

Peter Brown, another Black golfer, was the third highest money winner among Blacks, following Sifford and Elder. He won $30,000 in the San Diego Open in 1971.

Some other earlier Black professional golfers are Ted Rhodes, Bill Spillers, and Harold Donovant.

There are presently a number of Black professional golfers: Pete Brown, Ray Botts, Chuck Thome, Curtis Sifford, and George Johnson. Although Althea Gibson is best known as a tennis player, she was also a professional golfer. In 1968 she joined the Ladies Professional Golf Association, winning only $2,700 that year. Ethel Funches was more successful. She had played for about a decade when she won the championship at Lanston golf course in Washington, D.C. in 1968.

Professional tennis was also one of the last major sports that Blacks broke into. While many people know that Althea Gibson was the number one female tennis player in the world, the first Black to win the Wimbledon singles in England and the U.S. National singles, and was named Woman Athlete of the Year, she nevertheless did not play tennis professionally. Arthur Ashe is the first Black to play major professional tennis matches. In 1964 he was the first Black to play for the U.S. Davis Cup team. In 1968 he became the first Black male to win the U.S. National singles title. In 1968 he turned professional and signed a contract for $100,000. It was several years, however, before he won a major professional title. In 1975 he became the first Black to win the men's professional singles at Wimbledon. He also won the World Championship of Tennis tournament, with its $50,000 first prize that year. He was out of the tournament competition for most of 1977 due to surgery on his Achilles heel, and for the first time was not among the top ten players in the world. He was out again in 1978 for a neck injury and won only three tournaments. He did manage, however, to be among the top ten professional tennis players in the world. In 1979 Ashe suffered a mild heart attack and entered St. Lukes Hospital in New York, where he underwent quadruple bypass heart surgery. He announced his retirement from professional tennis in 1980 at age thirty-seven.

Although Blacks are involved in other professional sports such as wrestling, billiards, bowling, and hockey, we primarily focused on the six major sports: baseball, basketball, boxing, football, golf, and tennis. The major reason for excluding other sports was lack of significant literature. Since we plan to update this work at a later date, we hope then to include those sports that were omitted from this study.

This work is divided into eight parts. Part One deals with Major Reference Books in Baseball, Basketball, Boxing, Football, Golf, and Tennis. Some of the works include handbooks, encyclopedias, histories, registers, record books, almanacs, and guides. We want the user of this work to know that in many major reference works there are significant data on Black athletes. Part Two relates to General Books. This section discusses such topics as "The Greatest in Sports," "Big Business of Sports," "History of American Sports," "Sports in America," and "The World Almanac and Book of Facts." This section gives the reader a general overview of sports in the United States. Part Three is titled Major Black Reference Books. This section includes general Black reference materials on Black athletes and Blacks in sports in general. Part Four includes General Black Books. Part Five is devoted to books written by Black athletes in the various sports—baseball, basketball, boxing, football, golf, and tennis. Part Six relates to books about Black athletes in the various sports. Special attention was given to those works that were written for juvenile and young adult readers. Part Seven encompasses the largest section in this work and deals with articles: sports in general; individual sports; and articles by and about Black athletes. The latter articles make up the largest single group within this section. The appendixes include: Verticle

Files, Scrapbooks, Newspaper Clippings, Letters, Documents, and Doctoral Dissertations; Baseball Most Valuable Player Winners; NBA Most Valuable Player Winners; Black Boxing Champions; Blacks in the Baseball, Basketball, Boxing, and Football Halls of Fame; and the Black Athletes Hall of Fame. There is also a list of Black Athletes in Films. An extensive index rounds out this study.

While it would be impossible to acknowledge everyone that assisted us in this work, we must thank certain individuals and institutions: Miss Beverly Wilson for typing the complete manuscript; Mrs. Mary Smith of the Winston-Salem State University Library staff for doing computer searches and verifying some of the titles; Janie M. Harris for her assistance in organizing some of the titles and typing parts of the rough draft; and Janice L. Sims, Reference Librarian at the Moorland-Spingarn Research Center at Howard University for assisting us in locating missing books.

We would also like to acknowledge the assistance we received from the following library staffs: Winston-Salem State University, Wake Forest University, University of North Carolina at Greensboro, University of Tennessee at Knoxville, and Howard University's Moorland-Spingarn Research Center.

We take full responsibility for any errors of facts or omission, and welcome any corrections or additions. Any work of this nature can never be complete. We do, however, believe that given the limited availability of bibliographical works on Black professional athletes in the United States, this work is a major contribution in fulfilling a need that has not been met to date.

BLACK ATHLETES
IN THE UNITED STATES

1

Major Reference Books

BASEBALL

1. Alston, Walter and Don Weiskopf. The Complete Baseball Handbook.
   Over 500 Photographs. Boston: Allyn and Bacon, 1972. 567 pp.
   Various references are made to Black players.

2. Biesel, David, et al. Editors. The Baseball Encyclopedia: The
   Complete and Official Record of Major League Baseball. New York:
   Macmillan Publishing Co., 1976. 2142 pp. Various references are made
   to Black players throughout the book.

3. Boyle, Robert H. Sport - Mirror of American Life. Boston:
   Little, Brown and Co., 1963. One Chapter entitled "A Minority
   Group: The Negro Baseball Players," pp. 100-134.

4. Dickey, Glenn. The History of National League Baseball Since 1876.
   New York: Stein and Day, 1979. 308 pp. Various references are
   made to Black players.

5. Dickey, Glenn. The History of American League Baseball Since 1961.
   New York: Stein and Day, 1980. 319 pp. Various references are
   made to Black baseball players.

6. Jennison, Christopher. Wait 'Til Next Year: The Yankees, Dodgers,
   and Giants 1947-1957. New York: W.W. Norton and Co., 1974. 169
   pp. Various references are made to Black players.

7. Karst, Gene and Martin J. Jones, Jr. Who's Who in Professional
   Baseball. New Rochelle, New York: Arlington House, 1973.
   919 pp. Various references are made to Black players throughout
   the book.

8. Neft, David S. et al. Editors. The Sports Encyclopedia: Baseball.
   New York: Grosset and Dunlap, 1974. 478 pp. Various references
   are made to Black players throughout the book.

9. Neft, David S. et al. Editors. The Complete All-Time Pro Baseball Register. New York: Grosset and Dunlap, 1976. 372 pp. Various references are made to Black players.

10. Powers, James Joseph Aloysius. Baseball Personalities, the Most Colorful Figures of All Time. New York: R. Field, 1949. 320 pp. Various references are made to Black baseball players.

11. Shoemaker, Robert. The Best in Baseball. New York: Thomas Y. Crowell, 1974. 274 pp. Various references are made to Black baseball players.

12. Siwoff, Seymour, Editor. The Books of Baseball Records. New York: The Author, 1975. 352 pp. Various references are made to records set by Black baseball players.

13. Smith, Ken. Baseball's Hall of Fame. New York: Grosset and Dunlap, 1980. 230 pp. Black Baseball Hall of Famers are included in this work.

14. Smith, Robert Miller. Baseball. New York: Simon and Schuster, 1947. 362 pp. Various references are made to Black baseball players.

15. Turkin, Hy and S.C. Thompson. The Official Encyclopedia of Baseball. New York: A.S. Barnes, 1974. 737 pp. Various references are made to Blacks throughout this work.

16. Wallop, Douglass. Baseball: An Informal History. New York: W.W. Norton, 1969. 263 pp. Various references are made to Black baseball players.

17. Wayne, Bennett. Heroes of the Home Runs. Champaign, Il.: Garrard Publishing Co., 1973. 168 pp. Various references are made to Black baseball players.

BASKETBALL

18. Cummins, Gloria and Jim Cummins. Basketball by The Pros. New York: Van Nostrand Reinhold, 1976. Various references are made to Black basketball players throughout this work.

19. Goldpaper, Sam. Great Moments in Pro Basketball. New York: Grosset and Dunlap, 1977. 152 pp. Various references are made to Black players.

20. Gottehrer, Barry. Basketball Stars of 1965. New York: Pyramid Books, 1964. 158 pp. Various references are made to Black players.

21. Harris, Merv. On Court With the Superstars of The NBA. New York: Viking Press, 1973. 179 pp. Various references are made to Black superstars.

22. Hollander, Zander, Editor. <u>The Modern Encyclopedia of Basketball</u>. Garden City, New York: Doubleday and Co., 1979. 524 pp.

23. Hollander, Zander, Editor. <u>The Complete Handbook of Pro Basketball</u>. New York: New American Library, 1979.

24. Hollander, Zander, Editor. <u>Basketball's Greatest Games</u>. Englewood Cliffs, NJ: Prentice-Hall, 1971. 242 pp.

25. Mendell, Ronald L. <u>Who's Who in Basketball</u>. New Rochelle, New York: Arlington House, 1973. 248 pp. Various references are made to Blacks throughout the book.

26. Neft, David S. et al. Editors. <u>The Sport Encyclopedia: Pro Basketball</u>. New York: Grosset and Dunlap. 1975. 368 pp. Various references are made to Blacks throughout the book.

27. Paige, David. <u>Pro Basketball: An Almanae of Facts and Records</u>. Mankato, MN: Creative Education, 1977. Written for young adults. Various references are made to Blacks throughout the book.

28. Rosen, Charles. <u>God, Man and Basketball Jones: The Thinking Fan's Guide To Professional Basketball</u>. New York: Holt, Rinehart and Winston, 1979. 160 pp. Various references are made to Black professional basketball players throughout the book.

29. Rydell, Wendell. <u>Basketball</u>. New York: Abelard, 1971. 128 pp. Various references are made to Black basketball players.

BOXING

30. Carpenter, Harry. <u>Masters of Boxing</u>. New York; A.S. Barnes and Co., Inc., 1964. 245 pp. Discusses Sugar Ray Robinson, Jack Johnson, Henry Armstrong, Archie Moore, Joe Louis.

31. Durant, John. <u>The Heavyweight Champions</u>. New York: Hasting House Publisher, 1964. 176 pp. Various Black Heavyweights are discussed in this work. Written for young adults.

32. Durant, John. <u>The Heavyweight Champions</u>. New York: Hasting House, 1976. 244 pp. Sixth Edition Revised and Enlarged. Various Black champions are discussed: Jack Johnson, Joe Louis, Ezzard Charles, Joe Walcott, Floyd Patterson, Charles (Sonny) Liston, Muhammad Ali, Joe Frazier and George Foreman.

33. Fleisher, Nathaniel S. <u>The Heavyweight Championship, An Informal History of Heavyweight Boxing. From 1719 to the Present Day</u>. New York: Putman, 1949. 303 pp. Black champions are included in this work.

34 Golding, Louis. <u>The Bare - Knuckle Breed</u>. New York: Barnes, 1954. 231 pp. Tom Molyneux is included in this work. Molyneux fought Tom Cribb.

35 Heller, Peter. With an Introduction by Muhammad Ali. "In This
    Corner....!" Forty World Champions Tell Their Stories. New York:
    Simon and Schuster, 1973. Joe Louis, Henry Armstrong, Ike Williams,
    Sugar Ray Robinson, Archie Moore, Floyd Patterson, Emile Griffin
    are discussed.

36. Houston, Graham. Superfists: The Story of the World Heavyweight
    Champions. New York: Bounty Books, 1976. 176 pp. Black champions
    are also mentioned.

37. Johnston, Alexander. Ten - and Out! The Complete Story of The Prize
    Ring in America. With a foreword by Jack Dempsey. Revised and
    Enlarged Edition. New York: Washburn, 1936. 371 pp. Black prize
    fighters are also included in this work.

38. Liebling, Abbott Joseph. The Sweet Science. New York: Viking,
    1956. 306 pp. Black boxers such as Joe Louis and Archie Moore
    are included in this work.

39. McCallum, John D. The World Heavyweight Boxing Championship: A
    History. Radnor, PA.: Chilton Book Co., 1974. 393 pp. Jack
    Johnson, Joe Louis, Ezzard Charles, Joe Walcott, Floyd Patterson,
    Charles Sonny Liston, Muhammad Ali, Joe Frazier, George Foreman,
    are included.

40. McCallum, John D. The Encyclopedia of World Boxing Champions Since
    1882. Radnor, PA.: Chilton Book Co., 1975. 337 pp. Various refer-
    ences are made to Black boxers in this book.

FOOTBALL

41. Bennett, Tom, et al. Editors. The NFL's Official Encyclopedic
    History of Professional Football. New York: MacMillan Publishing
    Co., 1970. Various references are made to Black players through-
    out this work.

42. Ecker, Tom and Bill Calloway. Encyclopedia of Football. West
    Nyack, N.Y.: Parker Publishing Co., 1978. 318 pp. Various
    references are made to Blacks throughout this book.

43. Hank, Jack. Heroes of The NFL. New York: Random House, 1965.
    183 pp. Various references are made to Black players.

44. Heuman, William. Famous Pro Football Stars. New York: Dodd, Mead
    and Co., 1967. 153 pp. Various references are made to Black
    Players. Written for young adults.

45. Neft, David S. et al. Editors. The Sports Encyclopedia: Pro
    Football. New York: Grosset and Dunlap, 1974. 496 pp. Various
    references are made to Black players throughout the book.

46. Stainback, Berry. Football Stars of 1965. New York: Pyramid
    Books, 1965. 157 pp. Various references are made to Black
    players.

47. Zanger, Jack. Pro Football. New York: Pocket Books, 1966.
    277 pp. Various references are made to Black football players.

GOLF

48. Evans, Webster. Encyclopedia of Golf. New York: St. Martin's
    Press, 1974. 320 pp. References are made to Black golfers.

49. Stell, Donald and Peter Ryde. The Encyclopedia of Golf. New York:
    Viking Press, 1975. 480 pp. References are made to Black golfers.

50. Wind, Herbert. The Story of American Golf, Its Champions and Its
    Championships. New York: Knopf, 1975. 591 pp. References are
    made to Black golfers.

TENNIS

51. Robertson, Maxwell. The Encyclopedia of Tennis. New York: Viking
    Press, 1974. 392 pp. References are made to Black players.

2

General Books

52. Davis, Mac. *The Greatest in Sport*. New York: World, 1972. 160
    pp. Various references are made to Blacks in sports.

53. Durant, John, and Otto Behman. *Pictorial History of American
    Sports From Colonial Times to the Present*. 2d Revised Edition.
    New York: A.S. Barnes, 1962. 340 pp. Various references are
    also made to Blacks in sports.

54. Durso, Joseph. *The All-American Dollar: The Big Business of
    Sports*. Boston: Houghton Mifflin, 1971. 194 pp. Various re-
    ferences are made to Black players.

55. Hickok, Ralph. *New Encyclopedia of Sports*. New York. McGraw-Hill
    Book Co., 1977, 545 pp. Various references are made to Black
    sportsmen throughout the book.

56. Menke, Frank G. Revisions by Suzanne Treat. *The Encyclopedia of
    Sports*. Garden City, New York: Doubleday, 1977, 1132 pp.
    Various references are made to Blacks in sports.

57. Michener, James A. *Sports in America*. New York: Random House,
    1976. 466 pp. Various references are made to Black players.

58. *The World Almanac & Book of Facts For 1981*. New York; Newspaper
    Enterprise Associations, Inc., 1981. Various references are
    made to Black atheletes in the section entitled "Notable Sports
    Personalities."

59. Treat, Suzanne. *The Encyclopedia of Sports*. Cranbury, N.J.: A.S.
    Barnes & Co., 1975. 1125 pp. 5th Revised Edition. Various refer-
    ences are made to Black sportsmen throughout the book.

3

Major Black
Reference Books

60. Bontemps, Arna. Famous Negro Athletes. New York: Dodd, Mead & Co., 1964. 157 pp. The athletes include: Joe Louis, Sugar Ray Robinson, Jackie Robinson, Leroy Satchel Paige, Willie Mays, Jesse Owens, Wilton ("Wilt") Norman Chamberlain, James (Jim) Nathaniel Brown, Althea Gibson. This work was written for young people.

61. Chalk, Ocania. Pioneers of Black Sport: The Early Days of The Black Professional Athlete in Baseball, Basketball, Boxing and Football. New York: Dodd, Mead & Co., 1975. 305 pp.

62. Chalk, Ocania. Black College Sport. New York: Dodd Mead & Co., 1976. 376 pp. Many references are made to Blacks who became professional atheletes.

63. Editors of Ebony. The Negro Handbook. Chicago, IL: Johnson Publishing Co., 1966. Bobbie Barbee, "Sports, A Door Opener," pp. 339-351.

64. Editors of Ebony. Ebony Pictorial History of Black America. Chicago: Johnson Publishing Co., Inc., 1974. Vol. III Section 7 discusses "Sports", pp. 249-260.

65. Editors of Ebony. The Negro Handbook. Chicago, IL: Johnson Publishing Co., 1974. "Sports," pp. 463-476.

66. Editors of Ebony. The Ebony Success Library: 1,000 Successful Blacks. Vol. 1. Nashville, TN: Southwestern Co. by arrangement with Johnson Publishing Co., 1973. 341 pp. Many Black Athletes such as Hank Aaron, Kareem Abdul-Jabbar, Muhammad Ali, Arthur Ashe, Joe Black, etc., are included in this book.

67. Edwards, Harry. The Revolt of The Black Athlete. New York: Free Press, 1969, 202 pp.

68. Farr, Finis. Black Champion. Greenwich, CT: Fawcett Publications, 1964. 245 pp.

69. Fleischer, Nathaniel S. Black Dynamite : The Story of The Negro in The Prize Ring From 1782 to 1938. New York: C.J. O'Brien, Inc. 1938. 250 pp.

70. Henderson, Edwin B. The Negro in Sports. Washington, D.C.: Associated Publishers, Inc., 1939. 371 pp.

71. Henderson, Edwin B. The Negro in Sports. Washington, D.C.: Associated Publishers, Inc., 1949. Revised Edition.

72. Henderson, Edwin B. and The Editors of Sport Magazine. With an Introduction by Jackie Robinson. The Black Athlete: Emergence and Arrival. New York: Publishers Co., Inc., 1969. 306 pp.

73. Hughes, Langston and Milton Meltzer. A Pictorial History of The Negro in America. New York: Crown Publishers, Inc., 1968. Third Edition. There is a section entitled "Stars and Superstars: Black Americans in Sports," pp. 360-361. Various references are also made to Black professional athletes such as Joe Louis, Jackie Robinson, Muhammad Ali, etc.

74. Jones, Wally and Jim Washington. Black Champions Challenge American Sports. New York: David McKay, 1972. 180 pp.

75. Martin, Fletcher, Editor. Our Great Americans, The Negro Contribution to American Progress. Chicago; Gamma Corp., 1953. 96 pp. Black Athletes are included in this collection.

76. Matney, William C., Editor. Who's Who Among Black Americans. Vols. 1-10 Northbrook, IL: Who's Who Among Black Americans, Inc. 1976. 772 pp. Various references to Black athletes such as Henry L. Aaron, Kareem Abdul-Jabbar, Arthur Ashe, Joseph Black, Joe Louis, John Roseboro, Cazzie Russell and Gayle Sayers are included in this book.

77. Nelson, Robert L. The Negro in Athletics. New York: Service Bureau For Intercultural Education, 1940. 28 pp.

78. Olsen, Jack. The Black Athlete: A Shameful Story: The Myth of Integration in American Sport. New York: Time-Life Books, 1968, 223 pp.

79. Ploski, Harry A. and Warren Marr II, Editors. The Negro Almanac: A Reference Work On The Afro-American. New York: The Belwether Co., 1976. Section 17 is entitled, "The Black Amateur and Professional Athlete." pp. 661-711.

80. Ribalow, Harold Urie L. The Negro in American Sports. New York: N.P., 1954.

81. Smythe, Mabel M. The Black American Reference Book. Englewood Cliffs, N.J.: Prentice Hall, 1976. Chapter 30 discusses "The Black American in Sports." pp. 927-963.

82. Young, Andrew Sturgeon Nash. Negro Firsts in Sports. Chicago:
    Johnson Publishing Company, 1963. 301 pp.

4

General Black Books

BASEBALL

83. Holway, John. Voices From The Great Black Baseball Leagues. New York: Dodd, Mead & Co., 1975. Various Black professional baseball players are discussed: Hank Aaron, Ernie Banks, Joe Black, Roy Campanella, Larry Doby, Bob Gibson, Junior Gilliam, Elston Howard, Willie Mays, Don Newcombe, Leroy Satchel Paiege, Frank Robinson, Jackie Robinson, etc.

84. Picott, J. Rupert. Selected Black Sports Immortals. Washington, D.C.: Association For The Study of Afro-American Life and History, 1981. (Pamphlet).

85. Rust, Art. "Get That Nigger Off The Field!": A Sparkling, Informal History of The Black Man in Baseball. New York: Delacorte Press, 1976. 228 pp.

86. Young, Andrew Sturgeon Nash. Great Negro Baseball Stars and How They Made the Major Leagues. New York: A.S. Barnes and Company, 1953. 248 pp.

BOXING

87. Fox, Richard K. The Black Champions of Prize Ring: From Molineaux To Jackson. New York: R.K. Fox, 1890. 57 pp.

5

Books by Black Athletes

BASEBALL

HENRY AARON

88. Aaron, Henry (Hank) Louis. "Aaron, r.f." As told to Furman
Bisher. Forword by Furman Bisher. Cleveland: World Publishing
Co., 1968. 212 pp.

89. Aaron, Hank, et al. How To Hit and Run The Bases. New York:
Gosset, 1971. 92 pp. Written for young people.

90. Aaron, Henry (Hank) with Furman Bisher. Aaron. New York: Thomas
Y. Crowell Co., 1974. 236 pp. Revised Edition.

91. Aaron, Hank and Joel Cohen. Hitting The Aaron Way. Englewood
Cliffs, NJ: Prentice-Hall, 1974. 127 pp. Written for juvenile
readers.

ERNIE BANKS

92. Banks, (Ernest) Ernie and Jim Enright. "Mr. Cub." Foreword by
Warren C. Giles. Introductions by Jack Brickhouse and Jim
Enright. Chicago: Follett Publishing Co., 1971. 237 pp.

VIDA BLUE

93. Blue, Vida and Bill Libby. Vida: His Own Story. Englewood Cliff,
NJ: Prentice-Hall, 1972, 240 pp.

LOU BROCK

94. Brock, Lou and Franz Schilze. Stealing Is My Game. Englewood
Cliffs, NJ: Prentice-Hall, 1976. 206 pp.

ROY CAMPANELLA

95. Campanella Roy. It's Good To Be Alive. Boston: Little, Brown & Co., 1959. 306 pp.

CURT FLOOD

96. Flood, [Curtis]. Curt Charles with Richard Carter. The Way It Is. New York: Trident Press, 1971. 263 pp.

BOB GIBSON

97. Gibson, Bob. From Ghetto To Glory: The Story of Bob Gibson. Englewood Cliffs, NJ: Prentice-Hall, 1968. 200 pp.

ELSTON HOWARD

98. Howard, Elston. Catching. New York: Viking, 1966. 96 pp.

REGGIE JACKSON

99. Jackson, Reggie and Bill Libby. Reggie: A Season With a Superstar. Chicago: Playboy Press, 1975. 272 pp.

100. Jackson, Reggie and Joseph Cohen. Inside Hitting. Chicago: H. Regnery Co., 1975. 86 pp.

101. Jackson, Reggie. Reggie Jackson's Scrapbook. Robert Kraus, Editor. New York: Windmill Books, 1978. 120 pp.

RON LEFLORE

102. Leflore, Ron with Jim Hawkins. Breakout: From Prison To The Big Leagues. New York: Harper & Row, 1978. 180 pp.

WILLIE MAYS

103. Mays, Willie and Charles Einstein. Born to Play. New York: G.P. Putnam, 1955. 168 pp.

104. Mays, Willie. Willie Mays: My Life In and Out of Baseball. As told to Charles Einstein. New York: E.P. Dutton, 1966. 320 pp.

105. Mays, Willie. My Secrets of Playing Baseball. With Howard Liss. Photographs by David Sutton. New York: Viking Press, 1967. 89 pp.

LEROY PAIGE

106. Paige, Leroy and David Lipman. Maybe I'll Pitch Forever; A Great Baseball Player Tells the Hilarious Story Behind the Legend. Garden City, New York: Doubleday, 1962. 285 pp.

FRANK ROBINSON

107. Robinson, Frank with Al Silverman. My Life in Baseball. Garden City, New York: Doubleday, 1968. 225 pp.

108. Robinson, Frank. Frank: The First Year. New York: Holt, Rinehart and Winston, 1976. 259 pp.

JACKIE ROBINSON

109. Robinson, John (Jackie) Roosevelt. Jackie Robinson -My Own Story. As told by Jackie Robinson to Wendell Smith of the Pittsburgh Courier and the Chicago Herald American. New York: Greenberg Publishers, 1948. 172 pp.

110. Robinson, John (Jackie) Roosevelt. Baseball Has Done It. Charles Dexter, Editor. Philadelphia: J.B. Lippincott, 1964. 216 pp.

111. Robinson, John (Jackie) Roosevelt and Alfred Duckett. Breakthrough To The Big League: The Story of Jackie Robinson. New York: Harper & Row, Publishers, 1965. 178 pp.

112. Robinson, (John) Jackie (Roosevelt). I Never Had It Made. As told to Alfred Duckett. New York: Putnam's, 1972. 287 pp.

113. Robinson, Jackie. Jackie Robinson's Little League Baseball Book. Englewood Cliffs, NJ: Prentice-Hall, 1972. 135 pp.

JOHN ROSEBORO

114. Roseboro, John with Bill Libby. Glory Days With The Dodgers and Other Days With Others. New York: Atheneum, 1978. 297 pp.

WILLIE STARGELL

115. Stargell, Willie. Out of Left Field: Willie Stargell and The Pittsburgh Pirates. New York. Two Continents Publishing Group, 1976. 223 pp.

MAURY WILLS

116. Wills, (Maurice) Maury (Morning). It Pays To Steal. As Told to Steve Gardner. Introduction By Bobby Bragan. Englewood Cliffs, NJ: Prentice-Hall, 1963. 186 pp.

117. Wills, Maury. How To Steal a Pennant. New York: Putnam, 1976. 252 pp.

BASKETBALL

DICK BARNET

118. Barnet, Dick. Inside Basketball. Chicago: Regnery, 1971. 87 pp.

WILT CHAMBERLAIN

119. Chamberlain, Wilt and David Shaw. Wilt: Just Any Other 7-Foot Black Millionaire Who Lives Next Door. New York: MacMillan, 1973. 310 pp.

WALT FRAZIER

120. Frazier, Walt, and Joe Jares. Clyde. New York: Rutledge Books-Holt, Rinehart and Winston, 1970. 286 pp.

121. Frazier, Walt and Ira Berkow. Rockin' Steady: A Guide To Basketball and Cool. Englewood Cliffs, NJ: Prentice-Hall, 1974. 158 pp.

ELVIN HAYES

122. Hayes, Elvin. They Call Me "The Big E." Englewood Cliffs, NJ: Prentice-Hall, 1978. 169 pp.

SPENCER HAYWOOD

123. Haywood, Spencer and Bill Libby. Stand Up For Something: The Spencer Haywood Story. New York: Grosset & Dunlap, 1972. 248 pp.

EARL MONROE

124. Monroe, Earl and Wes Unseld. Basketball Skillbook. Ray Siegner, Editor. New York: Atheneum, 1973. 144 pp.

WILLIS REED

125. Reed, Willis and Phil Pepe. View From The Rim: Willis Reed On Basketball. New York: Lippincott, 1971. 208 pp.

CAZZIE LEE RUSSELL, JR.

126. Russell, Cazzie Lee, Jr. Me Cazzie Russell. Preface by the Publishers. Westwood, NJ: Fleming H. Revell, 1976. 122 pp.

BILL RUSSELL

127. Russell, Bill and Taylor Branch. Second Wind: The Memoirs of an Opinionated Man. New York: Random House, 1979. 265 pp.

LENNY WILKENS

128. Wilkens, Lenny. The Lenny Wilkens Story. New York: Paul S. Erikson, 1974. 174 pp.

BOXING

MUHAMMAD ALI

129. Ali, Muhammad with Richard Durham. The Greatest, My Own Story.
New York: Random House, 1975. 415 pp.

GEORGE DIXON

130. Dixon, George. A Lesson in Boxing, by George Dixon, Champion
Featherweight of the World. n. p. , 1893. 15 pp.

HENRY ARMSTRONG

131. Armstrong, Henry (Formerly Henry Jackson). Gloves Glory and God:
An Autobiography. Westwood, NJ: Fleming H. Revell, 1950.
256 pp.

HOGAN BASSEY

132. Bassey, Hogan. Bassey on Boxing, By the Former World Feather
Weight Champion. London: Nelson, 1963. 127 pp.

RUBIN CARTER

133. Carter, Rubin. The Sixteenth Round: From Number 1 Contender to
#45472. New York: Viking, 1974. 339 pp.

JACK JOHNSON

134. Johnson, Jack. Jack Johnson in the Ring and Out. With intro-
ductory articles by "Tad," Ed. W. Smith.. Damon Runyon, and Mrs.
Jack Johnson, special drawings by Edwin William Krauter. Chicago:
National Sports Publishing Co., 1927. 259 pp.

JOE LOUIS

135. Louis, Joe. How To Box. Edward J. Mallory, Editor.
Philadelphia: David McKay Co., 1948. 64 pp.

136. Louis, Joe. The Joe Louis Story. Written with the editorial
aid of Chester L. Washington and Haskell Cohen. New York:
Grosset and Dunlap, 1943. 197 pp.

ARCHIE MOORE

137. Moore, Archie. The Archie Moore Story. New York: McGraw-Hill
Book Company, Inc., 1960. 240 pp.

138. Moore, Archie Lee, and Leonard B. Pearl. Any Boy Can: The
Archie Moore Story. Foreword and afterward by Leonard B. Pearl.
Englewood Cliffs, NJ: Prentice-Hall, 1971. 263 pp.

FLOYD PATTERSON

139. Patterson, Floyd. Victory Over Myself. With Milton Gross. New
York: B. Geis Associates; Distributed by Random House, 1962.
244 pp.

SUGAR RAY ROBINSON

140. Robinson, Ray (formerly Smith, Walker, Jr.) with Dave Anderson.
Sugar Ray. New York: Viking Press 1970. 376 pp. Reprinted
New York: Signet Books - New American Library, 1971. 376 pp.

FOOTBALL

JAMES BROWN

141. Brown (James) Jimmy (Nathaniel) with Myron Cope. Off My Chest.
Garden City, NJ: Doubleday, 1964. 230 pp.

LARRY BROWN

142. Brown, Larry. I'll Always Get Up. New York: Simon and Schuster,
1973. 192 pp.

ROSEY GRIER

143. Grier, Rosey. Rosey Grier Needlepoint For Men. New York: Walker
& Co., 1973. 158 pp.

ARCHIE GRIFFIN

144. Griffin, Archie and Dave Diles. Archie-The Archie Griffin Story.
Graden City, New York: Doubleday & Co., 1977. 192 pp.

WALTER PAYTON

145. Payton, Walter. Sweetness. Chicago: Contemporary Books, 1978.

JOHNNY SAMPLE

146. Sample, (John) Johnny with Fred J. Hamilton and Sonny Schwartz.
Confessions of a Dirty Ball Player. Foreword by Joe Willie
Namath. New York: Dial Press, 1970. 343 pp.

GALE SAYERS

147. Sayers, Gale, with Al Silverman. I Am Third. Introduction by
Bill Cosby. New York: Viking Press, 1970. 238 pp.

148. Griese, Bob and Gale Sayers. Offensive Football. New York:
Atheneum, 1972. 176 pp.

O.J. SIMPSON

149. Simpson, O (renthal) J (ames), with Pete Axthelm. O. J. The
     Education of a Rich Rookie. New York: MacMillan, 1970. 255 pp.

EMLEN TUNNELL

150. Tunnell, Emlen with Bill Gleason. Footsteps of a Giant. Garden
     City, New York: Doubleday, 1966. 238 pp.

GOLF

151. Gibson, Althea. I Always Wanted To Be Somebody. Edward E.
     Fitzgerald, Editor. New York: Harper & Bros., 1958. 176 pp.

152. Gibson, Althea, with Richard Curtis. So Much To Live For.
     Introduction by Richard Curtis. New York: Putnam's, 1968.
     160 pp.

TENNIS

ARTHUR ASHE

153. Ashe, Arthur. Advantage Ashe. As told to Clifford George
     Gewecke, Jr. New York: Coward-McCann, Inc., 1967. 192 pp.

154. Ashe, Arthur with Frank Deford. Arthur Ashe: Portrait in Motion.
     New York: Houghton Mifflin, 1975. 272 pp.

6

Books about Black Athletes

BASEBALL

HENRY AARON

155. Baldwin, Stanley and Jerry Jenkins in Colloration with Hank Aaron. Bad Henry. Radnor, PA: Chilton Book Co., 1974. 205 pp.

156. Bardolph, Richard. The Negro Vanguard. New York: Vintage Books, 1961. Hank Aaron, pp. 456, 457, 458.

157. Braun, Thomas. The Hitters. Mankato, MN: Creative Education, 1976. Henry Aaron is discussed in this work. Written for young adults.

158. Burchard, Marshall & Sue Burchard. Sports Hero: Henry Aaron. New York: G.P. Putnam's, 1974. 96 pp. Written for juvenile readers.

159. Davidson, Donald with Jesse Outlaw. Caught Short. New York: Atheneum, 1976. Hank Aaron is included in this work.

160. Deegan, Paul J. Hank Aaron. Mankato, MN: Creative Education, 1974. 31 pp. Written for juvenile readers.

161. Eastern, Samuel. Henry Aaron, Home-Run King. Champaign, IL: Garrard Publishing Co., 1975. 96 pp. Written for young adults.

162. Golenbock, Peter. Dynasty: The New York Yankee, 1949-1964. Englewood Cliffs, NJ: Prentice-Hall, 1975. 394 pp. Hank Aaron, pp. 138, 173, 216, 217, 218, 219, 231, 234.

163. Gutman, Bill. Hank Aaron. New York: Grosset & Dunlap, 1973. 87 pp. Written for young adults.

164. Gutman, Bill. Modern Baseball Superstars. New York: Dodd, Mead & Co., 1973. 112 pp. Henry Aaron is included in this work written for young adults.

165. Haskins, James. <u>Babe Ruth and Hank Aaron</u>. New York. Lathrop, Lee & Shepard Co., 1974. 123 pp.

166. Hirshberg, Albert. <u>The Up-to-Date Biography of Henry Aaron: Quiet Superstar</u>. New York: G.P. Putnam, 1974. 189 pp. Written for juvenile readers.

167. Marsh, Irvin T. and Edward Ehre, Editors. <u>Best Sports Stories</u>. New York: E.P. Dutton & Co., 1973. Maury Allen, "Aaron Was The Big Noise," pp. 75-77.

168. Marsh, Irving T. and Edward Ehre, Editors. <u>Best Sports Stories</u>. New York: E.P. Dutton & Co., 1974. Al Cartwright, "The Drive On The Record (Henry Aaron)," pp. 90-92.

169. Marsh, Irving T. and Edward Ehre, Editors. <u>Best Sports Stories</u>. New York: E.P. Dutton & Co., 1975. Bob Hunter "Henry Aaron Was Able," pp. 64-68.

170. Mary, Julian. <u>Hank Aaron Clinches The Pennant</u>. Mankato, MN: Crestwood House, 1972. 45 pp. Written for juvenile readers.

171. McAdam, Robert. <u>Climb Any Mountain</u>. Glendale, CA: Bowmar, 1976. 58 pp. Hank Aaron is included in this work. Written for juvenile readers.

172. Milverstebt, F.M. <u>The Quiet Legend, Henry Aaron</u>. Milwaukee: Raintree Editions, 1974. Written for juvenile readers.

173. Money, Don. <u>The Man Who Made Milwaukee Famous: A Salute to Henry Aaron</u>. Milwaukee: Agape Publishers, 1976. 220 pp.

174. Morse, Ann. <u>Baseball's Record Breaker, Hank Aaron</u>. Mankato, MN: Creative Education, 1976. 30 pp. Written for juvenile readers.

175. Musick, Phil. <u>Hank Aaron: The Man Who Beat The Babe</u>. New York: Popular Library, 1974. 220 pp.

176. Plimpton, George. <u>Hank Aaron: One For The Record; The Inside Story of Baseball's Greatest Home Run</u>. New York: Bantam Books, 1974. 154 pp.

177. Rainbolt, Richard. <u>Baseball Home-Run Hitters</u>. Minneapolis: Lerner Publications Co., 1975. 71 pp. Henry Aaron is included in this collection written for juvenile readers.

178. Rywell, Martin, Editor. <u>Afro-American Encyclopedia</u>. North Miami, FL: Educational Book Publishers, Inc., 1974. Henry Louis "Hank" Aaron, Vol. 1, pp. 1-2.

179. Santa Barbara County Board of Education. <u>The Emerging Minorities in America</u>. Santa Barbara, CA: American Bibliographical Center - Clio Press, 1972. Henry Aaron, p. 5.

180. Schlossberg, Dan. Hammerin' Hank! New York: Stadia Sports
     Publishing Co., 1974. 158 pp.

181. Shapiro, Milton J. The Hank Aaron Story. New York: Julian
     Messner, 1961. 192 pp.

182. Voight, David Q. America Through Baseball. Chicago: Nelson-Hall,
     1976. Henry (Hank) Aaron, pp. 12, 13, 122, 124.

183. Young, Bernice. The Picture Story of Hank Aaron. New York:
     Julian Messner, 1974. 62 pp. Written for juvenile readers.

                        RICHIE ALLEN

184. Brosnan, Jim. Great Rookies of The Major Leagues. New York:
     Random House, 1966. Richie Allen, pp. 162-176, 180. Written
     for juvenile readers.

185. Rywell, Martin, Editor. Afro-American Encyclopedia. North Miami,
     FL: Educational Book Publishers, Inc. 1974. Richard Anthony
     Allen, Vol. 1, p. 120.

                        ERNIE BANKS

186. Libby, Bill. Ernie Banks: Mr. Cub. New York: G.P. Putnam's
     Sons, 1971. 171 pp. Written for juvenile readers.

187. May, Julian. Ernie Banks, Home Run Slugger. Mankato, MN:
     Crestwood House, 1973. 46 pp. Written for young adults.

188. Peterson, Robert. Only The Ball Was White. Englewood Cliffs, NJ:
     Prentice Hall, 1970. 406 pp. Baseball player Ernie Banks is
     discussed in this work.

189. Rywell, Martin, Editor. Afro-American Encyclopedia. North
     Miami, FL. Educational Book Publishers, Inc., 1974. Ernie Banks.
     Vol. 1, pp. 192-193.

                         JOE BLACK

190. Rywell, Martin, Editor. Afro-American Encyclopedia. North Miami,
     FL: Educational Book Publishers, Inc., 1974. Joe Black Vol. 1,
     p. 270.

191. Shapiro, Milton J. Heroes of the Bullpen: Baseball's Greatest
     Relief Pitchers. New York: Julian Messner, 1967. 186 pp. Joe
     Black is included in this collection.

                         VIDA BLUE

192. Bulter, Hal. Baseball's Champion Pitchers: The Cy Young Award
     Winners. New York: Julian Messner, 1974. 96 pp. Vida Blue is
     included in this collection written for young adults.

193. Demin, Richard. Vida (Blue). New York: Lancer, 1972. 173 pp.

194. Kowet, Don. Vida Blue: Coming Up Again. New York: G.P.
     Putnam's, 1974. 160 pp.

LOUIS BROCK

195. Braun, Thomas. The Hitters. Mankato, MN: Creative Education,
     1976. Lou Brock is discussed in this work. Written for young
     people.

196. Peterson, Robert. Only The Ball Was White. Englewood Cliffs, NJ:
     Prentice-Hall, 1970. 406 pp. Baseball player Lou Brock is dis-
     cussed in this work.

197. Rywell, Martin, Editor. Afro-American Encyclopedia. North Miami,
     FL: Educational Book Publishers, Inc., 1974. Louis Clark
     Brock, Vol. 2, pp. 397-398.

ROY CAMPANELLA

198. Golenbock, Peter. Dynasty: The New York Yankee, 1949-1964.
     Englewood Cliffs, NJ: Prentice-Hall, 1975. 394 pp. Roy
     Campanella, pp. 92, 95, 115, 116, 117, 157, 159, 161, 187, 189,
     190, 222, 237.

199. Marsh, Irving T. and Edward Ehre, Editors. Best Sports Stories.
     New York: E.P. Dutton & Co., 1956. Dick Seamon, "Big Man From
     Nicetown (Roy Campanella)," pp. 60-69.

200. Peterson, Robert. Only The Ball Was White. Englewood Cliffs, NJ:
     Prentice-Hall, 1970. 406 pp. Baseball catcher Roy Campanella
     is discussed in this work.

201. Rywell, Martin, Editor. Afro-American Encyclopedia. Noth Miami,
     FL: Educational Book Publishers, Inc., 1974. Roy Campanella,
     Vol. 2, pp. 515-516.

202. Santa Barbara County Board of Education. The Emerging Minorities
     in America. Santa Barbara, CA: American Bibliographical Center
     - Clio Press, 1972. Roy Campanella, p. 18.

203. Schoor, Gene. Roy Campanella, Man of Courage. New York: G.P.
     Putnam's, 1959. 190 pp.

204. Shapiro, Milton J. The Roy Campanella Story. New York: Julian
     Messner, 1958. 192 pp.

205. Shapiro, Milton J. Heroes Behind The Mask: America's Greatest
     Catchers. New York: Julian Messner, 1968. 191 pp. Roy
     Campanella is included in this collection.

206. Young, Dick. Roy Campanella. New York: Grosset. 1952. 184 pp.

ROD CAREW

207. Baston, Larry. Rod Carew. Mankato, MN: Creative Education,
     1977. 31 pp. Written for juvenile readers.

208. Baston, Larry. An Interview With Rod Carew. Mankato, MN: Creative Education, 1977. 31 pp. Written for juvenile readers.

209. Braun, Thomas. The Hitters. Mankato, MN: Creative Education, 1976. Rod Carew is discussed in this collection. Written for juvenile readers.

210. Burchard, Marshall. Sports Hero: Rod Carew. New York: G.P. Putnam's Son. 1978. 93 pp. Written for juvenile readers.

211. Gutman, Bill. More Modern Baseball Superstars. New York: Dodd, Mead, and Co., 1978. 128 pp. Rod Carew is included in this work.

212. Hahn, James. Rod Carew: A Promise and A Dream. St. Paul: EMC Corp., 1978.

213. Libby, Bill. Rod Carew: Master Hitter. New York: G.P. Putnam, 1976. 127 pp.

TOMMY DAVIS

214. Russell, Patrick. The Tommy Davis Story. Garden City, NY: Doubleday & Co., 1969. 143 pp.

LARRY DOBY

215. Peterson, Robert. Only The Ball Was White. Englewood Cliffs, NJ: Prentice-Hall, 1970. 406 pp. Larry Doby is discussed in this work.

216. Rywell, Martin, Editor. Afro-American Encyclopedia. North Miami, FL: Educational Book Publishers, Inc., 1974. Larry Doby, Vol. 3, pp. 701-702.

217. Smythe, Mabel M. The Black American Reference Book. Englewood Cliffs, NJ: Prentice-Hall, 1976. Larry Doby, p. 930.

LUKE EASTER

218. Peterson, Robert. Only The Ball Was White. Englewood Cliffs, NJ: Prentice-Hall, 1970. 406 pp. Luke Easter is included in this work.

219. Rywell, Martin, Editor. Afro-American Encyclopedia. North Miami, FL: Educational Book Publishers, Inc., 1974. Luscious "Luke" Easter, Vol. 3, p. 869.

CURTIS FLOOD

220. Rywell, Martin, Editor. Afro-American Encyclopedia. North Miami, FL: Educational Book Publishers, Inc., 1974. Curtis Charles Flood. Vol. 4, p. 961.

BOB GIBSON

221. Libby, Bill. Star Pitchers of the Major Leagues. New York: Random House, 1971. 142 pp. Bob Gibson is included in this work.

222. Lipman, David. Bob Gibson, Pitching Ace. New York: G.P. Putnam, 1975. 191 pp.

223. Marsh, Irving T. and Edward Ehre, Editors. Best Sports Stories. New York: E.P. Dutton & Co. 1968. Clark Nealon, "Gibson Puts On The Brakes," pp. 51-54.

224. Marsh, Irving T. and Edward Ehre, Editors. Best Sports Stories. New York: E.P. Dutton & Co., 1969. Bob Stevens, "Gibson Again," pp. 73-76.

225. Marsh, Irving T. and Edward Ehre, Editors. Best Sports Stories. New York: E.P. Dutton & Co., 1969. Mickey Herskowitz," Gibson Flails The Tigers," pp. 69-72.

226. Peterson, Robert. Only The Ball Was White. Englewood Cliffs, NJ: Prentice-Hall, 1970. 406 pp. Pitcher Bob Gibson is discussed in this work.

227. Shapiro, Milton J. Baseball's Greatest Pitchers. New York: Julian Messner, 1969. Bob Gibson, pp. 105-117.

228. Rywell, Martin, Editor. Afro-American Encyclopedia. North Miami, FL: Educational Book Publishers, Inc., 1924. Bob Gibson, Vol. 4, pp. 1060-1061.

229. Wesley, Charles H. The Quest For Equality: From Civil War To Civil Rights. New York: Published Co., 1976. Bob Gibson, p. 199.

ELSTON HOWARD

230. Golenbock, Peter. Dynasty: The New York Yankee, 1949-1964. Englewood Cliffs, NJ: Prentice-Hall, 1975. 394 pp. Ellie Elston Howard, pp. 139-146, 156, 160-166, 179, 188-195, 200-234, 304-322, 328-338, 346, 350-356, 364-376, 381.

231. Rywell, Martin, Editor, Afro-American Encyclopedia. North Miami, FL: Educational Book Publishers, Inc., 1974. Elston Gene "Ellie" Howard, Vol. 4, pp. 1235-1236.

232. Shapiro, Milton J. Heroes Behind The Mask: America's Greatest Catchers. New York: Julian Messner, 1968. 191 pp. Elston Howard is included in this collection.

REGGIE JACKSON

233. Allen, Maury. Reggie Jackson, The Three Million Dollar Man. New York: Harvey House, 1978. 62 pp.

234. Braun, Thomas. The Hitters. Mankato, MN: Creative Education,
     1976. Reggie Jackson is included in this work. Written for
     juvenile readers.

235. Burchard, Marshall. Sports Hero: Reggie Jackson. New York:
     Putnam's, Sons, 1975. 93 pp. Written for juvenile readers.

236. Burchard, Sue H. Sport Star: Reggie Jackson. New York:
     Harcourt Brace Jovanovich, 1976. Written for juvenile readers.

237. Gutman, Bill. The Picture Life of Reggie Jackson. New York:
     Watts, 1978. 48 pp.

238. Hahn, James. Reggie Jackson: Slugger Supreme. St. Paul: EMC
     Corp. 1978. Written for juvenile reader.

239. Halter, Jon C. Reggie Jackson, All Star in Right. New York:
     G.P. Putnam, 1975. 127 pp.

240. Libby, Bill. The Reggie Jackson Story. New York: Lothrop, Lee &
     Shepard. 1979. 224 pp. Written for juvenile readers.

241. Marsh, Irving T. and Edward Ehre, Editors. Best Sports Stories.
     New York: E.P. Dutton & Co., 1975. Murray Olderman "Reggie
     Jackson: Blood & Guts of The Fighting A's", pp. 85-91.

242. Marsh, Irving T. and Edward Ehre, Editors. Best Sports Stories.
     New York: E.P. Dutton, 1978. Thomas Boswell, "World Series:
     The Right-Field Sign Says "Reg-gie, Reg-gie, Reg-gie," pp. 1-3.

243. Rywell, Martin, Editor. Afro-American Encyclopedia. North Miami,
     FL: Educational Book Publishers, Inc., 1974. Reginald Martinez
     "Reggie" Jackson, Vol. 5, pp. 1297-1298.

244. Stone, Eddie. Reggie Jackson. Los Angeles: Holloway House
     Publishing Co., 1980. 96 pp.

245. Sullivan, George. Picture Story of Reggie Jackson. New York:
     Julian Messner, 1977. 63 pp. Written for young adults.

246. Vass, George. Reggie Jackson: From Baseball Superstar To
     Candy Bar. Chicago: Children's Press, 1979. Written for
     juvenile readers.

RON LEFLORE

247. Burchard, Marshall. Sports Hero: Ron LeFlore. New York: G.P.
     Putnam's 1979. 93 pp. Written for juvenile readers.

WILLIE MAYS

248. Bardolph, Richard. The Negro Vanguard. New York: Vintage Books,
     1961. Willie Mays, pp. 456, 457, 458.

249. Brosnan, Jim. Great Rookies of The Major Leagues. New York: Random House, 1966. Willie Mays, pp. 8, 84, 111, 116, 117, 118, 120, 121, 160, 161. Written for juvenile readers.

250. Devaney, John. Baseball's Youngest Big Leagues. New York: Holt, Rinehart, and Winston, 1969. 139 pp. Willie Mays is included in this collection.

251. Einstein, Charles. Willie Mays: Coast To Coast Giant. New York: G.P. Putnam, 1963. 191 pp.

252. Einstein, Charles. Willie's (Mays) Time: A Memoir. New York: J. B. Lippincott Co., 1979. 352 pp.

253. Franco, John M., Editor. Afro-American Contributors to American Life. Westerchester, IL: Benefic Press, 1970. Willie Howard Mays, pp. 166-175. Written for young adults.

254. Graham, Frank. Great Hitters of The Major Leagues. New York: Random House, 1959. 171 pp. Willie Mays is included in this collection.

255. Gross, M. Willie Mays, New York: N.P. 1966.

256. Gutman, Bill. Modern Baseball Superstars. New York: Dodd, Mead & Co., 1973. 112 pp. Willie Mays is included in this work written for young adults.

257. Hano, Arnold. Willie Mays, The Say-Hey Kid. New York: Bartholomew House, 1961. 159 pp.

258. Hano, Arnold. Willie Mays. New York: Grosset & Dunlap, 1966. 190 pp.

259. Hano, Arnold. Greatest Giants of Them All. New York: G.P. Putnam, 1967. 254 pp. Willie Mays is included in this collection.

260. Liss, Howard. The Willie Mays Album. New York: Hawthorn, 1966. 63 pp.

261. Marsh, Irving T. and Edward Ehre, Editor. Best Sports Stories. New York: E.P. Dutton & Co. 1968. Dick Young, "Prince Charming Takes Cinderella To the Ball Game (Willie Mays)," pp. 65-68.

262. Marsh, Irving, T. and Edward Ehre, Editor. Best Sports Stories. New York: E.P. Dutton & Co. 1970. Roger Kahn, "Willie Mays, Yesterday and Today," pp. 31-47.

263. Marsh, Irwing T. and Edward Ehre, Editors. Best Sports Stories. New York: E.P.Dutton & Co., 1974. Lou Chapman, "Mays Has The Last Laugh," pp. 41-54.

264. Marsh, Irving T. and Edward Ehre, Editors. Thirty Years of Best Sports Stories. New York: E.P. Dutton & Co., Inc., 1975. Roger Kahn, "Willie Mays, Yesterday and Today," pp. 260-277.

265. May, Julian. Willie Mays, Most Valuable Player Mankato. MN: Crestwood House, 1972. 47 pp. Written for young readers.

266. Peterson, Robert. Only The Ball Was White. Englewood Cliffs, NJ: Prentice-Hall, 1970. 406 pp. Willie Mays is discussed in this work.

267. Rainbolt, Richard. Baseball's Home - Run Hitters. Minneapolis: Lerner Publications Co., 1975. pp. 71. Willie Mays is included in this work written for juvenile readers.

268. Richardson, Ben. Great American Negroes. New York: Thomas Y. Crowell Co., 1945. Willie Mays, pp. 302-321.

269. Robinson, Wilhelmena S. Historical Afro-American Biographies. New York: Publishers, 1968. William (Willie) Howard Mays, p. 227.

270. Rywell, Martin, Editor. Afro-American Encyclopedia. North Miami, FL: Educational Book Publishers, Inc., 1974. Willie Mays, Vol. 6, pp. 1619-1620.

271. Schoor, Gene. Willie Mays: Modest Champion. New York: G.P. Putnam's, 1960. 187 pp.

272. Shapiro, Milton J. The Willie Mays Story. New York: Julian Messner, 1960. 192 pp.

273. Smith, Ken. The Willie Mays Story. New York: Greenberg, 1954. 94 pp.

274. Smith, Robert. Baseball in America. New York: Holt, Rinehart and Winston, 1961. Willie Mays, pp. 245, 246, 247, 248, 249, 250, 251, 252.

275. Sullivan, George. Willie Mays. New York: G.P. Putnam's 1973. 64 pp. written for juvenile readers.

276. Toppin, Edgar A. A Biographical History of Blacks in America Since 1528. New York: David McKay, 1971. Willie Mays, pp: 197, 241, 365, 366, 367.

277. Wesley, Charles H. The Quest For Equality: From Civil War To Civil Rigts. New York: Publishers Co., 1976. Willie Mays, p. 199.

WILLIE McCOVEY

278. Marsh, Irving T. and Edward Ehre, Editors. Best Sports Stories. New York: E.P. Dutton & Co., 1963. Jack Murphy, "When The World Stood Still (Willie McCovey)." pp. 17-19.

279. Rywell, Martin, Editor. Afro-American Encyclopedia. North Miami, FL: Educational Book Publishers, Inc., 1974. Willie Lee McCovey Vol. 5, pp. 1529-1530.

DON NEWCOMBE

280. Marsh, Irving T. and Edward Ehre, Editors. Best Sports Stories.
New York: E.P. Dutton & Co., 1957. Milt Gross, "The Long Ride
Home (Don Newcombe)," pp. 23-27.

281. Rywell, Martin, Editor. Afro-American Encyclopedia. North
Miami, FL: Educational Book Publishers, Inc., 1974. Don
"Newk" Newcombe, Vol. 7, pp. 1893-1894.

LEROY PAIGE

282. Bardolph, Richard. The Negro Vanguard. New York. Vintage Books,
1961. Leroy "Satchel Paige, pp. 270, 271.

283. Marsh, Irving T. and Edward Ehre, Editors. Best Sports Stories.
New York: E.P. Dutton & Co., 1955. Tex Maule, "Old Satch,"
pp. 98-100.

284. Peterson, Robert. Only The Ball Was White. Englewood Cliffs,
NJ: Prentice-Hall, 1970. 406 pp. Pitcher Leroy Satchel Paige
is discussed in this work.

285. Powers, James J. Baseball Personalities, The Most Colorful
Figures of All Times. New York: R. Field, 1949. Leroy Satchel
Paige is included in this collection.

286. Rubin, Robert. Satchel Paige: All-Time Baseball Great. New
York: G.P. Putnam's Sons, 1974. 157 pp. Written for young
adults.

287. Rywell, Martin, Editor. Afro-American Encyclopedia. North
Miami, FL: Educational Book Publishers, Inc., 1974. Leroy
Robert "Satchel" Paige, Vol. 7, pp. 1971-1972.

288. Santa Barbara County Board of Education. The Emerging Minorities
in America. Santa Barbara, CA: American Bibliographical Center
- Clio Press, 1972. Satchel Paige, p. 60.

289. Smith, Robert. Pioneers of Baseball. Boston: Little, Brown &
Co., 1978. 180 pp. "Leroy (Satchel) Paige, Old Man Moses," is
discussed in this work.

FRANK ROBINSON

290. Baston, Larry. Frank Robinson. Mankato, MN: Creative Education,
1974. 31 pp. Written for young adults.

291. Brosnan, Jim. Great Rookies of The Major Leagues. New York:
Random House, 1966. Frank Robinson, pp. 80-93, 158. Written
for juvenile readers.

292. Hirshberg, Albert. Frank Robinson: Born Leader. New York:
E.P. Putman's, 1973. 191 pp. Written for juvenile readers.

293. Liss, Howard. Triple Crown Winners. New York: Julian Messner, 1969. Frank Robinson, pp. 64-73. Written for juvenile readers.

294. Marsh, Irving T. and Edward Ehre, Editors. Best Sports Stories. New York: E.P. Dutton & Co., 1972. Joe Heiling, "Flat-Foot Frank (Robinson) Flies Home," pp. 64-67.

295. Marshall, Irving T. and Edward Ehre, Editors. Best Sports Stories. New York: E.P. Dutton & Co., 1975. Dick Young, "Now Comes The Big Test (Frank Robinson)" pp. 69-72.

296. Rywell, Martin, Editor. Afro-American Encyclopedia. North Miami, FL: Educational Book Publishers, Inc., 1974. Frank Robinson, Vol. 7, pp. 2248-2249.

297. Schneider, Russell J. Frank Robinson: The Making of a Manager. New York: Coward, McCann & Geohegan, Inc., 1976. 251 pp.

298. Voigt, David Q. American Through Baseball. Chicago: Nelson-Hall, 1976. Frank Robinson, pp. 122, 125.

299. Young, Bernice. The Picture Story of Frank Robinson. New York: Julian Messner, 1975. 60 pp.

JACKIE ROBINSON

300. Bardolph, Richard. The Negro Vanguard. New York: Vintage Books, 1961. Jackie Robinson, pp. 287, 328, 353, 453, 456, 457, 458.

301. Brosnan, Jim. Great Rookies of The Major Leagues. New York: Random House, 1966. Jackie Robinson, pp. 8-25, 79. Written for juvenile readers.

302. Cohen, Barbara. Thank You, Jackie Robinson. New York: Lothrop, Lee and Shepard Co., 1974. 125 pp. Written for juvenile readers.

303. Davis, Mac. 100 Greatest Baseball Heroes. New York: Grosset & Dunlap, 1974. 174 pp. Jackie Robinson is included in this collection.

304. Edwards, Harry. The Revolt of The Black Athlete. New York: Free Press. 1969. Jackie Robinson, pp. X, XVII, 27, 34, 119, 120.

305. Epstein, Samuel. Jackie Robinson: Baseball's Gallant Fighter. Champaign, IL: Garrard Publishing Co., 1974. 96 pp.

306. Franco, John, M. Editor. Afro-American Contributions to American Life. Westerchester, IL: Benefic Press, 1970. Jackie Robinson, pp. 148-157. Written for young adults.

307. Golenbock, Peter. Dynasty: The New York Yankee, 1949-1964.
     Englewood Cliffs, NJ: Prentice-Hall, 1975, 394 pp. Jackie
     Robinson, pp. ix, 8, 92-97, 115-117, 127, 125, 138, 143-145,
     155-161, 184-188.

308. Gutman, Bill. Famous Baseball Stars. New York: Dodd, Mead
     & Co., 1973. Jackie Robinson is included in this work.
     Written for juvenile readers.

309. Hirshberg, Albert, and Joe McKenney. Famous American Athletes
     of Today. Boston: Page, 1947. 382 pp. Jackie Robinson is
     included in this work.

310. Hughes, Langston. Famous American Negroes. New York: Dodd,
     Mead & Co., 1954. "Jackie Robinson - First Negro in Big League
     Baseball," pp. 139-144.

311. Mann, Arthur William. The Jackie Robinson Story. New York:
     Grosset, 1951. 120 pp.

312. Marsh, Irving T. and Edward Ehre, Editors. Best Sports Stories.
     New York: E.P. Dutton & Co. 1946. Al Laney, "Regardless of
     Race, Color Or- (Jackie Robinson)," pp. 270-276.

313. Marsh, Irving T. and Edward Ehre, Editor. Best Sports. New York:
     E.P. Dutton & Co., 1972. Joe Donnelly, " A Gilt-Edged Bond
     (Jackie Robinson)," pp. 281-283.

314. Marsh, Irving T. and Edward Ehre, Editors. Best Sports Stories.
     New York: E.P. Dutton & Co., 1973. Joe Gergen, "He Never Had It
     Made (Jackie Robinson)," pp. 259-260.

315. Peterson, Robert. Only The Ball Was White. Englewood Cliffs,
     NJ: Prentice-Hall, 1970. 406 pp. Jackie Robinson is dis-
     cussed in this work.

316. Olsen, James T. Jackie Robinson: Pro Ball's First Black Star.
     Mankato, MN: Creative Education, 1974. 29 pp. Written for
     juvenile readers.

317. Powers, James J. Baseball Personalities, The Most Colorful
     Figures of All Times. New York: R. Field, 1949. John "Jackie"
     Roosevelt Robinson is included in this work.

318. Robinson, Wilhelmena . Historical Afro-American Biographies.
     New York: Publishers, 1968. Jackie Robinson, pp. 244-245.

319. Reeder, Bill. Jackie Robinson. New York: A.S. Barnes and Co.,
     1950. 183 pp.

320. Rowan, Carl Thomas. Wait Till Next Year; the Life of Jackie
     Robinson. by Carl T. Rowan with Jackie Robinson. New York:
     Random House, 1960. 339 pp.

321. Rudeen, Kenneth. Jackie Robinson. New York: Thomas Y.
     Crowell, 1971. 41 pp. Written for young people.

322. Rywell, Martin, Editor. Afro-American Encyclopedia. North
     Miami, FL: Educational Book Publishers, Inc., 1974. Jack
     "Jackie" Roosevelt Robinson, pp. 2251-2252.

323. Santa Barbara County Board of Education. The Emerging Minorities
     in America. Santa Barbara, CA: American Bibliographical Center
     - Clio Press, 1972. Jackie Robinson, p. 67.

324. Schoor, Gener. Jackie Robinson, Baseball Hero. New York: G.P.
     Putnam's, 1958. 187 pp.

325. Shapiro, Milton J. Jackie Robinson of The Brooklyn Dodgers.
     New York: Julian Messner, 1973. 192 pp.

326. Smith, Robert. Baseball in America. New York: Holt, Rinehart
     and Winston, 1961. John, Roosevelt (Jackie) Robinson, pp. 227,
     228, 229, 230, 231, 232, 235.

327. Smith, Robert. Pioneers of Baseball. Boston: Little Brown &
     Co., 1978. 180 pp. "Jack Roosevelt (Jackie) Robinson, first
     Black across the line," is discussed in this collection.

328. Toppin, Edgar A. A Biographical History of Blacks in America
     Since 1528. New York: David McKay, 1971. Jackie Robinson,
     pp. 188, 290, 241, 401, 402, 403, 404.

329. Vass, George. Champions of Sports. Chicago: Reilly & Lee,
     1970. 202 pp. Jackie Robinson is included in this collection.
     Written for young adults.

330. Voight, David Q. America Through Baseball. Chicago: Nelson-
     Hall, 1976. Jackie Robinson, pp. 11, 12, 117, 118, 119, 120,
     121, 122.

331. Wesley, Charles H. The Quest For Equality: From Civil War
     To Civil Rights. New York: Publishers Co., 1976. Jackie
     Robinson, p. 199.

JOHN ROSEBORO

332. Rywell, Martin, Editor. Afro-American Encyclopedia. North Miami,
     FL: Educational Book Publishers, Inc., 1974. John Roseboro, Vol.
     8, pp. 2274-2275.

WILLIE STARGELL

333. Adelman, Bob. Out of Left Field: Willie Stargell and The
     Pittsburgh Pirates. Boston: Little, Brown & Co., 1974.

334. Libby, Bill. Willie Stargell: Baseball Slugger. New York:
     G.P. Putnam's & Sons, 1973. 160 pp. Written for young juvenile
     readers.

335. Rywell, Martin, Editor. Afro-American Encyclopedia. North
     Miami, FL: Educational Book Publishers, Inc., 1974. Wilver
     Dornel "Willie", Stargell, Vol. 9, p. 2562.

MOSES FLEETWOOD WALKER

336. Rywell, Martin, Editor. Afro-American Encyclopedia. North
     Miami, FL: Educational Book Publishers, Inc., 1974. Moses
     Fleetwood "Fleet" Walker. Vol. 9, p. 2732.

MAURICE WILLS

337. Marsh, Irving T. and Edward Ehre, Editors. Best Sports Stories.
     New York: E. P. Dutton & Co., 1971. Bill Libby, "Maurice
     Morning Willis At Twilight," pp. 56-67.

BASKETBALL

KAREEM ABDUL-JABBAR

338. Armstrong, Robert. The Centers. Mankato, MN: Creative
     Education, 1977. 47 pp. Kareem Abdul-Jabbar is included in this
     collection. Written for juvenile readers.

339. Burchard, Marshall and Sue Burchard. Sports Hero: Kareem
     Abdul-Jabbar. New York: Putnam, 1972. 111 pp. Written
     for juvenile readers.

340. Deegar, Paul J. Kareem Abdul-Jabbar. Mankato, MN: Creative
     Education, 1974. 31 pp. Written for juvenile readers.

341. Docuette, Eddie. The Milwaukee Bucks and The Remarkable Abdul-
     Jabbar. Englewood Cliffs, NJ: Prentice-Hall, 1974. 127 pp.

342. Edwards, Harry. The Revolt of The Black Athlete. New York:
     Free Press, 1969. Lew Alcindor (Kareem Abdul-Jabbar) pp.
     19, 49, 52, 53, 57, 71, 72, 76, 77, 107.

343. Gutman, Bill. Modern Basketball Superstars. New York: Dodd,
     Mead & Co., 1975. Kareem Abdul-Jabbar is included in this work.

344. Hano, Arnold. Kareem: Basketball Great. New York: G.P.
     Putnam, 1975. 159 pp. Written for juvenile readers.

345. Harvey, Merv. The Lonely Heroes: Professional Basketball's
     Great Centers. New York: Viking Press, 1975. 230 pp. There
     are individual chapters on the game's outstanding big men
     such as Kareem Abdul-Jabbar.

346. Haskins, James. From Lew Alcindor To Kareem Abdul-Jabbar.
     New York: Lothrop, Lee & Shepard, 1972. 96 pp. Written
     for young adults.

347. Haskins, James. From Lew Alcindor To Kareem Abdul-Jabbar.
     Revised Edition. New York: Lothrop, Lee & Shepard, 1978.
     144 pp. Written for young adults.

348. Jackson, Robert. Jabbar, Giant of The NBA. New York: Henry
Z. Walck, 1972, Revised Edition. 72 pp. Written for young
people.

349. Kleid, David. Pro-Basketball's Big Men. New York: Random
House, 1973. Kareem Abdul-Jabbar is discussed in this book.
Written for young people.

350. Lamb, Kevin. Kareem. Milwaukee: Raintree Editons, 1975.
Written for young adults.

351. Marsh, Irving T. and Edward Ehre, Editors. Best Sports Stories.
New York: E.P. Dutton & Co., 1972. Roy McHugh, "Nobody Roots
for Goliath (Lew Alcindor)," pp. 156-158.

352. Pepe, Phil. Stand Tall: The Lew Alcindor Story. New York:
Grosset & Dunlap. 1970, 206 pp.

353. Rainbolt, Richard. Basketball's Big Men. Minneapolis: Lerner
Publications Co., 1975. 77 pp. Kareem Abdul-Jabbar is included
in this collection. Written for juvenile readers.

354. Reilly, Sean. Meet The Centers. Mankato, MN: Creative
Education, 1977. 30 pp. Kareem Abdul-Jabbar is included in this
work written for young people.

355. Rywell, Martin, Editor. Afro-American Encyclopedia. North
Miami, FL: Educational Book Publisher, Inc., 1974. Kareem
Abdul Jabbar, Vol. 5, pp. 1285-1286.

356. Sabin, Louis. Stars of Pro Basketball. New York: Random
House, 1970. 144pp. Lew Alcindor (Kareem Abdul Jabbar) is
included in this work. Written for young adults.

357. Sabin, Louis. Hot Shots of Pro Basketball. New York: Random
House, 1974. 152 pp. Written for juvenile readers. Kareem
Abdul-Jabbar is included in this collection.

358. Santa Barbara County Board of Education. The Emerging Minorities
in America. Santa Barbara, CA: American Bibliographical Center
- Clio Press, 1972. Ferdinand Lewis Alcindor, Jr. (Kareem
Abdul Jabbar), p. 6.

359. Thacher, Alida. Kareem Abdul Jabbar. Milwaukee: Raintree
Editions, 1976.

360. Zavoral, Nolan. Sensitive Superstar, A Profile of Kareem Abdul
Jabbar. Milwaukee: Raintree Editions, 1975. Written for
young adults.

NATE ARCHIBAL

361. Armstrong, Robert. The Guards. Mankato, MN: Creative
Education, 1977. 47 pp. Nate Archibal is included in this collection. Written for juvenile readers.

362. Devaney, John. <u>Tiny: The Story of Nate Archibald</u>. New York:
     G.P. Putnam's Sons, 1977. 159 pp. Written for juvenile readers.

363. Greenfield, Jeff. <u>Tiny Giant: Nate Archibald</u>. Milwaukee:
     Raintree Editions, 1976. 47 pp. Written for juvenile readers.

364. Marsh, Irving T. and Edward Ehre, Editors. <u>Best Sports Stories</u>.
     New York: E.P. Dutton & Co., 1974. Bob Greene, "Nate Archibald
     Is Ten Feet Tall," pp. 125-137.

365. McAdam, Robert. <u>The Skillful Rider</u>. Glendale, CA: Bowmar, 1976.
     Nate Archibald is included in this work.

DICK BARNETT

366. Rywell, Martin, Editor. <u>Afro-American Encyclopedia</u>. North Miami
     FL: Educational Book Publisher, Inc., 1974. Dick Barnett, Vol. 1
     p. 203.

ELGIN BAYLOR

367. Berger, Phil. <u>Heroes of Pro Basketball</u>. New York: Random House,
     1968. 173 pp. Elgin Baylor is included in this collection.

368. Heuman, William. <u>Famous Pro Basketball Stars</u>. New York:
     Dodd, Mead & Co., 1970. 121 pp. Elgin Baylor is included
     in this work.

369. Rainbolt, Richard. <u>Basketball's Big Men</u>. Minneapolis: Lerner
     Publications Co., 1975. 77 pp. Elgin Baylor is included in
     this list.

370. Rywell, Martin, Editor. <u>Afro-American Encyclopedia</u>. North
     Miami, FL: Educational Book Publishers, Inc. 1974. Elgin
     Baylor, Vol. 1, p. 214.

WALT BELLAMY

371. Hollander, Zander. <u>Great Rookies of Pro Basketball</u>. New York:
     Random House, 1967. 172. pp. Walt Bellamy is discussed in this
     work written for juvenile readers.

372. Rywell, Martin, Editor. <u>Afro-American Encyclopedia</u>. North Miami,
     FL: Educational Book Publishers, Inc., 1974. Walter "Bells"
     Bellamy, Vol. 1 p. 232.

DAVE BING

373. Armstrong, Robert. <u>The Guards</u>. Mankato, MN: Creative Education,
     1977. 47 pp. Dave Bing is included in this collection. Written
     for juvenile readers.

374. Rywell Martin, Editor. <u>Afro-American Encyclopedia</u>. North,
     Miami, FL: Educational Book Publishers, Inc., 1974. David
     Bing, Vol. 1 p. 264.

WILT CHAMBERLAIN

375. Allen, Maury. The Record Breakers. Englewood Cliffs, NJ: Prentice-Hall, 1968. "Wilt Chamberlain: Feat of The Century," pp. 33-47. Shot 100 points in a professional basketball game.

376. Bergen, Phil. Heroes of Pro Basketball. New York: Random House, 1968. 173 pp. Wilt Chamberlain is included in this collection.

377. Etter, Les. Basketball Superstars: Three Great Pros. Champaign, IL: Wilt Chamberlain is included in this collection written for young adults.

378. Gutman, Bill. Modern Basketball Superstars. New York: Dodd, Mead & Co., 1975. Wilt Camberlain is included in this collection.

379. Harris, Merv. The Lonely Heroes: Professional Basketball's Great Centers. New York: Viking Press, 1975. 130 pp. There are individual chapters on the fame's outstanding big men such as Wilt Chamberlain.

380. Heaslip, George. Wilt Chamberlain: A Winner. Mankato, MN: Creative Education, 1973. 31 pp. Written for young readers.

381. Heuman, William. Famous Pro Basketball Stars. New York: Dodd, Mead & Co., 1970. 121 pp. Wilt Chamberlain is included in this work. Written for young adults.

382. Liss, Howard. Strange But True Basketball Stories. New York: Random, 1972. 152 pp. Wilt Chamberlain is included in this work written for young adults.

383. Kleid, David. Pro-Basketball's Big Men. New York: Random House, 1973. Wilt Chamberlain is included in this work. Written for juvenile readers.

384. Marsh, Irving T. and Edward Ehre, Editors. Best Sports Stories. New York: E.P. Dutton & Co., 1972. Roy McHugh, "Nobody Roots For Goliath (Wilt Chamberlain)," pp. 156-158.

385. Rainbolt, Richard. Basketball's Big Men. Minneapolis: Lerner Publications Co., 1975. 77 pp. Wilt Chamberlain is discussed in this work. Written for juvenile readers.

386. Robinson, Wilhelmena S. Historical Afro-American Biographies. New York: Publishers Co., 1976. Wilton (Wilt) Chamberlain, pp. 171-174.

387. Rudeen, Kenneth. Wilt Chamberlain. New York: Thomas Y. Crowell, 1970. 32 pp. Written for young people.

388. Rywell, Martin, Editor. Afro-American Encyclopedia. North Miami, FL: Educational Book Publishers, Inc., 1974. Wilt Norman "The Stilt" Chamberlain, Vol. 2, pp. 558-559.

389. Santa Barbara County Board of Education. The Emerging Minorities in America. Santa Barbara, CA: American Bibliographical Center - Clio Press, 1972. Wilt Chamberlain, p. 20.

390. Sullivan, George. Wilt Chamberlain. New York: Grosset & Dunlap, 1966. 186 pp.

391. Toppin, Edgar A. A Biographical History of Blacks in America Since 1528. New York: David McKay, 1971. Wilt Chamberlain pp. 196, 241, 266, 267.

392. Wesley, Charles H. The Quest For Equality: From Civil War To Civil Rights. New York: Publishers Co., 1976, Wilt Chamberlain, p. 199.

JULIUS ERVING

393. Aaseng, Nathan . Basketball High Flyers. Minneapolis: Lerner Publications Co., 1979. Julius Erving is included in this work.

394. Armstrong, Robert. The Forwards. Mankato, MN: Creative Education, 1977. 46 pp. Julius Erving is included in this collection. Written for juvenile readers.

395. Bell, Marty. The Legend Dr. J: The Story of Julius Erving. New York: Coward, McCann & Geoghegan, 1975. 224 pp.

396. Bortstein, Larry. Dr. J-Dave Cowens. New York: Grosset & Dunlap, 1974. Written for juvenile readers.

397. Bortstein, Larry. Julius Erving. Mankato, MN: Creative Education, 1976. Written for juvenile readers.

398. Braun, Thomas. Julius Erving. Mankato, MN: Creative Education, 1976, 31 pp. Written for juvenile readers.

399. Burchard, Marshall. Sports Hero: The Story of Julius Erving. New York: G.P. Putnam's Sons, 1976. 89 pp. Written for juvenile literature readers.

400. Gergen, Joe. Dr. J.: The Story of Julius Erving. New York: Scholastic Book Services, 1975. Written for juvenile readers.

401. Gutman, Bill. Modern Basketball Superstars. New York: Dodd, Mead & Co., 1975. Julius Erving is included in this collection.

402. Gutman, Bill. Superstars of the Sports World. New York: Julian Messner, 1978. 96 pp. A short biography of Julius Erving is included in this collection.

403. Haskins, James. Doctor J: A Biography of Julius Erving. Garden City, New York: Doubleday & Co., 1975. 88 pp. Written for young adults.

404. Jacobs, Linda. Julius Erving: Doctor J and Julius. St. Paul: EMC Corp., 1976. 38 pp.

405. Rywell, Martin, Editor. Afro-American Encyclopedia. North
     Miami, FL: Educational Book Publishers, Inc., 1974 Julius
     "Dr. J." Erving, Vol. 3, pp. 905-906.

406. Sabin, Louis. Hot Shots of Pro Basketball. New York: Random
     House, 1974: 152 pp. Written for juvenile readers. Julius
     Erving is included in this work.

407. Sabin, Louis. The Fabulous Dr. J.: All Time All Star. New
     York: G.P. Putnam 1976.

408. Thomas, Donzell. Dr. "J." Los Angelos: Holloway House
     Publishing Co. 1980. 96 pp.

WALT FRAZIER

409. Armstrong Robert. The Guards. Makato, MN: Creative Education,
     1977, 47 pp. Walt Frazier is included in this collection.
     Written for juvenile readers.

410. Batson, Larry. Walt Frazier. Mankato, MN: Creative Education,
     1977. 31 pp. Written for juvenile readers.

411. Burchard, Sue H. Sports Star: Walt Frazier. New York: Harcourt
     Brace Jovanovich, 1975. 63 pp. Written for juvenile readers.

412. Gutman, Bill. Modern Basketball Superstars. New York: Dodd,
     Mead & Co., 1975. Walt Frazier is included in this work.

413. Sabin, Louis. Hot Shots of Pro Basketball. New York: Random
     House, 1974. 152 pp.: Written for juvenile readers. Walt
     Frazier is included in this work.

414. Sabin, Louis. Stars of Pro Basketball. New York: Random House,
     1970. 144 pp. Walt Frazier is included in this book written
     for young adults.

415. Sabin, Louis. The Picture Story of Walt Frazier. New York:
     Julian Messner, 1976. 61 pp. Written for juvenile readers.

416. Sabin, Louis. Walt Frazier, No. 1 Guard of The NBA. New York:
     G.P. Putnam, 1976. 124 pp. Written for juvenile readers.

ARTIS GILMORE

417. Sabin, Louis. Hot Shots of Pro Basketball. New York: Random
     House, 1974. 152 pp. Written for juvenile readers. Artis
     Gilmore is included in this collection .

418. Rywell, Martin, Editor. Afro-American Encyclopedia. North Miami,
     FL: Educational Book Publishers, Inc. 1974. Artis Gilmore,
     Vol. 4, p. 1066.

CONNIE HAWKINS

419. Sabin, Louis. Stars of Pro Basketball. New York: Random House,
     1970. 144 pp. Connie Hawkins is included in this work.
     Written for young people.

420. Rywell, Martin, Editor. Afro-American Encyclopedia. North
     Miami, FL: Educational Book Publishers, Inc. 1974. Connie
     Hawkins, Vol. 4, p. 1156.

421. Wolf, David. Foul: The Connie Hawkins Story. New York: Holt,
     Rinehart & Winston, 1972. 400 pp.

ELVIN HAYES

422. Aaseng, Nathan. Basketball High-Flyers. Minneapolis: Lerner
     Publications Co. 1979. Elvir Hayes is included in this col-
     lection.

423. Rywell, Martin, Editor. Afro-American Encyclopedia. North Miami,
     FL: Education Book Publishers, Inc., 1974. Elvin "Big E" Hayes
     Vol. 4, p. 1158.

424. Sabin, Louis. Stars of Pro Basketball. New York: Random House,
     1970. 144 pp. Elvin Hayes, is included in this collection.
     Written for young adults.

SPENCER HAYWOOD

425. Rywell, Martin, Editor. Afro-American Encyclopedia. North Miami,
     FL: Educational Book Publishers, Inc., 1974. Spencer Haywood,
     Vol. 4, pp. 1166

426. Sabin, Louis. Hot Shots of Pro Basketball. New York: Random
     House, 1974. 152 pp.: Written for juvenile readers. Spencer
     Haywood is included in this work.

427. Sabin, Louis. Stars of Pro Basketball. New York: Random
     House, 1970. 144 pp. Spencer Haywood is included in this work.
     Written for young people.

EARVIN JOHNSON

428. Dodd, Garet. Magic Johnson. Los Angeles: Holloway House
     Publishing Co. 1980. 96 pp.

BOB LANIER

429. Gutman, Bill. Walton, Thompson, Lanier, Collins. New York:
     Tempo, 1977. 184 pp.

430. Rubin, Bob. Great Centers of Pro Basketball. New York: Random
     House, 1975. Bob Lanier is discussed in this work. Written for
     juvenile readers.

431. Rywell, Martin, Editor. Afro-American Encyclopedia. North Miami,
     FL: Educational Book Publishers, Inc., 1974. Bob Lanier, Vol. 5,
     pp. 1441-1442.

MOSES MALONE

432. Aaseng, Nathan. Basketball High Flyers. Minneapolis: Lerner
     Publications Co., 1979. Moses Malone is included in this work.

BOB McAdoo

433. Aaseng, Nathan. Basketball High Flyers. Minneapolis: Lerner
     Publications Co., 1979. Bob McAdoo is included in this work.

434. Armstrong, Robert. The Centers. Mankato, MN: Creative
     Education, 1977. 47 pp. Bob McAdoo is included in this
     collection. Written for juvenile readers.

435. Haskins, James. Bob McAdoo, Superstar. New York: Lothrop, Lee
     & Shepard, 1977. Written for juvenile readers.

436. O'Reilly, Sean. Meet The Centers. Mankato, MN: Creative
     Education, 1977. 30 pp. Bob McAdoo is included in this work
     written for juvenile readers.

437. Rubin, Bob. Great Centers of Pro Basketball. New York: Random
     House, 1975. Bob McAdoo is discussed in this collection. Written
     for juvenile readers.

438. Tuttle, Anthony. Bob McAdoo. Mankato, MN: Creative Education,
     1976. 31 pp. Written for juvenile readers.

GEORGE McGINNIS

439. Armstrong, Robert. The Forwards. Mankato, MN: Creative Educa-
     tion, 1977. 46 pp. George McGinnis included in this collection.
     Written for juvenile readers.

440. Armstrong, Robert. George McGinnis. Mankato, Minn: Creative
     Education, 1977. 31 pp. Written for juvenile readers.

441. Haskins, James. George McGinnis: Basketball Superstar. New
     York: Hastings House, 1978. Written for juvenile readers.

442. Sabin, Louis. Hot Shots of Pro Basketball. New York: Random
     House, 1974. 152 pp. Written for juvenile readers. George
     McGinnis is included in this collection.

EARL MONROE

443. Hollander, Zander. Great Rookies of Pro Basketball. New York:
     Random House, 1969. 172 pp. Earl Monroe is included in this
     collection. Written for juvenile readers.

444. Jackson, Robert B. Earl The Pearl: The Story of Earl Monroe.
New York: Henry Z. Walck, 1969. 63 pp. Written for young
people.

445. Jackson, Robert B. Earl The Pearl: The Story of Earl Monroe.
Revised Edition. New York: Henry Z. Walck, 1974. 72 pp.
Written for young people.

446. Rywell, Martin, Editor. Afro-American Encyclopedia. North
Miami: FL: Educational Book Publishers, Inc., 1974. Earl
"The Pearl" Monroe, Vol. 6, p. 1677.

WILLIS REED

447. Fox, Larry. Willis Reed: Take-Charge Man of the Knicks. New
York: Gosset, 1970. 176 pp.

448. Rainbolt, Richard. Basketball's Big Men. Minneapolis: Lerner
Publications Co., 1975. 77 pp. Willis Reed is discussed in this
collection. Written for juvenile readers.

449. Rywell Martin, Editor. Afro-American Encyclopedia. North Miami,
Fl: Educational Book Publishers, Inc., 1974. Willis Reed,
Vol. 8. p. 2193.

OSCAR ROBERTSON

450. Berger, Phil. Heroes of Pro Basketball. New York: Random House,
1968. 173 pp. Oscar Robertson is included in this collection.

451. Berkow, Ira. Oscar Robertson: The Golden Year, 1964. Englewood
Cliffs, NJ: Prentice-Hall, 1971. 204 pp.

452. Etter, Les. Basketball Superstars: Three Great Pros. Champaign,
IL: Garrard Publishing Co., 1974. 96 pp. Oscar Robertson is
included in this book for young readers.

453. Heuman, William. Famous Pro Basketball Stars. New York: Dodd,
Mead & Co., 1970. 121 pp. Oscar Robertson is included in this
work.

454. Rywell, Martin, Editor. Afro-American Encyclopedia. North Miami
FL: Educational Book Publishers, Inc., 1974. Oscar Palmer
"Big O". Robertson, Vol. 8, p. 2244.

CAZZIE RUSSELL

455. Rywell, Martin, Editor. Afro-American Encyclopedia. North Miami,
FL: Educational Book Publishers, Inc., 1974. Cazzie Lee Russell,
Vol 8, p. 2288.

BILL RUSSELL

456. Berger, Phil. Heroes of Pro Basketball. New York: Random House,
1968. 173 pp. New York: Random House, 1968. 173 pp. Bill
Russell is included in this collection.

457. Deegan, Paul J. Bill Russell. Mankato, MN: Creative Education, 1973. 31 pp. Written for juvenile readers.

458. Edwards, Harry. The Revolt of The Black Athlete. New York: Free Press, 1969. Bill Russell, pp. 32, 23, 39, 72, 120.

459. Harris, Merv. The Lonely Heroes: Professional Basketball's Great Centers. New York: Viking Press, 1975. 230 pp. There are individual chapters on the games outstanding big men, such as Bill Russell.

460. Hirshberg, Albert. Basketball's Greatest Stars. New York: G.P. Putnam's & Sons, 1963. 191 pp. Bill Russell is included in this work.

461. Hirshberg, Albert. Bill Russell of The Boston Celtics. New York: Julian Messner Co., 1963. 191 pp.

462. Kleid, David. Pro Basketball's Big Men. New York: Random House, 1973. Bill Russell is discussed in this work. Written for juvenile readers.

463. Marsh, Irving T. and Edward Ehre, Editors. Best Sports Stories. New York: E.P. Dutton & Co. 1964. Gilbert Rogin, "Playing A Child's Game (Bill Russell)," pp. 33-44.

464. Marsh, Irving T. and Edward Ehre, Editors. Best Sports Stories. New York: E.P. Dutton & Co., 1969. George Kiseda, "The Proud Old Men Didn't Collapse (Bill Russell)," pp. 203-206.

465. Rainbolt, Richard. Basketball's Big Men. Minneapolis: Lerner Publications, Co., 1975. 77 pp. Bill Russell is included in this work.

466. Rywell, Martin, Editor. Afro-American Encyclopedia. North Miami, FL: Educational Book Publishers, Inc., 1974. William "Bill" Felton Russell, Vol. 8, pp. 2291-2293.

467. Santa Barbara County Board of Education. The Emerging Minorities in America. Santa Barbara, CA: American Bibliographical Center - Clio Press, 1972. Bill Russell, p. 68.

468. Toppin, Edgar A. A Biographical History of Blacks in America Since 1528. New York: David McKay, 1971. Bill Russell, pp. 196, 241, 405, 406, 407, 408.

469. Wesley, Charles H. The Quest For Equality: From Civil War To Civil Rights. New York: Publishers Co., 1976. Bill Russell, p. 199.

MAURICE STOKES

470. Hollander, Zander. Great Rookies of Pro Basketball. New York: Random House, 1969, 172 pp. Maurice Stokes is included in this work. Written for juvenile readers.

471. Rywell, Martin, Editor. Afro-American Encyclopedia. North
     Miami, FL: Educational Book Publishers, Inc., 1974. Maurice
     Stokes, Vol. 9, p. 2573.

DAVID THOMPSON

472. Armstrong, Robert. The Forwards. Mankato, MN: Creative
     Education, 1977. 46 pp. David Thompson is included in this
     collection. Written for juvenile readers.

NATE THURMOND

473. Harris, Merv. The Lonely Heroes: Professional Basketball's
     Great Centers. New York: Viking Press, 1975. 230 pp. There
     are indivudal chapters on the game's outstanding big men such
     as Nate Thurmond.

474. Rywell, Martin, Editor. Afro-American Encyclopedia. North
     Miami, FL: Educational Book Publishers, Inc., 1974. Nate
     Thurmond, Vol. 9, p. 2627.

WES UNSELD

475. Armstrong, Robert. The Centers. Mankato, MN: Creative
     Education, 1977. 47 pp. Wes Unseld's included in this
     collection. Written for juvenile readers.

476. Hollander, Zander. Great Rookies of Pro Basketball. New York:
     Random House, 1969. 172 pp. West Unsel is included in this work.
     Written for juvenile readers.

477. Rubin, Bob. Great Center of Pro Basketball. New York: Random
     House, 1975. Wes Unseld is included in this work. Written for
     juvenile readers.

478. Rywell, Martin, Editor. Afro-American Encyclopedia. North Miami,
     FL: Educational Book Publishers, Inc., 1974. Wes Unseld, Vol. 9,
     p. 2704.

LENNY WILKENS

479. Rywell, Martin, Editor. Afro-American Encyclopedia. North Miami,
     FL: Educational Book Publishers, Inc., 1974. Lenny Wilkens,
     Vol. 9, pp. 2810-2811.

BOXING

MUHAMMAD ALI

480. Atyeo, Don. Blood & Guts: Violence in Sports. New York:
     Paddington Press, Ltd. 1979 Muhammad Ali, pp. 127, 128, 129,
     147, 148, 166, 179, 181, 330, 363, 368, 369.

481. Atyeo, Don and Felix Dennis. The Holy Warrior: Muhammad Ali.
     New York: Simon & Schuster, 1975. 112 pp.

482. Bockris, Wylie. Ali. New York: Freeinay Press, 1974.

483. Bortstein, Larry. Ali. New York: Tower Books, 1971. 173 pp.

484. Burchard, Marshall. Sports Hero: Muhammad Ali. New York:
     G.P. Putnam's Sons, 1975. 89 pp. Written for juvenile readers.

485. Carpenter, Harry. Boxing: A Pictorial History. Chicago:
     Regnery co., 1975 190 pp. "Foreword" by Muhammad Ali.

486. Contrell, John. Muhammad Ali Who Once Was Cassius Clay. New
     York: Funk and Wagnalls, 1968. pp. 363.

487. Edwards, Audry. Muhummad Ali: The People's Champ. Boston:
     Little, Brown, and Co., 1977. 181 pp.

488. Edwards, Harry. The Revolt of The Black Athlete. New York:
     Free Press, 1969. Muhammad Ali, pp. 31, 58, 63, 74, 89, 90.

489. Fisher, Art and Neal Marshall. Garden of Innocents. New York:
     E.P. Dutton, 1972. 186 pp. Discusses the "fight of the century,"
     between Muhammad Ali and Joe Frazier.

490. Hoskins, Robert. Muhammad Ali. Los Angeles: Holloway House
     Publishing Co., 1979. 96 pp.

491. Lardner, Rex. Ali: Again The Champion!. New York: Grosset and
     Dunlap, 1974.

492. Lipsyte, Robert. Free To Be Muhammad Ali. New York: Harpers &
     Row, 1978. 124 pp.

493. Mailer, Norman. King of The Hill. New York: New American
     Library, 1971. 93 pp. Mainly about the Ali-Frazier fight of
     1971.

494. Mailer, Norman. The Fight (Muhammad Ali vs. George Foreman).
     Boston: Little, Brown & Co., 1975. 239 pp.

495. Marsh, Irving T. and Edward Ehre, Editors. Best Sports Stories.
     New York: E.P. Dutton & Co., 1963. Myron Cope, "Feats of Clay,"
     pp. 25-38.

496. Marsh, Irving T. and Edward Ehre, Editors. Best Sports Stories.
     New York: E.P. Dutton & Co., 1968. Ray Grody, "The Torture
     Chamber (Muhammad Ali)," pp. 23-25.

497. Marsh, Irving T. and Edward Ehre, Editors. Best Sports Stories.
     New York: E.P. Dutton & Co., 1971. Bill Lee, "Those Three
     Terrible Left Hooks (Muhammad Ali)," pp. 197-201.

498. Marsh, Irving T. and Edward Ehre, Editors. Best Sports Stories.
New York: E.P. Dutton & Co., 1972. Bill Lee, "The First Beating
of His Life (Muhammad Ali), " pp. 159-163.

499. Marsh, Irving T. and Edward Ehre, Editors. Best Sports Stories.
New York: E.P. Dutton & Co., 1973. Leonard Gardner, "Pain
and Violence As A Way of Life (Muhammad Ali)," pp. 168-182.

500. Marsh, Irving T. and Edward Ehre, Editors. Best Sports Stories.
New York: E.P. Dutton & Co., 1974. Dave Anderson, "The Greatest
Is Now The Tiredest (Muhammad Ali)," pp. 177-179.

501. Marsh, Irving T. and Edward Ehre, Editors. Best Sports Stories.
New York: E.P. Dutton & Co., 1975. Will Grimsley, "Muhammad
Ali: Athlete, Folk Hero, World Social Force," pp. 164-167.

502. Marsh, Irving T. and Edward Ehre, Editors. Best Sports Stories.
New York: E.P. Dutton & Co., 1975. Peter Bonventre and Peter
Axthelm," Ali-You Gotta Believe! ," pp. 159-163.

503. Marsh, Irving T. and Edward Ehre, Editors. Best Sports Stories.
New York: E.P. Dutton, 1978. John Shulian, "No Garden Party
For Ali," pp. 52-54.

504. Okpaku, Joseph. Superfight II. New York. Third Press, 1974.
126 pp. Second Fight between Muhammad Ali and Joe Frazier.

505. Olsen Jack. Black Is Best: The Riddle of Cassius Clay. New
York: Dell, 1967. 255 pp.

506. Olsen, James T. Muhammad Ali: "I Am The Greatest". Minnesota:
Creative Education, 1974. 30 pp. Written for juvenile readers.

507. Rywell, Martin, Editor. Afro-American Encyclopedia. North
Miami, FL: Educational Book Publishers, Inc., 1974. Muhammad
Ali, Vol. 1, pp. 110-113.

508. Schulberg, Budd. Loser and Still Champion: Muhammad Ali.
Garden City, NY: Doubleday & Co., 1974. 168 pp.

509. Sheed, Wilfred. Muhammad Ali: A Portrait in Words and
Photographs. New York: Thomas Y. Crowell, 1975. 255 pp.

510. Sullivan, George. The Cassius Clay Story. New York: Fleet
Publishing Cop., 1964. 116 p.

511. Torres, Jose. Sting Like A Bee. New York: Abelard-Schuman,
1971. 248 pp. Book discusses Muhammad Ali.

512. Vecsey, George. Frazier/Ali. New York: Scholastic Book
Services, 1972. 144 pp.

513. Wilson, Beth P. Muhammad Ali. New York: G.P. Putnams, 1974.
62 pp. Written for young adults.

HENRY ARMSTRONG

514. Bromberg, Lester. Boxing's Unforgettable Fights. New York: Ronald Press Co., 1962. 351 pp. Henry Armstrong, pp. 227, 230, 248, 250, 251, 252, 253, 256.

515. Carpenter, Harry. Masters of Boxing. New York: A.S. Barnes & Co., Inc., 1964. "Fight The Good Fight" (Henry Armstrong, born 1912).

516. Marsh, Irving T. and Edward Ehre, Editors. Best Sports Stories. New York: E.P. Dutton & Co., 1953. Harold Rosenthal," The Ten Months That Shook The Boxing World (Henry Armstrong)," pp. 494-201.

517. Myrdal, Gunnar. An American Dilemma: The Negro Problem and Modern Democracy. New York: Harper & Row, Publishers, 1944. Henry Armstrong, pp. 734, 903n, 988.

518. Rywell, Martin, Editor. Afro-American Encyclopedia. North Miami, FL: Educational Book Publishers, Inc., 1974. Henry "Hank" Armstrong. Vol. 1, pp. 161-162.

HOGAN BASSEY

519. Rywell, Martin, Editor. Afro-American Encyclopedia. North Miami, Fl: Educational Book Publishers, Inc., 1974. Hogan "Kid" Bassey, Vol. 1, p. 211.

RUBIN CARTER

520. Marsh, Irving T. and Edward Ehre, Editors. Best Sports Stories. New York: E.P. Dutton & Co., 1964. Leonard Shecter "The Baleful Look of a New Liston (Rubin Carter)," pp. 186-196.

521. Rywell, Martin, Editor. Afro-American Encyclopedia. North Miami, FL: Educational Book Publishers, Inc., 1974. Rubin "Hurricane" Carter, Vol. 2, p. 544.

EZZARD CHARLES

522. Bromberg, Lester. Boxing's Unforgettable Fights. New York: Ronald Press Co., 1962. 351 pp. Ezzard Charles, pp. 291, 302, 303, 304, 305, 314, 316, 338.

523. Marsh, Irving T. and Edward Ehre, Editors. Best Sports Stories. New York: E.P. Dutton & Co., 1952. Jerry Cohen, "It Happened (Ezzard Charles)," pp. 214-216.

524. Marsh, Irving T. and Edward Ehre, Editors. Best Sports Stories. New York: E.P. Dutton & Co., 1959. Bill Rives, "202 Pounds of Hollow Shell (Ezzard Charles)," pp. 162-163.

525. Marsh, Irving T. and Edward Ehre, Editors. Best Sports Stories. New York: E.P. Dutton & Co. 1951. James P. Dawson, "Bombed Bombed (Ezzard Charles)," pp. 23-27.

526. Rywell, Martin, Editor. Afro-American Encyclopedia. North
     Miami: FL: Educational Book Publishers, Inc., 1974. Ezzard
     Charles. Vol. 2, pp. 562-563.

GEORGE DIXON

527. Rywell, Martin, Editor. Afro-American Encyclopedia. North
     Miami, FL: Educational Book Publishers, Inc. 1974. George
     "Little Chocolate" Dixon, Vol. 3, p. 779.

TIGER FLOWERS

528. Rywell, Martin, Editor. Afro-American Encyclopedia. North
     Miami, FL: Educational Book Publishers, 1974. Tiger Flowers,
     Vol. 4, pp. 965-966.

GEORGE FOREMAN

529. Marsh, Irving T. and Edward Ehre, Editors. Best Sports Stories.
     New York: E.P. Dutton & Co. 1973, Leonard Gardner, "Pain and
     Violence As A Way of Life (George Foreman)," pp. 168-182.

530. Marsh, Irving T. and Edward Ehre, Editors. Best Sports Stories.
     New York: E.P. Dutton & Co., 1974. Eddie Muller, "It Took
     Him 4 Minutes 35 Seconds (George Foreman)," pp. 172-176.

531. Marsh, Irving T. and Edward Ehre, Editors. Best Sports Stories.
     New York: E. Dutton & Co., 1974. Will Grimsley, "The Square
     Who Became Champion (George Foreman)," pp. 180-183.

532. Rywell, Martin, Editor. Afro-American Encyclopedia. North Miami,
     FL: Educational Book Publishers, Inc., 1974. George Foreman, Vol.
     4 pp. 973.

BOB FOSTER

533. Rywell, Martin, Editor. Afro American Encyclopedia. North Miami,
     FL: Educational Book Publishers, Inc. 1974. Bob Foster,
     Vol, 4, p. 983

JOE FRAZIER

534. Marsh, Irving T. and Edward Ehre, Editors. Best Sports Stories.
     New York: E.P. Dutton & Co., 1969. Roy McHugh, "(Emile)
     Griffith Wore His Tuxedo... Frazier Ran Out of Words," pp. 191-
     193.

535. Marsh, Irving T. and Edward Ehre, Editors. Best Sports Stories.
     New York: E.P. Dutton & Co., 1972. Bill Lee, "The First Beating
     of His Life (Joe Frazier)," pp. 159-163.

536. Marsh, Irving T. and Edward Ehre, Editors. Best Sports Stories.
     New York: E.P. Dutton & Co.. 1972. David Wolf, "How They Got
     Joe Frazier To The Fight," pp. 167-178.

551. Lardner, John. White Hope and Other Tigers. Philadelphia:
     J.P. Lippincott, 1951. 190 pp. Jack Johnson is discussed in
     this book.

552. Lardner, Rex. Legendary Champions. New York: American Heritage,
     1972. Jack Johnson, pp. 180-184.

553. Lucas, Bob. Black Gladiator: A Biography of Jack Johnson. New
     York: Dell, 1970, 189 pp.

554. Rice, Harold. Within The Ropes. New York: Stephen-Paul, 1946.
     Jack Johnson, pp. 108-115.

555. Roberts, Randy. Jack Dempsey: The Manassa Mauler. Baton Rouge:
     Louisiana State University Press, 1979. 310 pp. Jack Johnson,
     pp. 20, 21, 26, 27, 28, 34, 39, 59, 51, 54, 56, 64, 141, 142,
     268.

556. Rogers, Joel A. World's Great Men of Color. Vol. 2. New York:
     J.A. Rogers, 1947. "Jack Johnson: World Heavyweight Champion
     and Demolisher of "The White Hope," pp. 474-489.

557. Rywell, Martin, Editor. Afro-American Encyclopedia. North
     Miami, FL: Educational Book Publishers, Inc., 1974. Jack
     Johnson, Vol, 5, pp. 1342-1343.

558. Santa Barbara County Board of Education. The Emerging Minorities
     in America. Santa Barbara, CA: American Bibliographical Center
     -Clio Press, 1972. Jack Johnson, p. 45.

559. Toppin, Edgar A. A Biographical History of Blacks in America
     Since 1528. New York: David McKay, 1971. Jack Johnson pp.
     159, 333, 334, 335.

560. Van BenBergh, Tony. The Jack Johnson. London: Hamilton, 1956.

RALPH JONES

561. Bromberg, Lester. Boxing's Unforgettable Fights. New York:
     Ronald Press Co., 1962. 351 pp. Ralph ("Tiger") Jones, pp. 321,
     322, 323, 324, 325.

562. Rywell, Martin, Editor. Afro-American Encyclopedia. North Miami,
     FL: Educational Book Publishers, Inc., 1974. Ralph "Tiger" Jones,
     Vol. 5, p. 1377.

JOHN HENRY LEWIS

563. Rywell, Martin, Editor. Afro-American Encyclopedia. North
     Miami, FL: Educational Book Publishers, Inc., 1974. John
     Henry Lewis, Vol. 5, p. 1469.

SONNY LISTON

564. Marsh, Irving T. and Edward Ehre, Editor. Best Sports Stories. New York: E.P. Dutton & Co., 1963. Jesse Abramson, "2 Minutes 6 Seconds After 2 years (Sonny Liston)," pp. 126-129.

565. Marsh, Irving T. and Edward Ehre, Editors. Best Sports Stories. New York: E.P. Dutton & Co. 1965. Jack Murphy "The Champ Behind The Mask (Sonny Liston)," pp. 197-203.

566. Rywell, Martin, Editor. Afro-American Encyclopedia. North Miami, FL: Education Book Publishers, Inc., 1974. Charles "Sonny" Liston, Vol. 5, pp. 1491-1492.

567. Young, Andrew Sturgeon Nash. Sonny Liston: The Champ Nobody Wanted. Chicago: Johnson Publishing Company, 1963. 224 pp.

JOE LOUIS

568. Astor, Gerald. "... And A Credit To His Race": The Hard Life and Times of Joseph Louis Barrow, A.K.A. Joe Louis. New York: Saturday Review Press E.P. Dutton & Co., Inc., 1974. 275 pp.

569. Bardolph, Richard. The Negro Vanguard. New York: Vintage Books, 1961. Joe Louis, pp. 262, 270, 295, 453, 454, 455.

570. Bell, Norman. The Fighting Life of a Fighter: How Joe Louis Became the World's Greatest Heavyweight. London: The War Fact Press. 1943. 65 pp.

571. Bromberg, Lester. Boxing's Unforgetable Fights. New York: Ronald Press Co., 1962. 351 pp. Joe Louis pp. 218-228, 237-246, 259, 261-270, 280-285, 302, 304, 315, 338, 339.

572. Carpenter, Harry. Masters of Boxing. New York: A.S. Barnes & Co., Inc., 1964. "Headmaster" (Joe Louis, born 1914).

573. Deusen, John George Van. Brown Bombers: The Story of Joe Louis. Philadelphia: Dorrance & Co., 1940. 163 pp.

574. Edmonds, Anthony O. Joe Louis: Grand Rapids, Mich: Eerdmans, 1973. 112 pp.

575. Embree, Edwin Rogers. 13 Against The Odds. New York: Viking Press, 1944. Joe Louis, pp. 534-545.

576. Every, Edward Van. Joe Louis. New York: Frederick A. Stokes Co., 1936.

577. Fleishcher, Nathaniel S. The Louis Legend: The Amazing Story of the Brown Bomber's Rise To The Heavyweight Championship of The World and His Retirement From Boxing. New York: N.P., 1956. 181 pp.

578. Heyn, Ernest V. Twelve Sport. Immortals. New York: Bartholomew House, 1949. One section entitled "Brown Bomber, The Saga of Joe Louis" is included in this collection.

579. Jones, Claudias. Lift Every Voice for Victory!: Joe Louis. New York: New Age Publishers, Inc. 1942. 14 pp.

580. Kaese, Harold. Famous American Athletes of Today. Boston: Page, 1938. Joseph "Joe" Louis, pp. 133-160.

581. Kessler, Gene. Joe Louis, The Brown Bomber. Racine, WI: Whitman, 1936. 237 pp.

582. Libby, Bill. Joe Louis: The Brown Bomber. New York: Random House, 1980, 224 pp. Written for juvenile readers.

583. Marsh, Irving T. and Edward Ehre, Editors. Best Sports Stories. New York: E.P. Dutton & Co., 1949. James P. Dawson, "Potent Punch Joe Louis". pp. 185-192.

584. Marsh, Irving T. and Edward Ehre, Editors. Best Sports Stories. New York: E.P. Dutton & Co. 1951. James P. Dawson, "Bomber Bombed (Joe Louis)," pp. 23-27.

585. Marsh, Irving T. and Edward Ehre, Editors. Best Sports Stories. New York: E.P. Dutton & Co. 1952. Joseph C. Nichols, "Joe Louis Was Knocked Out Last Night," pp. 211-213.

586. Marsh, Irving and Edward Ehre, Editors. Best Sports Stories. New York: E.P. Dutton & Co. 1966. Morris Siegel, "The Born Loser (Joe Louis), " pp. 144-146.

587. McAdam, Robert. Viva Gonzalez. Glendale, CA: Bourmar, 1972, 63 pp. A short biography of Joe Louis is included. Written for young people.

588. Miller, Margery. Joe Louis: American. New York: A.A. Wyn Publisher, 1945. 181 pp.

589. Miller, Margery. Joe Louis: American. Revised Edition. New York: Hill and Wang, 1961. 198 pp.

590. Myrdal, Gunnar. An American Dilemma: The Negro Problem and Modern Democracy. New York: Harper & Row, Publishers, 1944. Joe Louis, pp. 734, 903n, 988, 1184, 1396.

591. Nagler, Barney. Brown Bomber: The Pilgrimage of Joe Louis. New York: World, 1972. 236 pp.

592. Rice, Grantland. The Tumult and The Shouting: My Life in Sports. New York: A.S. Barnes & Co., 1954. Joe Louis, pp. 133, 248, 249, 250.

593. Richardson, Ben. Great American Negroes. New York: Thomas Y. Crowell Co., 1945. Joe Louis pp. 278-290.

594. Robinson, Wilhelmena S. Historical Afro-American Biographies.
     New York: Publishers, 1968. Joe Louis, pp. 223-224.

595. Rogers, Joel A. World's Great Men of Color. Vol. 2. New York:
     J.A. Rogers, 1947." Joe Louis: The Superman of the Prize
     Ring," pp. 530-534.

596. Rywell, Martin, Editor. Afro-American Encyclopedia.   North
     Miami, FL: Educational Book Publishers, Inc., 1974. Joe
     "Brown Bomber" Louis, Vol. 5, pp. 1504-1505.

597. Santa Barbara County Board of Education. The Emerging Minorities
     in America. Santa Barbara, CA: American Bibliographical Center-
     Clio Press, 1972. Joe Louis, p. 53.

598. Scott, Neil. Joe Louis: A Picture Story of His Life.
     New York: Greenberg, 1947. 126 pp.

599. Silverman, Al. More Sports Titans of the 20th Century. New York:
     G.P. Putnam Sons, 1969. 224 pp. Joe Louis is included in this
     work.

600. Toppin, Edgar A. A Biographical History of Blacks in America
     Since 1528. New York: David McKay, 1971. Joe Louis, pp. 186,
     241, 306, 354, 355, 356, 357, 358.

601. Vitale, Rugio. Joe Louis: Biography of Champion. Los Angeles:
     Holloway House Publishing Co., 1979. 224 pp.

602. Wesley, Charles H. The Quest For Equality: From Civil War To
     Civil Rights. New York: Publishers Co., 1976. Joe Louis, p.
     199.

ARCHIE MOORE

603. Bromberg, Lester. Boxing's Unforgettable Fights. New York:
     Ronald Press, Co., 1962. 351 pp. Archie Moore, pp. 331, 332,
     333, 334, 335, 336.

604. Carpenter, Harry. Masters of Boxing. New York: A.S. Barnes
     & Co., Inc., 1964. "Wizard of Oz...And Pounds" (Archie Moore,
     born ca. 1913).

605. Marsh, Irving T. and Edward Ehre, Editors. Best Sports Stories.
     New York: E.P. Dutton & Co., 1959. Jesse Abramson, "The Perils
     of Archie (Moore)," pp. 25-27.

606. Marsh, Irving T. and Edward Ehre, Editors. Best Sports Stories.
     New York: E.P. Dutton & Co., 1960. Irv Goodman, "Archie Moore's
     Secret," pp. 158-166.

607. Rywell, Martin, Editor. Afro-American Encyclopedia. North Miami,
     FL: Educational Book Publishers, Inc., 1974. Archie Moore, Vol.
     6, pp. 1681-1682.

FLOYD PATTERSON

608. Bromberg, Lester. Boxing's Unforgettable Fights. New York:
     Ronald Press Co., 1962. 351 pp. Floyd Patterson, pp. 337,
     338, 339, 340, 341, 342, 343.

609. Marsh, Irving T. and Edward Ehre, Editors. Best Sports Stories.
     New York: E.P. Dutton & Co., 1957. Paul O'Neil, "The Heavyweight
     Champion (Floyd Patterson)," pp. 143-154.

610. Marsh, Irving T. and Edward Ehre, Editors. Best Sports Stories.
     New York: E.P. Dutton & Co., 1959. Arthur Daley, "Courage and
     Fortitude Were Not Enough (Floyd Patterson)," pp. 153-157.

611. Marsh, Irving T. and Edward Ehre, Editors. Best Sports Stories.
     New York: E.P. Dutton & Co., 1960. Jesse Abramson, "The Right
     Was The Might (Floyd Patterson)," pp. 139-142.

612. Marsh, Irving T. and Edward Ehre, Editors. Best Sports Stories.
     New York: E.P. Dutton & Co. 1960. Gay Talese, "The Beaten
     (Floyd Patterson)," pp. 143-144.

613. Marsh, Irving T. and Edward Ehre, Editors. Best Sports Stories.
     New York: E.P. Dutton & Co., 1963. Milton Gross, "The Long
     Journey Home (Floyd Patterson)," pp. 130-133.

614. Marsh, Irving T. and Edward Ehre, Editors. Best Sports Stories.
     New York: E.P. Dutton & Co. 1963. Jesse Abramson, "2 Minutes
     6 Seconds After 2 years (Floyd Patterson)," pp. 126-129.

615. Marsh, Irving T. and Edward Ehre, Editors. Best Sports Stories.
     New York: E.P. Dutton & Co., 1964. John P. Carmichael, "Only
     Four Seconds More (Floyd Patterson)," pp. 163-164.

616. Marsh, Irving T. and Edward Ehre. Editors. Best Sports Stories.
     New York: E.P. Dutton & Co., 1965. Gay Talese, "The Loser
     (Floyd Patterson)," pp. 173-190.

617. Newcombe, Jack. Floyd Patterson Heavyweight King. New York:
     Bartholemew, 1961. 159 pp.

618. Rywell, Martin, Editor. Afro-American Encyclopedia. North Miami,
     FL: Educational Book Publishers, Inc. 1974. Floyd Patterson,
     Vol. 7, pp. 1986-1987.

BILL RICHARD

619. Rywell, Martin, Editor. Afro-American Encyclopedia. North
     Miami, FL: Educational Book Publishers, Inc., 1974. Bill
     Richmond, Vol. 8, p. 2230.

620. Smythe, Mabel M., Editor. The Black American Reference Book.
     Englewood Cliffs, NJ: Prentice-Hall, Inc., 1976. Bill
     Richmond, p. 946.

SUGAR RAY ROBINSON

621. Bardolph, Richard. The Negro Vanguard. New York: Vintage Books,
     1961. Sugar Ray Robinson, pp. 453, 454, 455.

622. Bromberg, Lester. Boxing's Unforgettable Fights. New York:
     Ronald Press Co., 1962. 351 pp. Sugar Ray Robinson, pp. 306-
     311, 321, 322, 323, 324.

623. Carpenter, Harry. Masters of Boxing. New York: A.S. Barnes &
     Co. Inc., 1964 "Sweet Prince - Sour King" (Sugar Ray Robinson,
     born 1920), pp. 52-65.

624. Graziano, Rocky with Rowland Barber. Somebody Up There Likes
     Me. New York: Simon & Schuster, 1955. 376 pp. Sugar Ray
     Robinson, pp. 1,2, 3, 309, 360, 361, 362.

625. Marsh, Irving T. and Edward Ehre, Editors. Best Sports Stories.
     New York: E.P. Dutton & Co., 1951. Marshall Smith, "Sugar
     Ray Robinson," pp. 156-164.

626. Marsh, Irving T. and Edward Ehre, Editors. Best Sports Stories.
     New York: E.P. Dutton & Co., 1952. Harry Keck, "Sugar and
     Turpin," pp. 221-223.

627. Marsh, Irving T. and Edward Ehre, Editors. Best Sports Stories.
     New York: E.P. Dutton & Co., 1957. Bill Roeder, "But Robinson
     Looked," pp. 85-86.

628. Marsh, Irving T. and Edward Ehre, Editors. Best Sports Stories.
     New York: E.P. Dutton & Co., 1953. Jesse Abramson, "Melted
     Sugar (Ray Robinson)," pp. 19-23.

629. Marsh, Irving T. and Edward Ehre, Editors. Best Sports Stories.
     New York: E.P. Dutton & Co., 1956. Bill Leiser, "Forget He
     "Was" (Sugar Ray)," pp. 174-176.

630. Marsh, Irving T. and Edward Ehre, Editors. Best Sports Stories.
     New York: E.P. Dutton & Co., 1965. Dave Anderson, "The
     Longest Day of Sugar Ray," pp. 35-48.

631. Marsh, Irving T. and Edward Ehre, Editors. Best Sports Stories.
     New York: E.P. Dutton & Co., 1966. Jesse Abramson, "(Sugar
     Ray) Robinson's Pipe Dream," pp. 23-25.

632. Robinson, Wilhemena S. Historical Afro-American Biographies.
     New York: Publishers, 1968. Ray (Sugar Ray) Robinson, p. 246.

633. Rywell, Martin, Editor. Afro-American Encyclopedia. North Miami,
     FL: Educational Book Publishers, Inc., 1974. Ray "Sugar
     Ray" Robinson. Vol. 8, p. 2256.

634. Wesley, Charles H. The Quest For Equality: From Civil War To
     Civil Rights. New York: Publishers Co., 1976. Sugar Ray
     Robinson, p. 199.

54   BLACK ATHLETES IN THE UNITED STATES

BATTLING SIKI

635. Cunard, Nancy, Editor. Negro: An Anthology. New York:
Frederick Ungar Publishing Co., 1970. Battling Siki, pp. 209-
211.

636. Rywell, Martin, Editor. Afro-American Encyclopedia. North
Miami, FL: Educational Book Publishers, Inc., 1974. Battling
Siki, Vol. 8, pp. 2343-2344.

DICK TIGER

637. Marsh, Irving T. and Edward Ehre, Editors. Best Sports Stories.
New York: E.P. Dutton & Co., 1972. Bob Waters, "(Dick) Tiger
Took Wisdom With Him," pp. 164-622.

638. Rywell, Martin, Editor. Afro-American Encyclopedia. North
Miami, FL: Educational Book Publishers, Inc., 1974. Dick
Tiger Vol. 9, pp. 2629-2630.

JOSE TORRES

639. Rywell, Martin, Editor. Afro-American Encyclopedia. North
Miami, FL: Educational Book Publishers, Inc., 1974. Jose
Torres, Vol. 9, p. 2367.

RANDOLPH TURPIN

640. Rywell, Martin, Editor. Afro-American Encyclopedia. North Miami,
FL: Educational Book Publishers, 1974. Randolph "Rand" Turpin,
Vol. 9, pp. 2670-2671.

JERSEY JOE WALCOTT

641. Bromberg, Lester. Boxing's Unforgettable Fights. New York:
Ronald Press Co., 1962. 351 pp. Jersey Joe Walcott, pp. 282,
283, 299, 302, 304, 305, 313, 314, 315, 316, 317, 318, 319, 338.

642. Marsh, Irving T. and Edward Ehre, Editors. Best Sports Stories.
New York: E.P. Dutton & Co., 1952. Jerry Cohen, "It Happened
(Jersey Joe Walcott)," pp. 214-216.

643. Marsh, Irving T. and Edward Ehre, Editors. Best Sports Stories.
New York: E.P. Dutton & Co., 1953. James P. Dawson," ...
And New Champion (Jersey Joe Walcott)," pp. 161-165.

644. Rywell, Martin, Editor. Afro-American Encyclopedia. North
Miami, FL: Educational Book Publishers, Inc., 1974. Jersey
Joe Walcott, Vol. 9, pp. 2728-2729.

FOOTBALL

JIM BROWN

645. Allen, Maury. The Record Breakers. Englewood Cliffs, NJ:
     Prentice-Hall, 1968. "Jimmy Brown: Measure of a Man," pp. 104-
     117. He scored 237 yards gained in two separate games.

646. Hollander, Zander, Compiler. Great Moments in Pro Football. New
     York: Random House, 1969. 174 pp. "Jim Brown's Repeat
     Performance" by J. Zanger is discussed in this work.

647. Issacs, Stan. Jim Brown, The Golden Years. Englewood Cliffs,
     N.J: Prentice Hall, 1970. 150 pp.

648. Klein, Larry. Jim Brown; The Running Back. New York: G.P.
     Putnam's, Sons, 1965. 158 pp.

649. May, Julian. Jim Brown: Runs With The Ball. Mankato, MN:
     Crestwood House 1972. 47 pp. Written for juvenile readers.

650. Rainbolt, Richard. Football's Rugged Running Backs! Minneapolis:
     Lerner Publications Co., 1975. 71 pp. Jim Brown is included in
     this book written for juvenile readers.

651. Robinson, Wilhelmena S. Historical Afro-American Biographies.
     New York: Publishers, 1968. James Nathaniel Brown, pp. 169-
     170.

652. Terzian, James P. and Jim Benagh. The Jimmy Brown Story. New
     York: Julian Messner, 1964.

653. Toback, James. Jim: The Author's Self-Centered Memoir on The
     Great Jim Brown. Garden City, NY: Doubleday & Co. 1971.
     133 pp.

654. Rywell, Martin, Editor. Afro-American Encyclopedia. North
     Miami, FL: Educational Book Publishers, Inc., 1974. Jimmy
     Brown, Vol. 2, pp. 421-422.

655. Santa Barbara County Board of Education. The Emerging Minorities
     in America. Santa Barbara, CA: American Bibliographical Center-
     Clio Press, 1972. Jim Brown, p. 15.

656. Toppin, Edgar A. A Biographical History of Blacks in America
     Since 1528. New York: David McKay, 1971. Jim Brown, pp. 196,
     241, 259.

657. Wesley, Charles H. The Quest For Equality: From Civil War To
     Civil Rights. New York: Publishers Co., 1976. Jim Brown,
     p. 199.

LARRY BROWN

658. Libby, Bill. Star Running Backs of The NFL. New York: Random House, 1971. p. 144 pp. Larry Brown is included in this work.

659. Marsh, Irving T. and Edward Ehre, Editors. Best Sports Stories. New York: E.P. Dutton & Co., 1974. Ray Diginger, "Larry Brown: King of The Hill," pp. 29-35.

660. Rywell, Martin, Editor. Afro-American Encyclopedia. North Miami, FL: Educational Book Publishers, Inc., 1974. Larry Brown, Vol. 2, p. 434.

WILLIE DAVIS

661. Anderson, Dave. Great Defensive Players of the NFL. New York: Random House, 1967. 176 pp. Willie Davis is included in this collection.

662. McAdams, Robert. Viva Gonzalez. Glendale, CA: Bowmar, 1972. 63 pp. A short biography of Willie Davis is included. Written for young people.

663. Rywell, Martin, Editor. Afro-American Encyclopedia. North Miami, FL: Educational Book Publishers, Inc., 1974. Willie Davis, Vol. 3, p. 728.

TONY DORSETT

664. Biffle, Marcia McKenna. Tony Dorsett. New York: Simon & Schuster, 1980. Written for juvenile readers.

665. Conrad, Dick. Tony Dorsett, From Heisman To Super Bowl in One Year. Chicago: Children Press, 1979. Written for juvenile readers.

CHUCK FOREMAN

666. Morse, Charles. The Running Backs. Mankato, MN: Creative Education, 1975. 47 pp. Chuck Foreman is discussed in this work written for young people.

667. Thorne, Ian. Meeting The Running Backs. Mankato, MN: Creative Education, 1975. 30 pp. Chuck Foreman is included in this work.

JOE GREENE

668. Atyeo, Don. Blood & Guts: Violence in Sports. New York: Paddington Press, Ltd., 1979. "Mean" Joe Greene, pp. 219, 332, 368.

669. Burchard, Sue H. "Mean" Joe Greene. New York: Harcourt Brace Javanovich, 1976. 64 pp. Written for juvenile readers.

670. Fox, Larry. Mean Joe Greene and the Steelers Front Four. New York: Dodd, Mead, 1975. 241 pp.

671. Rubin, Bob. <u>All-Stars of the NFL</u>. New York: Random House,
     1976. 153 pp. Joe Greene is included in this collection.
     Written for juvenile readers.

672. Rywell, Martin, Editor. <u>Afro-American Encyclopedia</u>. North
     Miami, FL: Educational Book Publishers, Inc., 1974. Joe
     "Mean" Greene Vol. 4, p. 1087.

ROSEY GRIER

673. Marsh, Irving T. and Edward Ehre, Editors. <u>Best Sports Stories</u>.
     New York: E.P. Dutton & Co., 1969. Bill Libby, "He Was a
     Very Special Person." (Roosevelt "Rosey" Grier)," pp. 274-281.

674. Rywell, Martin, Editor. <u>Afro-American Encyclopedia</u>. North
     Miami, FL: Educational Book Publishers, Inc., 1974. Roosevelt
     "Rosey," Grier, Vol. 4, p. 1094.

ARCHIE GRIFFIN

675. Dolan, Edward F. and Richard B. Lyttle. <u>Archie Griffin</u>. Garden
     City, New York: Doubleday & Co., Inc., 1977. 113 pp. Written
     for young adults.

FRANCO HARRIS

676. Braun, Thomas. <u>Franco Harris</u>. Mankato, MN: Creative Education,
     1975. Written for young adults.

677. Burchard, Sue H. <u>Sports Star: Franco Harris</u>. New York:
     Harcourt Brace Jovanovich, 1976. 64 pp. Written for juvenile
     readers.

678. Gutman, Bill. <u>Football Superstars of the 1970s</u>. New York.
     Julian Messner, 1975. 191 pp. Franco Harris is included in
     this collection written for young adults.

679. Gutman, Bill. <u>Superstars of the Sports World</u>. New York: Julian
     Messner, 1978. 96 pp. A short biography of Franco Harris is
     included in this work.

680. Hahn, James. <u>Franco Harris: The Quiet Ironman</u>. St. Paul: EMC
     Corp., 1978.

681. Sullivan, George. <u>On The Run, Franco Harris</u>. Milwaukee:
     Raintree Editions, 1976. 47 pp. Written for juvenile readers.

BOB HAYES

682. Coan, Howard. <u>Great Pass Catchers in Pro Football</u>. New York:
     Julian Messner, 1971. 192 pp. Bob Hayes is included in this
     collection written for young adults.

683. Devaney, John. <u>Star Pass Receivers of the NFL</u>. New York:
     Random House, 1972. 153 pp. Bob Hayes is included in this
     collection.

684. Lipman, David and Ed Wilks. The Speed King: Bob Hayes of The
     Dallas Cowboys. New York: G.P. Putnam's Sons, 1971. 188 pp.

685. Rywell, Martin, Editor. Afro-American Encyclopedia. North
     Miami, FL: Educational Book Publishers, Inc., 1974. Robert
     "Bob" Lee Hayes, Vol. pp. 1160-1162.

686. Santa Barbara County Board of Education. The Emerging Minorities
     in America. Santa Barbara, CA: American Bibliographical Center
     - Clio Press, 1972. Bob Hayes, p. 38.

DAVE JONES

687. Anderson, Dave. Great Defensive Players of The NFL. New York:
     Random House, 1967. 176 pp. Dave "Deacon," Jones is included
     in this collection.

688. Libby, Bill. Life in The Pit: The Deacon Jones Story. Garden
     City, New York: Doubleday and Co., 1970. 208 pp.

689. Rywell, Martin, Editor. Afro-American Encyclopedia. North
     Miami, FL: Educational Book Publishers, Inc., 1974. David
     "Deacon," Jones Vol. 5, pp. 1365-1366.

GENE LIPSCOMBE

690. Marsh, Irving T. and Edward Ehre, Editors. Best Sports Stories.
     New York: E.P. Dutton & Co., 1964. Edward Linn, "The Sad End
     of Big Daddy, (Lipscomb)," pp. 113-123.

691. Marsh, Irving T. and Edward Ehre, Editors. Thirty Years of Best
     Sports Stories. New York: E.P. Dutton & Co., Inc., 1975.
     Edward Linn, "The Sad End of Big Daddy (Lipscombe)," pp. 187-197.

692. Rywell, Martin, Editor. Afro-American Encyclopedia. North
     Miami, FL: Educational Book Publishers, Inc., 1974. Gene
     "Big Daddy" Lipscombe, Vol. 5, pp. 1490-1491.

JAMES MARSHALL

693. Rywell Martin, Editor. Afro-American Encyclopedia. North
     Miami, FL: Educational Book Publishers, Inc., 1974. James
     Lawrence Marshall, Vol. 6, p. 1577

694. Thorne, Ian. Meet The Defensive Linemen. Mankato, MN: Creative
     Education, 1975. James Marshall is included in this work written
     for young people.

OLLIE MATSON

695. Rainbolt, Richard. Football's Rugged Running Backs. Minneapolis:
     Lerner Publications Co., 1975. 71 pp. Ollie Matson is discussed
     in this work that was written for young adults.

696. Rywell, Martin, Editor. Afro-American Encyclopedia. North Miami,
     FL: Educational Book Publishers, Inc., 1974. Ollie Matson, Vol.
     6. p. 1606.

LENNY MOORE

697. Rainbolt, Richard. Football's Rugged Running Backs. Minneapolis:
     Lerner Publications Co., 1975. 71 pp. Lenny Moore is included
     in this collection. Written for young people.

698. Rywell, Martin, Editor. Afro-American Encyclopedia. North Miami,
     FL: Educational Book Publishers, Inc., 1974. Lenny Moore,
     Vol. 6, pp. 1685-1686.

MERCURY MORRIS

699. Morse, Charles. The Running Backs. Mankato, MN: Creative
     Education, 1975. 47 pp. Mercury Morris is discussed in this
     work written for young adults.

700. Rywell, Martin, Editor. Afro-American Encyclopedia. North
     Miami, FL: Educational Book Publishers, Inc., 1974. Eugene
     "Mercury" Morris, Vol. 6, p. 1693.

ALAN PAGE

701. Batson, Larry. Alan Page. Mankato, MN: Creative Education,
     1974. 31 pp. Written for juvenile readers.

702. Rywell, Martin, Editor. Afro-American Encyclopedia. North
     Miami, FL: Educational Book Publishers, Inc., 1974. Alan
     Cedric Page, Vol. 7, p. 1970.

703. Thorne, Ian. Meet The Defensive Linemen. Mankato, MN:
     Creative Education, 1975. Alan Page is included in this book
     written for juvenile readers.

WALTER PAYTON

704. Conrad, Dick. Walter Payton, The Running Machine. Chicago:
     Children Press, 1979. 42 pp. Written for juvenile readers.

JOHN SAMPLE, JR.

705. Rywell, Martin, Editor. Afro-American Encyclopedia. North
     Miami, FL: Educational Book Publishers Inc., 1974, John B.
     Sample, Jr. Vol. 8, pp. 2306-2307.

CHARLIE SANDERS

706. Devaney, John. Star Pass Receivers of the NFL. New York:
     Random House, 1972. 153 pp. Charlie Sanders is included in
     this collection.

707. Rywell, Martin, Editor. Afro-American Encyclopedia. North Miami, FL: Educational Book Publishers, Inc., 1974. Charlie Sanders, Vol. 8, p. 2309.

GALE SAYERS

708. Collins, David R. Football Running Backs. Champaign, IL: Garrard Publishing Co., 1976. 96 pp. Gale Sayers is included in this work. Written for juvenile readers.

709. Marsh, Irving T. and Edward Ehre, Editors. Best Sports Stories. New York: E.P. Dutton & Co. 1970. Al Silverman, "Gale Sayers: The Hard Road Back," pp. 120-131.

710. Rainbolt, Richard. Football's Rugged Running Backs. Minneapolis: Lerner Publications Co., 1975. 71 pp. Gale Sayers is included in this work written for young adults.

711. Rywell, Martin, Editor. Afro-American Encyclopedia. North Miami, FL: Educational Book Publishers, Inc., 1974. Gayle Sayers, Vol. 8, p. 2315.

O.J. SIMPSON

712. Baker, Jim. O.J. Simpson. New York: Grosset & Dunlap, 1974. 145 pp.

713. Baker, Jim. O.J. Simpson's Most Memorable Games. New York: G.P. Putnam, 1978. 288 pp.

714. Burchard, Marshall & Sue Burchard. Sports Hero: O.J. Simpson. New York: G.P. Putnam's & Sons, 1975. 95 pp. Written for juvenile readers.

715. Fox, Larry. The O.J. Simpson Story: Born To Run. New York: Dodd, Mead & Co., 1974. 173 pp.

716. Gutman, Bill. O.J.. New York: Grosset & Dunlap, 1974. 95 pp.

717. Gutman, Bill. Football Superstars of The 1970s. New York: Julian Messner, 1975. 191 pp. O.J. Simpson is included in this work written for young people.

718. Hill, Ray. O.J. Simpson. New York: Random House, 1975. 153 pp. Written for young adult.

719. Libby, Bill. Star Running Backs of the NFL. New York: Random House, 1971. 144 pp. O.J. Simpson is included in this collection.

720. Morse, Ann. Football's Great Running Back, O.J. Simpson. Mankato, MN: Creative Education, 1976. 30 pp. Written for juvenile readers.

721. Morse, Charles. The Running Backs. Mankato, MN: Creative Education, 1975. 47 pp. O.J. Simpson is included in this work. Written for young adults.

722. Rubin, Bob. All-Stars of the NFL. New York: Random House, 1976. 153 pp. O.J. Simpson is included in this work. Written for juvenile readers.

723. Rywell, Martin, Editor. Afro-American Encyclopedia. North Miami, FL: Educational Book Publishers, Inc., 1974. O.J. Simpson, Vol. 8, pp. 2348-2349.

724. Santa Barbara County Board of Education. The Emerging Minorities in America. Santa Barbara, CA: American Bibliographical Center - Clio Press, 1972. Orenthal James (O.J.) Simpson, p. 71.

725. Thorne, Ian. Meet The Running Backs. Mankato, MN: Creative Education, 1975. 30 pp. O.J. Simpson is included in this collection. Written for juvenile readers.

C.A. "BUBBA" SMITH

726. Marsh, Irving T. and Edward Ehre, Editors. Best Sports Stories. New York: E.P. Dutton & Co., 1973. Larry L. King, "The Beasts of Baltimore (Bubba Smith)," pp. 101-116.

727. Rywell, Martin, Editor. Afro-American Encyclopedia. North Miami, FL: Educational Book Publishers, Inc., 1974. C.A. "Bubba" Smith, Vol. p. 2514.

728. Thorne, Ian. Meet The Defensive Linemen. Mankato, MN: Creative Education, 1975. Bubba Smith is included in this work written for juvenile readers.

WOODY STRODE

729. Rywell, Martin, Editor. Afro-American Encyclopedia. North Miami, FL: Educational Book Publishers, Inc., 1974. Woody Strode, Vol. 9, p. 2577.

OTIS TAYLOR

730. Devaney, John. Star Pass Receivers of The NFL. New York: Random House, 1972. 153 pp. Otis Taylor is included in this collection.

731. Rywell, Martin, Editor. Afro-American Encyclopedia. North Miami, FL: Educational Book Publishers, Inc., 1974. Otis Taylor, Vol. 9. pp. 2600-2601.

EMLEN TUNNEL

732. Rywell, Martin, Editor. Afro-American Encyclopedia. North Miami, FL: Educational Book Publishers, Inc., 1974. Emlen Tunnell Vol. 9, pp. 2656-2657.

PAUL WARFIELD

733. Devaney, John. Star Pass Receivers of the NFL. New York: Random House, 1972. 153 pp. Paul Warfield is included in this collection.

734. Rywell, Martin, Editor. Afro-American Encyclopedia. North Miami, FL: Educational Book Publishers, Inc. 1974. Paul Warfield, Vol. 9 pp. 2742-2743.

KENNY WASHINGTON

735. Rywell, Martin, Editor. Afro-American Encyclopeida. North Miami, FL: Educational Book Publishers, 1974. Kenny Washington, p. 2765.

GOLF

RAY BOTTS

736. Smythe, Mabel M. Editor. The Black American Reference Book. Englewood Cliffs, NJ: Prentice Hall, 1976. Ray Botts, p. 956.

PETER BROWN

737. Smythe, Mabel M., Editor. The Black American Reference Book. Englewood Cliffs, NJ: Prentice-Hall, 1976. Peter Borwn, p. 956.

HAROLD DONOVANT

738. Smythe, Mabel M., Editor. The Black American Reference Book. Englewood Cliff, NJ: Prentice-Hall, 1976. Harold Donovant, p. 956.

LEE ELDER

739. Jacobs, Linda. Lee Elder: The Daring Dream. St. Paul, MN: EMC Corp., 1976. 39 pp. Written for young adults.

740. Rywell, Martin, Editor. Afro-American Encyclopedia. North Miami, FL: Educational Book Publishers, Inc. 1974. Elder, Lee Vol. 3, p. 879.

741. Smythe, Mabel M., Editor. The Black American Reference Book. Englewood Cliffs, NJ: Prentice-Hall, 1976. Lee Elders, p. 956.

ALTHEA GIBSON

742. Robinson, Wilhelmena S. Historical Afro-American Biographies. New York: Publishers, 1968. Althea Gibson, pp. 194-195.

743. Santa Barbara County Board of Education. The Emerging Minorities
     in America. Santa Barbara, CA: American Bibliographical Center
     - Clio Press, 1972. Althea Gibson, p. 35.

744. Smythe, Mabel M., Editor. The Black American Reference Book.
     Englewood Cliffs, NJ: Prentice-Hall, 1976. Althea Gibson,
     p. 956.

745. Toppin, Edgar A. A Biographical History of Blacks in America
     Since 1528. New York: David McKay, 1971. Althea Gibson,
     pp. 197, 241, 305, 306, 307.

746. Wesley, Charles H. The Quest For Equality: From Civil War To
     Civil Rights. New York: Publishers Co., 1976 Althea Gibson,
     p. 199.

GEORGE JOHNSON

747. Editors of Ebony. Ebony Handbook. Chicago: Johnson Publishing
     Co., 1974. George Johnson, p. 476.

748. Smythe, Mabel M., Editor. The Black American Reference Book.
     Englewood Cliffs, NJ: Prentices Hall, 1976. George Johnson,
     p. 956.

CHARLES OWENS

749. Editors of Ebony. Ebony Handbook. Chicago: Johnson Publishing
     Co., 1974. Charles Owens, p. 476.

CHARLES SIFFORD

750. Editors of Ebony. Ebony Handbook. Chicago: Johnson Publishing
     Co., 1975. Charles Sifford, p. 4762.

751. Rywell, Martin, Editor. Afro-American Encyclopedia. North
     Miami, FL: Educational Book Publishers, Inc., 1974. Charles
     Sifford, Vol. 8 p. 2343.

752. Smythe, Mabel M., Editor. The Black American Reference Book.
     Englewood Cliffs, NJ: Prentice-Hall, 1976. Charles Sifford,
     p. 956.

CURTIS SIFFORD

753. Smythe, Mabel M., Editor. The Black American Reference Book.
     Englewood Cliffs, NJ: Prentice-Hall, 1976. Curtis Sifford,
     p. 956.

CHUCH THOME

754. Smythe, Mabel M., Editor. The Black American Reference Book.
     Englewood Cliffs, NJ: Prentice-Hall, 1976. Chuch Thome,
     p. 956.

TENNIS

ARTHUR ASHE

755. Higdon, Hal. Champions of The Tennis Court. Englewood Cliffs, NJ: Prentice-Hall 1971. 60 pp. Arthur Ashe is included in this book written for young adults.

756. Jacobs, Linda. Arthur Ashe: Alone in the Crowd. St. Paul, MN: EMC Corp., 1976. 38 pp. Written for juvenile readers.

757. McAdam, Robert. Chief Cloud of Dust. Glendale, CA: Bowmar, 1972. 63 pp. Arthur Ashe is included in this work for young adults.

758. Toppin, Edgar A. A Biographical History of Black in America Since 1528. New York: David McKay, 1971. Arthur Ashe, pp. 241, 249, 250.

759. Santa Barbara County Board of Education. The Emerging Minorities in America. Santa Barbara, CA: American Bibliographical Center-Clio Press, 1972. Arthur Ashe, pp. 7-8.

7

Articles

SPORTS IN GENERAL
A SELECTED LIST

760. Bannister, Jr. Frank T. "Sports." Ebony, 25 (January 1980), 30.

761. Bannister, Jr. Frank T. "Search For White Hope Threatens Black Athletes." Ebony, 35 (February 1980), 130-2+.

762. "Black Athletes Need More Support.." The Voice of Hope, (April 14, 1970).

763. "Black Athlete Victimized At An Early Age." Pittsburgh Courier, (September 21, 1978).

764. "Black Hall of Fame Adds 21 More To Its Inductees." Jet, 50 (April 8, 1976), 53.

765. "The Black Athlete Speaks Out." Opportunities for the College Graduate, Annual Edition 1971.

766. Bradley, B. "Is Too Much Sex Ruining Our Athletes." Sepia, 7 (July 1959), 64-66.

767. Brooks, A.N. D. "Democracy Through Sports." Negro History Bulletin, 15 (December 1951), 56+.

768. Burwell, B. "Batting, Betting and Bouncing Into Business." Black Enterprise, 10 (November 1979), 31-36+.

769. "Charles, Schmeling, Wills Picked for Hall of Fame." Jet, 39 (January 28, 1971), 53.

770. "Color-Blind Stopwatch." Nation, 191 (September 3, 1960), 101.

771. Deford, Frank. "The Power of the Press." Sports Illustrated, 22 (March 29, 1965), 21-24.

772. Edwards, H. "Sport Within The Veil: The Triumphs, Tragedies and Challenges of Afro-American Involvement." American Academy of Political and Social Science Annual, 445 (September 1979), 116-27.

773. Eitzen, Stanley and Norman Yetman. "Black Americans in Sports Unequal Opportunity for Equal Ability." Civil Rights Digest, (August, 1972).

774. "Entertaining Athletes: Negro Sport Stars." Ebony, 21 (December 1965), 39-40+.

775. Fisher, A. L. "Best Way Out of the Ghetto". Phi Delta Kappan, 60 (November 1978), 240.

776. Graves, E.G. "Right Kind of Excellence." Black Enterprise, 10 (November 1979), 9.

777. Harlow, Alvin F. "Unrecognized Stars." Esquire, 10 (September 1938), 75.

778. Henderson, Edwin. "The Black Man as Athlete." Carolina Peacemaker, (June 13, 1970).

779. Holway, John. "Before You Could Say Jackie Robinson, Black Players." Look, 85 (July 13, 1971), 46-50.

780. "I Am Strong, I Am Quick." Ebony, 27 (August 1972), 150-4.

781. Jesse Owens Narrates The Black Athlete." Philadelphia Tribune, (March 30, 1971).

782. Kane, J. "Assessment of Black Is Best." Sports Illustrated, 34 (January 18, 1971), 72-6+.

783. King, A. "Batters, Boxers, and Runners: Sporting Quiz." Essence, 9 (October 1978), 44.

784. Lewis, W. S. "Pioneers of the Sporting Life." Encore, 8 (November 19, 1979), 24-6.

785. Mitchell, E.D. "Racial Traits in Athletics." American Physical Educational Review, 27 (March-May 1922), 93-9; 147-52, 197-206.

786. "Negro Athletes and Civil Rights." Sepia, 13 (June 1964), 35-39

787. "Negro Stars on the Playing Fields of America." Literary Digest, 119 (March 2, 1935), 32.

788. "Off-Season Athletes In Off-Beat Jobs." Ebony, 17 (May 1962), 68-69.

789. "Off Season Pursuits Prepare Pros For The Future." Ebony, 34 (December 1978), 150-2+.

790. "$100,000 - A Year Superstars." Ebony, 25 (June 1970), 128-130+.

791. Peterson, R. "Josh Gibson Was The Equal of Babe Ruth, But...;
     Negro Players." New York Times Magazine, (April 11, 1971),
     12-13+.

792. "Place in the Sun: Negro Players." Time, 57 (May 14, 1951),
     91-3.

793. "PV Clinic and Coca-Cola Honor Top Sports Figures." Sepia,
     12 (October 1963), 67-70.

794. Robinson, E. and A. Morissett. "International Goodwill Through
     Sports." Liberation, 5 (July-August 1960), 28-29.

795. "Round Table Discussion: The Negro In American Sport." Negro
     History Bulletin, 24 (November 1960), 27-31.

796. Scully, G.W. "Economic Discrimination In Professional Sports."
     Law and Contemporary Problems, 38 (Winter 1973), 67-84.

797. Slater, J. "Stardom: The New Generation's Elusive Dream."
     Ebony, 33 (August 1978), 152-41.

798. "Sports". Negro History Bulletin, 18 (February, 1955), 120-22.

799. "Sports Are Color Blind." America, 99 (August 16, 1958), 503.

800. "Sports: They Set The Pace In 1947." Opportunity, 26 (Spring
     1948), 83.

801. Tobin, R. L. "Sports As An Integrator." Saturday Review, 50
     (January 21, 1967), 32.

802. "Top Athletes of the 1970's." Jet, 57 (January 3, 1980), 48-53.

803. Vining, D.R., Jr. and J.F. Kerrigan. "Application of the Lexis
     Ratio to the Detection of Racial Quotas in Professional Sports:
     A Note." American Economist, 22 (Fall, 1978), 71-5.

804. Ward, W. "Low and Inside: Views From The Arena." Nation,
     200 (May 10, 1965), 508-10.

805. "Where Negroes Have Struck It. Rich." U.S. News And World Report,
     63 (December 11, 1967), 71.

806. Yetman, Norman R. and D. Stanley Eitzen. "Black Americans In
     Sports: Unequal Opportunity For Equal Ability." Civil Rights
     Digest, (August 1972), 21-34.

807. Young, Andrew S. Are Today's Athletes Too Dull?" Negro Digest,
     11 (July 1962), 13-20.

808. Young, Whitney. "The Black Athlete" Carolina Times,
     (March 13, 1971).

INDIVIDUAL SPORTS
A SELECTED LIST

BASEBALL

809. Adderton, Donald. "Weren't Black Players Ready For A Black Boss." Jet, 52 (August 11, 1977), 18-19+.

810. "All-Stars." Jet, 4 (June 17, 1971), 53.

811. "Annual Baseball Roundup: Bandits of the Base Paths." Ebony, 28 (June 1973), 124-126+.

812. "Annual Baseball Roundup: How Much Is A Ball Player Worth." Ebony, 32 (June 1977), 153-156+.

813. "Annual Baseball Roundup:1965: The Year of The Pitchers. Ebony, 20 (June 1965), 152-158+.

814. "Annual Baseball Roundup, The Last of the Big Bats." Ebony, 26 (June 1971), 92-94+.

815. "Annual Baseball Roundup: The Sluggers and The Hitters." Ebony, 33 (June 1978), 170-172+.

816. "Annual Baseball Roundup: Where Are the Catchers: Position Glorified By Roy Campanella Is Now Shunned by Players." Ebony, 29 (June 1974), 142-144+.

817. Barbee, B. "Annual Baseball Roundup, 1965: The Year of the Pitchers." Ebony, 20 (June 1965), 152-58.

818. Barbee, B. "Baseball's Untouchables." Ebony, 19 (June 1964), 153-154+.

819. "Baseball Business." Crisis, 61 (October 1934), 301.

820. "Baseball Jump Into Its 2nd Century." Sepia, 18 (June 1969), 70-62.

821. "Baseball Round-up." Sepia, 14 (May 1965), 64-69.

822. "Baseball Roundup 1966: Year of the Holdouts." Ebony, 21: (June 1966). 120-122+.

823. "Baseball's Young Turks." Sepia, 15 (September 1966), 56-60.

824. "Black Baseball's History To Be Preserved in Hall." Winston-Salem Journal, (November 7, 1980).

825. "Black Stars Rap On Issues After Putting A Roar In Tiger Stadium." Jet, 41 (July 29, 1971), 52-54.

826. "Blacks' Owning Team "Unrealistic." Journal and Sentinel, (February 15, 1970).

827. Boyle, Robert H. "The Private World of the Negro Ballplayer." Sports Illustrated, 12 (March 21, 1960), 16-19.

828. "Branch Rickey Discusses The Negro in Baseball Today." Ebony, 12 (May 1957), 38-44.

829. Brawley, Benjamin. "The Baseball." Crisis, 77 (December 1970), 409-410.

830. Brower, William A. "Time For Baseball To Erase The Blackball." Opportunity, 20 (June 1942), 164-67.

831. "Brown Bombers." Time, 78 (July 21, 1961), 60.

832. Brown, D. "Negro In Baseball." Negro History Bulletin, 15 (December 1951), 51-52.

833. Dodson, D.W. "Integration of Negroes In Baseball." Journal of Educational Sociology, 28 (October 1954), 73-82.

834. Elliat, Jeffrey M. "It's Time To Take The Racism Out Of Pro Baseball." Sepia, 26 (December 1977), 28-33.

835. "End of An Era for Negroes on Baseball." Ebony, 16 (June 1961), 36-40.

836. "Fact Chart on Negro Major League Players." Ebony, 19 (June 1964), 156.

837. "Funny Men of Baseball." Sepia, 14 (August 1965), 60-64.

838. "Future 'Jackie Robinsons' Amateur Teams Will Supply Major Leagues With New Crop of Negro Stars." Ebony, 7 (May, 1952), 120+.

839. Greenberg, Peter S. "Wild In The Stands." Black Sports, 7 (March 1978), 8-9+.

840. Gwartney, J. and C. Haworth. "Employer Cost and Discrimination: The Case of Baseball." Journal of Political Economy, 82 (July 1974), 873-81.

841. "Hall to Stay Open to Negro Stars." Winston-Salem Journal, (September 4, 1977).

842. Hartnett, G. "Negroes Are A Big Factor In Baseball's Success." Sepia, 8 (May 1960), 76-78.

843. Hicks, J. H. "St. Louis: Is It The Toughest Town For Negro Baseball Players?" Crisis, 57 (October 1950), 573-76.

844. "History of the Negroes In the World Series." Ebony, 12 (October 1957), 93-96.

845. "How Much Is A Player Worth?" Ebony, 27 (June 1972), 152-162+.

846. "It's Baseball Season Again." Black Sports, 4 (April 1975), 5.

847. Izenberg, Jerry. "World Series That Almost Wasn't." Black Sports, 6 (February 1977), 20-25+.

848. Kisner, Ronald E. "Are Baseball Owners Too Racist To Hire A Black Manager." Jet, 46 (August 15, 1974), 48-50+.

849. Kisner, Ronald E. "Another Season For Records Seen For '73 Baseball." Jet, 44 (April 19, 1973), 48-50+.

850. Kisner, Ronald E. "Baseball Score On Black Managers: A.L. 2, N.L.O." Jet, 54 (August 3, 1978), 48+.

851. Kisner, Ronald E. "Honors Highlight '75 All Star Baseball Classic." Jet, 48 (July 31, 1975), 52-53.

852. Kisner, Ronald E. "It's Baseball Season Again." Black Sports, 4 (April 1975), 5.

853. Kisner, Ronald E. "Problems Of Baseball Wives." Jet, 50 (April 22, 1976), 21-23+.

854. Kisner, Ronald E. "White Widow of Baseball League Pioneer Writes Book About Saga." Jet, 51 (March 3, 1977), 46-48.

855. Kisner, Ronald E. "World Series: A Game Business." Jet, 51 (November 4, 1976), 52-53.

856. Kisner, Ronald. "World Series Ends Baseball's Hottest Season." Jet, 41 (October 14, 1971), 52-56.

857. Lacy, S. "Let's Look At The Record; the Negro In The Major Leagues." Our World, 9 (April 1954), 40-43.

858. "Last Year For Big Bonus Babies." Ebony, 22 (November 1966), 120-22.

859. Leggett, William. "The Rampaging Twins Want The Series Too."
Sports Illustrated, 23 (October 4, 1965), 26-28.

860. Mann, J. "The Battle of San Francisco." Sports Illustrated, 23
(August 30, 1965), 12-15.

861. Markus, B. "Do Black Ball Players Last Longer." Sepia, 2
(August 1971), 24-28+.

862. Medoff, Marshall H. "Racial Segregation In Baseball, The Economic
Hypotheses." Journal of Black Studies, 6 (June 1976), 393-400.

863. Medoff, Marshall H. "Reappraisal of Racial Discrimination Against
Blacks in Professional Baseball." Review of Black Political
Economy, 5 (Spring 1975), 259-68.

864. Mogull, R.G. "Salary Discrimination in Major League Baseball."
Review of Black Political Economy, 5 (Spring 1975), 269-79.

865. "Negro Baseball Players in Japan." Ebony, 8 (October 1953),
101-2.

866. "Negro Baseball Players In Japan; Trio of Flashy American Stars
Make Hanky Braves Best Japanese Team." Ebony, 8 (October 1953),
101-102+.

867. "The Negro Comes of Age in Baseball." Ebony, 14 (June 1959),
41-46.

868. "Negro in Baseball: 1962, Year of the Big Money." Ebony, 17
(June 1962), 81-82.

869. "Negro On The Farm." Newsweek, 26 (November 5, 1945), 94-5.

870. "Negro Players in Major League Baseball." Crisis, 44 (April 1937),
112.

871. "Negroes In The Major Leagues." Ebony, 15 (June 1960), 99-106.

872. "Negroes' Role In Baseball." Sepia, 17 (April 1968), 10-14.

873. Ortiz, Carlos. "Can The Mets Afford To Pass Up Any More Black
Players." Black Sports, 6 (October 1976), 10-12+.

874. Pinkney, Ron. "New Wellspring For Baseball-Black Colleges."
Encore, 4 (July 7, 1975), 44-45.

875. Pinkney, Ron. "What's Happening In The American League." Encore,
4 (April 21, 1975), 38.

876. "Place In The Sun: Negro Players." Time, 57 (May 14, 1951),
91-93.

877. Roche, John, "Golden Age of Baseball." Twin City Sentinel,
(October 25, 1972).

878. "The Rube and Smokey Joe: Black Baseball Greats." _Dawn Magazine_, (September 1977), 12-14+.

879. "San Francisco's Most Colorful Team." _Ebony_, 15 (July 1960), 103-7.

880. "Scouting Reports: American and National Baseball Leagues." _Sports Illustrated_, 6 (April 15, 1957), 45-83.

881. "Scouting Reports: American and National Baseball Leagues, 1960." _Sports Illustrated_, 12 (April 11, 1960), 28-62.

882. "Scouting Reports: Baseball 1959, American and National Leagues." _Sports Illustrated_, 10 (April 18, 1959), 32-87.

883. "Scouting Reports: 1958 National and American Baseball Leagues." _Sports Illustrated_, 8 (April 14, 1958), 39-77.

884. Smith, W. "Most Prejudiced Teams In Baseball." _Ebony_, 8 (May 1953), 111-141.

885. "Sports in Action." _The New Courier_, (August 15, 1970).

886. Stevens, Jo Ann. "Yankee Pleasure Dome Adds Glitter To Ghetto." _Black Sports_, 5 (April 1976), 50-52.

887. "10 Top Negro Rookies." _Our World_, 6 (August 1951), 30-31.

888. Unger, Norman. "The Princes and the Paupers." _Ebony_, 34 (June 1979), 150-54+.

889. Veeck, B. "Are There Too Many Negroes In Baseball." _Ebony_, 15 (August 1960), 25-28+.

890. Ward, W. "Low and Inside: Views From the Arena" _Nation_, 200 (May 10, 1965), 509-10.

891. Weaver, B.L. "Black Press and the Assault on Professional Baseball's Color Line, October 1945-April 1947." _Phylon_, 40 (December 1979), 303-17.

892. Winterich, J.J. "Playing Ball: Negroes In Organized Baseball." _Saturday Review of Literature_, 28 (November 24, 1945), 12.

893. "World Series, 1958." _Sports Illustrated_, 9 (October 13, 1958), 14-21.

894. Young, Andrew S. "Baseball History Lesson." _Sepia_, 27 (July 1978), 62-66.

895. Young, Andrew S. "Baseball's Top Ten All-Time Black Stars." _Sepia_, 2 (June 1971), 26-33.

896. Young, Andrew S. "Giants of Baseball's Democracy League." _Sepia_, 8 (October 1960), 73-75.

897. Young, Andrew S.   "Sepia's Major League Baseball Preview."   <u>Sepia</u>, 13 (May 1964), 72-77.

BASKETBALL

898. "All-Stars." Jet, 4 (June 17, 1971), 53.

899. "Annual Basketball Roundup: It's Still A Big Man's Game." Ebony, 28 (January 1973), 83-86+.

900. Baltimore, C. H. "Negro in Basketball." Negro Historical Bulletin, 15 (December 1951), 49-50.

901. Banks, Lacey J. "Milwaukee Bucks, An Instant Dynasty." Ebony, 26 (January 1971), 83-86+.

902. Barron, Allan P. "Coaching In The National Basketball Association." Black Sports, 5 (May 1976), 4.

903. Brower, William A. "Five Black Coaches In Pro Basketball." Sepia, 23 (December 1974), 53-56+.

904. "Bucks Bounce Way Toward NBA Crown." Jet, 39 (January 14, 1971), 54-55.

905. Devaney, John. "Pro Basketballs Hidden Fear". Negro Digest, 15 (May 1964), 54-62.

906. "Have Scandals Doomed Negro Cagers." Our World, 6 (December 1951), 70-73.

907. Kisner, Ronald E. "Basketball's Best Men in Biggest Battle For Crown." Jet, 42 (March 3, 1972), 51-57.

908. Louis, Robert. "Three Things The Cleveland Cavaliers Are Not." Black Sports, 6 (April 1977). 26-30.

909. McDonnell, Joe. "Mysterious Philadelphia 76ers." Sepia, 27 (December 1978), 52-56+.

910. McFadden, Jerome. "Black Basketball Stars In Europe." Sepia, 23 (July 1974), 32-37.

911. Markus, B. "The World's Highest Paid Black Athletes." Sepia, 2 (May 1971), 2-27.

912. Mogull, R.G. "Racial Discrimination in Professional Basketball." American Economist, (September 1974), 11-15.

913. "Negroes in Pro Basketball." Ebony, 14 (February 1959), 55-58.

914. "New NBA." Black Sports, 6 (October 1976), 20-22+.

915. "Pro Basketball." Sports Illustrated, 25 (October 24, 1966), 40-52.

916. "Pro Basketball: NBA vs ABA, Prosperity." Ebony, 23 (January 1968), 64-66+.

917. "Pro Basketball, 1957-1958." Sports Illustrated, (November 7, 1957), 48-51.

918. "Pro Basketball Roundup." Ebony, 19 (January 1964), 71-72.

919. "Pro Basketball Roundup: The Year of the Center." Ebony, 33 (January 1978), 51-52+.

920. "Professional Basketball's Dream Team." Ebony, 16 (March 1976), 54-56.

921. Rhoden, Bill. "ABA Superstars Join The NBA." Ebony, 32 (January 1977), 88-92.

922. Rhoden, Bill. "Annual Basketball Roundup: Pros Donate Talent To Help Black Youth." Ebony, 31 (January 1976), 106-108+.

923. Riley, Clayton. "Close Encounters of the NBA Kind." Black Sports, 7 (March 1978), 16+.

924. Roberts, Ozzie. "Players Profit From War Between The Leagues." Ebony, 29 (January 1974), 80+.

925. Schwartz, Barbara. "Summer Basketball Guide." Black Sports, 4 (June 1975), 31-34.

926. Spander, Art. "Warriors". Black Sports, 6 (January 1977), 48+.

927. Tax, J. "The Test of the Nation's Best: Basketball Title Tournament." Sports Illustrated, 12 (March 14, 1960), 39-42.

928. "10 Blacks and Barry." Black Sports, 4 (March 1975), 42-43+.

929. "What Causes Pro Basketball Violence." Sepia, 26 (February 1978), 81.

BOXING

930. Adderton, Donald. "While The Stars, Superstars and Crowd Sparkle In Stadium." Jet, 51 (October 14, 1976), 54-55.

931. Barron, Allan P. "Boxing." Black Sports, 6 (February 1977), 4.

932. Bobb, Scott F. "How Zaire Landed The Big Fight." Sepia, 23 (September 1974), 59-62.

933. "Boxing's Best To Gamble On Las Vegas 'Supercard'." Jet, 57 (October 4, 1979), 50.

934. "Boxing Monopoly Puts On the Squeeze." Sports Illustrated, 3 (January 24, 1955), 24-26.

935. Dempsey, Jack. "Why Negroes Rule Boxing." Ebony, 5 (February 1950), 58-60+.

936. Hare, Nathan. "Psychology of Great Black Boxers." Ebony, 32 (January 1977), 68-70+.

937. Hare, Nathan. "A Study of the Black Fighter." Black Scholar, 3 (November 1971), 2-8.

938. Jack, B. "Maybe Somebody Did Rob Me, but I Don't Know Who." Sports Illustrated, 1 (November 19, 1954), 18-20.

239. "How Mobsters Control Boxing." Our World, 6 (December 1951), 32-35.

940. Jackson, W.H. "Negro In Boxing." Negro History Bulletin, 15 (December 1951), 53-54.

941. Jacobs, M. "Have Negroes Killed Boxing?" Ebony, 5 (May 1950), 29-32+.

942. Kisner, Ronald. "Big Fight That May End Loser's Career." Jet 45 (September 26, 1974), 50-53.

943. Kisner, Ronald. "Zaire Postscript Ali Out Duels Foe For Crown."
     Jet, 47 (November 14, 1974), 52-54.

944. Kisner, Ronald. "Zaire City Ready For Big Bout." Jet, 47
     (October 31, 1974), 52-56.

945. Massaquoi, H.J. "Should Boxing Be Abolished?" Ebony, 17
     (June 1962), 44-46.

946. Nipson, Herb. "Plan to Save Boxing." Ebony, 19 (May 1964),
     59-60.

949. "Pictorial Highlights as Veteran Boxers Hit Come Back Trail,"
     New Courier, (May 22, 1971).

950. Quarles, Benjamin. "Peter Jackson Speaks of Boxers." Negro
     History Bulletin, 18 (November 1954), 39-40.

951. Schulberg, B. "Boxing's Dirty Business Must Be Cleaned Up Now."
     Sports Illustrated, (November 1, 1954), 11-12.

952. "Should Boxing Be Abolished?" Ebony, 10 (January 1955), 34-36.

953. Simms, Gregory. "There Are Many Styles To Pick From Among
     Boxing's Top Ten Heavyweight Contenders." Jet, 54 (May 18, 1978),
     48-49.

954. Ward, Arch. "Negroes in the Golden Gloves." Ebony, 6
     (March 1951), 86-92.

955. "Why Negroes Rule Boxing." Our World, 6 (November 1951), 48-52.

FOOTBALL

956. " The Pros See Them: Time's Propicked All-America." Time, 88 (December 9, 1966), 65-66.

957. Banks, Lacey J. "Annual Football Roundup, Case For The Defense." Ebony, 27 (November 1971), 170-172+.

958. Banks, Lacey J. "Vikings Front Four," Ebony, 25 (January 1970), 83-86+.

959. Baron, Allan. "Legalized Gambling on Pro Football Games." Black Sports, 9 (November 1976), 4.

960. Bingham, William. "A Season for Sophomores." Sports Illustrated, 13 (October 31, 1960), 53-54.

961. Brower, William A. "Has Professional Football Closed the Door?" Opportunity, 18 (December 1940), 375-77.

962. Brower, William A. "Negro Players on White Gridirons." Opportunity, 19 (October 1941), 307-8.

963. "Brown Bombers." Time, 78 (July 21,1961), 60.

964. "Cleveland Browns: Football's Most Democratic Team." Ebony, 11 (December 1955), 104-8.

965. Eitzen, D.S. and D.C. Sanford. "Segregation of Blacks By Playing Position in Football: Accident or Design?" Social Science Quarterly, 55 (March 1975), 948-59.

966. "Falcons Rush 'Best Ever'." Atlanta Journal and Constitution, (September 6, 1970).

967. "Football Honor Roll." Crisis, 46 (November 1939), 337.

968. "Football Roundup." Ebony, 19 (November 1963), 70-72.

969. "Football's Most Democratic Team; Multi-Racial Cleveland Browns Boast of Nine Winning Seasons." Ebony, 11 (December 1955), 104+.

970. Gilmar, S. "All-Star Pro Team: A Prediction for 1966." Esquire, 66 (October 1966), 88-90.

971. Henderson, Edwin B. "The Season's Football." Crisis, 10 (February 1915), 193-95.

972. "History Repeats Itself in Miami." Sepia, 11 (March 1962), 22-23.

973. "Is This The Year of the Giants?" Our World, 10 (November 1955), 72-74.

974. Jones, P.W.L. "All-Time Negro Football Team." Crisis, 44 (January 1937), 16-21.

975. "Last Year For the Big Bonus Babies." Ebony, 22 (November 1966), 120-122.

976. "Los Angeles Rams." Sepia, 13 (November 1964), 58-62.

977. Markus, B. "The World's Highest Paid Black Athletes." Sepia, 2 (May 1971), 2-27.

978. Maule, Tex. "Run For The Money: Pro Football Superstars." Sports Illutrated, 7 (November 7, 1957), 20-25.

979. Maule, Tex and M.H. Sharnik. "National Football League." Sports Illustrated, 23 (September 13, 1965), 46-71.

980. Nace, E. "Negro Grid Stars, Past and Present." Opportunity, 17 (September 1939), 272-3.

981. "New Faces In Pro Football." Our World, 7 (December 1952), 62-64.

982. The Pigskin Club: A Washington "Who's Who," Negro History Bulletin, 36 (March 1963), 191-94.

983. "Pro Football Is Murder." Our World, 8 (November 1953), 76-79.

984. "Pro Football Roundup." Ebony, 19 (November 1963), 70-72.

985. "Pro Football Stars From Negro Colleges." Ebony, 20 (October 1965), 57-58.

986. Rhoden, Bill. "Annual Football Roundup: The Rookies." Ebony, 32 (December 1976), 100-104.

987. Ribowsky, Mack. "Why is Everybody Picking on the Poor Defensive Backs." Black Sports, 9 (December 1976), 23-26.

988. Robinson, Louie. "New Football Stars in the Old South." Ebony, 23 (December 1967), 25-38.

989. "The Running Fame Is On." Ebony, 27 (November 1972), 194-28+.

990. Shrake, Edward. "American Football League." Sports Illustrated, 23 (September 13, 1965), 72-79.

991. "Sports Classic Integrates Miami Beach." Sepia, 12 (March 1963), 75-79.

992. "Sport." Negro History Bulletin, 16 (May 1953), 183.

993. Streator, G.W. "Negro Football Standards." Crisis, 38 (March 1931), 85-86.

994. "Super Sunday Marked by Tourists, Pagentry, Topsy-Turvy Game." Jet, 39 (February 4, 1971), 52.

995. Stowers, C. "Pro Football Capital of America." Sepia, 2 (October 1971), 46-51.

996. "Three Blacks Enshrined In Halls of Fame for Baseball and Football." Jet, 41 (February 24, 1972), 56.

997. "Top Negro Stars In Pro Football." Sepia, 12 (November 1963), 75-78.

998. White, A. "Can Negroes Save Pro-Football?" Our World, 5 (December 1950), 60-65.

999. White, Dwight. "Rap with Pittsburgh Steelers Front Four." Black Sports, 5 (February 1976), 32-36.

1000. Wilkins, Roy. "Negro Stars on Big Grid Teams." Crisis, 43 (December 1936), 362-63.

GOLF

1001. "After 38 Years, Blacks Still Not Invited To Masters." Jet, 42 (May 4, 1972), 52-53.

1002. "Black Women In Golf." Sepia, 19 (January 1970), 46-49.

1003. "Flint Tees Off, Vehicle City Golf Club Interracial Tourney Is Biggest in the U.S." Our World, 9 (November 1954), 28-33.

1004. "Golf Course Discrimination (Looking and Listening)." Crisis, 67 (August-September 1960), 440-441.

1005. "Is Golf Necessary? The Atlanta Decision." Time, 67 (January 2, 1956), 14.

1006. "Lady Pros Seek Golf Glory." Ebony, 26 (July 1971), 16-18+.

1007. "Road Is Rocky For Black Female (Rene Powell) Golf Pros." Jet, 51 (October 28, 1976), 52.

1008. "Social Side of Golf." Sepia, 11 (September 1962), 53-56.

1009. "Swingers" Our World, 10 (December 1954), p. 64-66.

1010. "Tee Time For The Black Athlete." Sepia, 18 (April 1969), 66-68.

1011. "United Golfers Association National Championship and Tours For Negro Players." New York Times, (August 25, 1968), Section 5, p. 3.

1012. Williams, L.J. "Negro In Golf." Negro History Bulletin, 15 (December 1951), 52-53+.

TENNIS

1013. Barron, Allan P. "Upsurge in Tennis." Black Sports, 5
      (October 1975), 4.

1014. "Blacks Making Little Progress." Winston-Salem Journal,
      (September 20, 1976).

1015. Carrington, Ray. "Black Professional Tennis Tour." Black
      Collegian, 7 (March 1977), 68-69.

1016. "Celebrity Tennis For Black Charities." Jet, 50 (July 29, 1976),
      52-55.

1017. Henderson, Edwin B. "Negro In Tennis." Negro History Bulletin,
      15 (December 1951), 54.

1018. Kisner, Ronald. "How Celebrities Use Tennis To Get Money For
      Blacks." Jet, 48 (July 17, 1975), 52-55.

1019. Norman, G.F. "Colored Tennis Champions." Crisis, 31
      (November 1925), 18.

1020. Norman, G.F. "The American Tennis Association." Crisis, 29
      (November 1924), 22.

1021. Provost, Herb. "Art of Pitch and Catch." Black Sports, 6
      (July 1976), 17.

ARTICLES BY BLACK ATHLETES
A SELECTED LIST

BASEBALL

VIDA BLUE

1022. Blue, Vida. "Next Year Is Going To Be Different." Ebony, 27
       (October 1972), 132-142+.

ROY CAMPANELLA

1023. Campanella, Roy. "I'll Walk Again." Saturday Evening Post,
       231 (July 26, 1958), 13-15; (August 2, 1958), 26-27.

1024. Campanella, Roy. "How I Catch A Ball Game." Saturday Evening
       Post, 228 (May 26, 1956), 33.

DOCK ELLIS

1025. Hall, Donald and Dock Ellis.   "Dock Ellis: Maverick Citizen
       In The Country of Baseball." Black Sports, 6 (May 1977), 35-44.

JACKIE ROBINSON

1026. Robinson, John Roosevelt [Jackie] "Best Advice I Ever Had."
       Reader's Digest, 72 (May 1958), 214-16.

1027. Robinson, Jackie. "My Son's Story: Excerpt From I Never Had It
       Made." McCalls, 100 (October 1972), 135-41.

1028. Robinson, John Roosevelt. "Speaking Out." Saturday Evening
       Post, 236 (August 10, 1963), 10.

1029. Robinson, John Roosevelt. "There's Only One Way To Beat the
       Yankees." Life, 55 (October 4, 1963), 106A-12.

1030. Robinson, John Roosevelt. "Why I'm Quiting Baseball." Look,
      21 (February 22, 1955), 78.

                        MAURY WILLS

1031. Wills, Maury. "Why Lou Brock Is A Great Base Stealer." New York
      Times, (August 7, 1977), p. 2. sec. 5.

                        BASKETBALL

                    KAREEM ABDUL-JABBAR

1032. Alcindor, Lew and Patrick William Salva. "Kareem Abdul-Jabbar:
      Best Man In His Game." Sepia, 27 (March 1978), 47-50.

1033. Langlais, Rudy and Lewis Alcindor. "Kareem Abdul-Jabbar...
      Interview." Black Sports, 5 (January 1976), 10-14+.

                    WILT CHAMBERLAIN

1034. Chamberlain, Wilt and B. Ottum. "My Life In A Bush League."
      Sports Illustrated, 22 (April 12, 1965), 32-34; (April 19, 1965),
      38-41.

1035. Chamberlain, Wilt. "Pro Basketball Has Ganged Up On Me." Look,
      24 (March 7, 1960), 51-55.

1036. Chamberlain, Wilt. "Why I Am Quitting College." Look, 22
      (June 10, 1958), 91-94.

                        BILL RUSSELL

1037. Maule, Tex and Bill Russell. "I Am Not Worried About Ali."
      Sports Illustrated, 26 (June 1967), 18-21.

1038. Russell, Bill. "I Don't Have To Prove A Thing." Negro Digest,
      13 (March 1964), 12-21.

1039. Russell, Bill. "I Was A 6'9" Babe in the Woods." Saturday
      Evening Post, 230 (January 18, 1958), 25.

1040. Russell, Bill and Branch Taylor. "Family Heroes [Excerpt From
      Second Wind: The Memoirs of An Opinonated Man]." Essence, 11
      (June 1980), 76-7+.

1041. Russell, Bill and B. Ottum. "Psych and My Other Tricks: Stars
      of World Champion Boston Celtics." Sports Illustrated, 23
      (October 25, 1965), 32-34.

BOXING

MUHAMMAD ALI

1042. Clay, Cassius. "I'll Chop That Big Monkey To Pieces." Life, 54 (February 15, 1963), 62A+.

1043. Clay, Cassius. "I'm A Little Special." Sports Illustrated, 20 (February 24, 1964), 14-15.

1044. Clay, Cassius. "I'm The Greatest: Poem." Life, 54 (February 15, 1963), 62B-63.

1045. Clay, Cassius. "Integration: As Negro Champ Views It; Excerpts From News Conference." U.S. News and World Report, 56 (March 16, 1964), 20.

1046. Muhammad Ali. "I Am The Master of My Destiny". Crawdaddy, (February 1975), 54.

1047. Muhammad Ali. "My Mother Right or Wrong." McCalls, (May 1971), 110.

EZZARD CHARLES

1048. Charles, Ezzard. "How I'll Beat Rocky Marciano." Ebony, 9 (June 1954), 27-32.

1049. Charles, Ezzard. "I Was Jinxed by Joe Louis." Ebony, 6 (October 1951), 114-16.

JOE FRAZIER

1050. Frazier, Joe. "Cassius Who?" Ebony, 27 (May 1972), 68-76+.

JOE LOUIS

1051. Louis Joe. "Fidel and the U.S. Negro." Time, 75 (June 6, 1960), 36.

1052. Louis, Joe. "I'd Do It All Over Again." Ebony, 11 (November 1955), 65-70.

1053. Louis, Joe. "Oh, Where Did My Money Go?" Saturday Evening Post, 223 (January 7, 1956), 22-23.

1054. Louis, Joe. "Why I Retired: Brown Bomber's Exclusive Story." New York Age, (March 5, 1945), 1.

1055. Louis, Joe. "Why I Quit." Ebony, 5 (December 1949), 61-70.

1056. Louis, Joe. "Why I'm Fighting Again: Ex-Champ Tells Why He Is Returning To The Ring For Heavyweight Title Fight With Ezzard Charles." Ebony, 5 (October, 1950), 15-18.

ARCHIE MOORE

1057. Moore, Archie. "My Rocky Road to Rocky." Look, 19
(September 6, 1955), 94-99, (September 20, 1955), 80-82.

1058. Moore, Archie "The Secret of My Diet." Sports Illustrated, 13
(July 4, 1960), 27-29.

FLOYD PATTERSON

1059. Gross, M. and Floyd Patterson. "I Want to Destroy Clay." Sports
Illustrated, 21 (October 19, 1964), 42-44.

1060. "Patterson, Floyd. "Cassius Clay Must Be Beaten." Sports
Illustrated, 23 (October 11, 1965), 78-80+.

1061. Patterson, Floyd. "In Defense of Cassius Clay." Esquire, 66
(August, 1966), 55-8.

1062. Patterson, Floyd. "The Floyd Patterson I Know I Am." Sports
Illustrated, 14 (March 27, 1961), 28-33.

1063. Patterson, Floyd. "I Live With Myself: Patterson-Liston Fight."
Sports Illustrated, 19 (August 5, 1963), 27.

1064. Patterson, Floyd. "I Want My Title Back: Johanson-Patterson
Rematch." Ebony, 14 (September 1959), 47.

1065. Patterson, Floyd. "My Greatest Ambition, Financial Security."
Ebony, 12 (March 1957), 59-62.

1066. Patterson, Floyd. "With A Bit of Fear." Sports Illustrated, 18
(September 17, 1962), 18-23.

SUGAR RAY ROBINSON

1067. Robinson, Ray. "Why I'm the Bad Boy of Boxing." Ebony, 6
(November 1950), 72-74.

FOOTBALL

JIM BROWN

1068. Brown, Jim. "How I Play Fullback." Sports Illustrated,
13 (September 26, 1960), 53-57.

1069. Brown, Jim and Myron Cope. "Jimmy Brown's Own Story." Look, 27
(October 20, 1964), 104-12.

TENNIS

ARTHUR ASHE

1070. Ashe, Arthur. "Don't Tell Me How To Think." Black Sports, 5
      (August 1975), 34-37.

1071. Ashe, Arthur. "I'm Simply Me." Newsweek, 64 (September 7, 1964)
      53.

1072. Ashe, Arthur. "Why Me?" Ebony, 35 (November 1979), 44+.

ARTICLES ABOUT INDIVIDUAL
BLACK ATHLETES
A SELECTED LIST

BASEBALL

HANK AARON

1073. "A. Daley Comment." New York Times, (July 10, 1973), p. 51.

1074. "Aaron Clouts No. 715 on 1st Swing in Game." Winston-Salem Journal, (April 9, 1974).

1075. Aaron, Gaile. "Hank Aaron Day In Milwaukee Spawns Tender Thoughts." Jet, 51 (October 7, 1976), 46-47.

1076. "Aaron Hammers No. 700; 14 Shy of Babe." Winston-Salem Journal and Sentinel, (July 22, 1973).

1077. "Aaron Predicted His Baseball Future." Chicago Defender, (April 13, 1974).

1078. "Aaron Remembers Flag-Winning H.R." Winston-Salem Journal, (July 14, 1976).

1079. "Aaron Says He's Even Money to Hit 715 HRS." The Philadelphia Tribune, (May 4, 1971).

1080. "Aaron to Stay." Winston-Salem Journal, (October 15, 1975).

1081. "Aaron Withdraws Suit; Company Representative Say New Agreement Has Been Reached." New York Times, (May 24, 1973), p. 62.

1082. "Anderson Article On Fame And Continuing Round of Celebrations, Fetes and Appearances For Henry Aaron." New York Times, (June 20, 1974), p. 51.

1083. "Annual Baseball Roundup, the Last of the Big Bats." Ebony, 26 (June, 1971), 92-4+.

1084. "Aaron Blasts Baseball For Barring Blacks From Management."
Washington Post, (March 7, 1974), p. 4 sec. C.

1085. "Article On Henry Aaron Following His Hitting Record 715th Home
Run." New York Times, (April 9, 1974), p. 50.

1086. "Artificial Rhubard." Time, 103 (March 25, 1974), 93.

1087. "Atlanta Braves Announce On July 26 That They Will Continue
To Give Money To Fans Who Return Baseballs Hit by Hank Aaron..."
New York Times, (July 27, 1973), p. 22.

1088. "Atlanta, Georgia Mayor Maynard Jackson's Proposal To Rename
Atlanta Stadium After Henry Aaron Hits Snag." New York Times,
(May 2, 1974), p. 68.

1089. "Atlanta On Edge." Newsweek, 74 (September 19, 1969), 129-30.

1090. "Autobiography Reviewed." Washington Post, (October 27, 1974),
p. 18, sec. D.

1091. "Babe Ruth Derby." Time, 97 (May 10, 1971), 58+.

1092. "Babe, Willie and Hank." Newsweek, 77 (May 10, 1971), 67.

1093. "Baseball's Hero." Economist, 251 (April 13, 1974), 56.

1094. "Biographical Sketch: Real Name Is Henry Louis Aaron." New York
Times, (May 18, 1970), p. 42.

1095. "Biography By George Plimpton Reviewed." Washington Post,
(October 27, 1974), p. 18 sec. D.

1096. "Book Aaron by Henry Aaron With Furman Bisher, Reviewed by
Roger Kahn." New York Times, (June 2, 1974), p. 6.

1097. Book Bad Henry by Henry Aaron, Stan Baldwin and Jerry Jenkins
Reviewed by Roger Kahn." New York Times, (June 2, 1974), p. 6.
sec. 7.

1098. "Braves Owner Try For A Better Score." Business Week, (April
6, 1974), 23.

1099. Buckley, T. "Packaging of A Home Run." New York Times Magazine,
(March 31, 1974), 22.

1100. "Cartoon Shows The Babe Watching 715." Washington Post,
(April 10, 1974), p. 18, sec. A.

1101. "Catch Me If You Can." Winston-Salem Journal,
(February 1, 1970).

1102. "Chasing The Babe," Newsweek, 81 (June 4, 1974), 67 (August
13, 1973), 52-4+.

1103. "Chicago Honors Hank Aaron While Atlanta Is Too Busy Hating Him For His Homers." Jet, 44 (June 21, 1973), 48-49.

1104. Clarke, Norm. "Aaron Slams No. 714 to Tie Ruth." Winston-Salem Journal, (April 5, 1974).

1105. Cohane, T. "Portrait of a Hitter: Hank Aaron." Look, 24 (July 19, 1960), 406-40d.

1106. Collins, B. "Hank Aaron: Record-Breaking Year?" Saturday Evening Post, 244 (Summer 1972), 83+.

1107. "Computer at Georgia State University. Predicts That Aaron Will Probably Break Record Next Season..." New York Times, (August 2, 1973), p. 42.

1108. Cunningham, George. "Hank As Mother Hen: Young Atlanta Team Looks To 'The Hank' For Leadership." Black Sports, 5 (April 1976), 30-31+.

1109. "Curtain Closes on Aaron's Glorious Career." Jet, 51 (October 21, 1976), 53.

1110. "Dr. Anderson Comments." New York Times, (January 22, 1974), p. 45.

1111. "Delinger Column on Comparing Hank Aaron and Sadaharu." Washington Post, (September 7, 1977), p. 1, sec. D.

1112. "Does Not Attend Luncheon at Which He Was To Be Honored for 715th Home Run; Send Telegram Explaining Reasons." Washington Post, (January 29, 1980), p. 3a Sec. D.

1113. "Downing in Vanishing Act." Twin City Sentinel, (April 1974).

1114. Editorial-Home Run Achievement Praised." Washington Post, (April 6, 1974), p. 14 sec. A.

1115. "Editorial on Hank Aaron and Walter Alston." Washington Post, (October 11, 1976), p. 26, sec. A.

1116. "Files Suit In Manhattan Supreme Court. N.Y.C. on May 17 Charging that Lever Bros. Reneged on Contract..." New York Times, (May 18, 1973), p. 25.

1117. Fimrite, R. "End of the Glorious Ordeal." Sports Illustrated, 40 (April 15, 1974), 20-3.

1118. Furlong, W.B. "Panther At The Plate: Hank Aaron." New York Times Magazine, (September 21, 1958), 43.

1119. "Georgia Lt. Governor Lester G. Maddox, Following Meeting With Atlanta Braves Baseball Player Henry Aaron." New York Times, (January 31, 1974), p. 38.

1120. "Grammas to Get Milwaukee Job." Winston-Salem Journal, (November 10, 1975).

1121. Gulliver, H. "Women Behind Hank Aaron's Smashing Success." Todays Health, 52 (April 1974), 22-5+.

1122. "Hall of Fame Is Waiting." Winston-Salem Journal, (July 10, 1974).

1123. "Hank Aaron." Crisis, 83 (February 1976), 41.

1124. "Henry Aaron, Attending Ceremony In Atlanta, GA on September 29, Say He Is Undecided on Retirement." New York Times, (September 20, 1974), p. 48.

1125. "Henry Aaron Breaks Ty Cobb's Major League Record By Playing in His 3,034th Game." New York Times, (July 21, 1974), p. 4, sec. 5.

1126. "Hank Aaron-Editorial." Crisis, 83 (February 1976), 41.

1127. "Hank Aaron Eyes Ruth Homer Mark." Chicago Daily Defender, (March 14, 1970).

1128. "Hank Finds His Dream." Twin City Sentinel, (January 24, 1974).

1129. "Hank Aaron Hits His 695th and 696th Career Home Runs on July 8 in New York City." New York Times, (July 9, 1973), p. 45.

1130. "Hank Aaron Hits His 700th Career Home run on July 21 in Atlanta." New York Times, (July 22, 1973), p. 1, sec. 5.

1131. "Hank Aaron Hits 702 on August 16." New York Times, (August 17, 1973), p. 21.

1132. "Hank Aaron Knocks Barriers To Commercial $$ For Blacks." Jet, 44 (May 17, 1973), 54.

1133. "Hank Aaron Pockets $600,000 As He Aims To Rip Ruth's Record." Jet, 41 (March 16, 1972), 51-52.

1134. "Hank Aaron Postpones His Date With Destiny Until Next Season." Jet, 44 (October 18, 1973), 78-80.

1135. "Hank Aaron Say New Baseballs Go Farther." Jet, 57 (June 9, 1977), 48.

1136. "Hank Aaron Says That When He Retires As Baseball Player He Hopes To Be Offered A Position In Front Office." New York Times, (August 8, 1973), p. 30.

1137. "Hank Aaron Steals All-Star Thunder." Jet, 44 (August 9, 1973), 52-53.

1138. "Hank Aaron Takes A Swing At Racist Air In Baseball." Jet, 56 (August 16, 1979), 50.

1139. "Hank Aaron Tells Atlanta, Ga. Court on October 30 That His Ex-Wife Has Not Allowed Him Reasonable Visitation Rights With His 4 Children." New York Times, (October 1973), p. 52.

1140. "Hank Aaron Wastes No Time." Newsweek, 83 (April 15, 1974), 72.

1141. "Hank Aaron's 648th." Newsweek, 79 (June 12, 1972), 70.

1142. "Hanks No. 44 Retired As He's Honored By Braves." Jet, 52 (May 5, 1977), 52+.

1143. Harrison, Claude. "Mays, Aaron and Banks Last of the Old Guard." Philadelphia Tribune, (May 26, 1970).

1144. "Henry Aaron Has Been Invited By President Ford To White House Dinner on October 2 in Honor of Japanese Emperor Hirohito." New York Times, (September 19, 1975), p. 48.

1145. "Henry Aaron Interviewed," Washington Post, (September 30, 1976), p. 1. sec. D.

1146. "Henry Aaron of Atlanta Braves Says He will Retire After This Season If He Hits 42 Home Runs and Breaks Babe Ruth's Career Record of 714." New York Times, (March 15, 1973), p. 54.

1147. "Henry Aaron Says That He Will Announce Within 10 days Whether He Will Return For Another Season for Baseball." New York Times, (October 4, 1974), p. 46.

1148. "Henry Aaron Signs $1-million, 5-yr. Contract With Magnavox Company on January 21." New York Times, (January 22, 1974), p. 61.

1149. "Henry Aaron To Retire After '74 Season and Join Atlanta Braves Front Office." New York Times, (May 12, 1974), p. 25, sec. 5.

1150. "Henry Aaron's Golden Autumn." Time, 102 (September 24, 1973), 73-4+.

1151. "The High and The Mired: Hank Aaron." Sports Illustrated, 10 (May 25, 1959), 24.

1152. "Hits 703rd." New York Times, (August 13, 1983), 15.

1153. "Hits 704th: Home Run Is Also Aaron's 1,378th Career Extra Base Hit." New York Times, (August 19, 1973), p. 1, sec. 5.

1154. "Hits 714th Home Run." Washington Post, (April 5, 1974), p. 6. sec. D.

1155. "Hits 715th Home Run." Washington Post, (April 9, 1974), p. 1 sec. D.

1156. "Home-Run Hysteria." Time, 103 (April 8, 1974), 57-8.

1157. "Home Run King Sets New Goals." Washington Post, (April 9, 1974), p. 1, sec. D.

1158. "Honored By Georgia Legislature." Washington Post, (January 31, 1974), p. 6, sec. D.

1159. "Honored In U.S. House Ceremonies." Washington Post, (June 14, 1974), p. 3. sec. D.

1160. "I'm Just Happy It's Over. Twin City Sentinel, (April 9, 1974).

1161. "Interview With Hank Aaron." Black Enterprise, 5 (December 1974), 49-51+.

1162. "It's Almost Over With." Time, 103 (April 15, 1974), 68.

1163. "It Comes Naturally: Hank Aaron." Newsweek, 53 (June 15, 1959), 94.

1164. "J.J. O'Connor Reviews NBC TV Program On Aaron's Career." New York Times, (October 23, 1973), p. 95.

1165. Kisner, Ronald E. "Aaron Aims His Bat To Break Ruth's Record." Jet, 42 (April 13, 1973), 46-48+.

1166. Kisner, Ronald E. "Hammering Hank Aaron's Human Side." Jet, 44 (August 30, 1973), 14-17+.

1167. Kisner, Ronald E. "Hank Aaron Discusses Racism and His Race For Ruth's Record." Jet, 44 (July 19, 1973), 52-56.

1168. Kisner, Ronald E. "Hank Aaron: His Honeymoon and His Home Life Today." Jet, 45 (December 13, 1973), 69-77.

1169. Kisner, Ronald E. "Hank Aaron On Top Alone." Jet, 46 (April 25, 1974), 4-6+.

1170. Kisner, Ronald E. "Hank Aaron Will Play For Milwaukee Braves Lose Out." Jet, 47 (November 7, 1974), 53.

1171. Leggett, William. "Hank Becomes A Hit." Sports Illustrated, 31 (August 18, 1969), 10-13.

1172. Legget, William. "Henry Raps One For History." Sports Illustrated, 32 (May 25, 1970), 20-2.

1173. Leggett, William. "Poised For the Golden Moment." Sports Illustrated, 40 (April 8, 1974), 46-8.

1174. Leggett, William. "Tortured Road To 715." Sports Illustrated, 38 (May 28, 1973), 28-3+.

1175. "Letter To Henry Aaron-Editorial." Crisis, 80 (October 1973), 258.

1176. McDonald, D. "Henry Aaron, Superstar." Reader's Digest, 104
      (April 1974), 183-4+.

1177. Mann, Arthur J. "Danger With A Double." Sports Illustrated, 23
      (September 20, 1965), 36-7.

1178. Masin, H.L. "Homer of the Braves." Senior Scholastic, 91
      (September 21, 1967), 28.

1179. "Mattigo Enterprises, Inc. File $3-Million Suit in NYS
      Supreme Court, NYC on October 17." New York Times,
      (October 18, 1973), p. 59.

1180. "Milwaukee's Newest Darling." Ebony, 11 (September 1956), 83-86.

1181. Montague, John. "Aaron's Memory Hazy About 1951 Trip To Twin
      City." Twin City Sentinel, (April 10, 1974).

1182. Montague, John. "Moment Frozen in History." Winston-Salem
      Journal, (April 9, 1974).

1183. "Mrs. Babe Ruth In Telephone Interview..." New York Times,
      (July 27, 1973), p. 22.

1184. "Mrs. Barbara Lucas Aaron, Former Wife of Henry Aaron Asks Fulton
      County (Ga.) Court To Increase Her Alimony Payments." New York
      Times, (June 5, 1974), p. 34.

1185. "NYC Mayor Beame Declares June 18 Henry Aaron Day in New York
      City." New York Times, (June 19, 1974), p. 47.

1186. Nipson, Herb. "Hank Aaron: Pursuing Ruth's Record, Star
      Worries About Wins." Ebony, 28 (September 1973), 144-146+.

1187. "No Biz Like Show Biz." Newsweek, 83 (March 25, 1974), 88.

1188. Norwood, Beverly. "Hank Waits and Waits." Winston-Salem
      Journal, (September 1, 1973).

1189. Norwood, Beverly. "Aaron: No More Home Run Goals. Just Help
      Braves Win." Winston-Salem Journal, (April 10, 1974).

1190. "Not Better Hitter Than Aaron, Japan's OH Says." Jet, 51
      (October 28, 1976), 49.

1191. "Number 715, After The Ball Was Over." Newsweek, 83
      (April 22, 1974), 69.

1192. Perry, Harmon. "Hank Aaron's Four Children Didn't Attend
      Historic Game." Jet, 46 (April 25, 1974), 55-56.

1193. "Pictured After Hitting No. 715." Washington Post, (April 9,
      1974), p. 1, sec. A.

1194. "Pleasing the Babe." Winston-Salem Journal, (April 4, 1974).

1195. Plimpton, George. "Final Twist of the Drama." Sports
      Illustrated, 40 (April 22, 1974), 82-6+.

1196. Poinsett, Alex. "Hank Aaron Nobody Knows." Ebony, 29
      (July 1974), 31-4+.

1197. "Quest for No. 715." Time, 102 (July 9, 1973), 53.

1198. "Reggie Smith Comments On Hank Aaron's Attempt To Set Major
      League Career Home Run Record." New York Times, (July 16, 1973),
      p. 37.

1199. "R. Smith Comments On Hank Aaron's Pursuit of Record." New York
      Times, (August 6, 1973), p. 27.

1200. "Ryoichi Shibusawa Article On Sadaharu OH: Hank Aaron."
      Washington Post, (September 11, 1977), p. 3, sec. D.

1201. Saladino, Tom. "Atlanta Sports Capital of World Monday."
      Journal & Sentinel, (April 7, 1974).

1202. "Salute To Henry Aaron." Washington Post, (September 19, 1976),
      p. 2, sec. D.

1203. Schoener, C.J. "One of World's Few Authentic Heroes." Twin City
      Sentinel, (June 9, 1974).

1204. Shearer, Ed. "Aaron is Hounded Daily by Fans, Reporters."
      Twin City Sentinel, (April 3, 1974).

1205. Shearer, Ed. "Hank Aaron Once Failed Try Out With Dodgers."
      Twin City Sentinel, (April 1, 1974).

1206. Shearer, Ed. "Hank: It Just Didn't Work." Winston-Salem
      Journal, (October 1, 1973).

1207. Shearer, Ed. "Thomson's 1954 Injury Gave Aaron His Big Chance."
      Twin City Sentinel, (April 2, 1974).

1208. "Signs Contract With Magnavox Corporation." Washington Post,
      (January 22, 1974), p. 2, sec. D.

1209. "Small Men, Big Bats: Ernie Banks and Hank Aaron." Ebony, 15
      (May 1960), 85-90.

1210. "Sport." Time, 103 (April 22, 1974), 63.

1211. "Students Say Hank Better, Not Older." Jet, 45 (February 28,
      1974), 48-49.

1212. "T. Buckley Comments On Try For Record; Aaron's Baseball Career
      Reviewed." New York Times, (July 26, 1973), p. 39.

1213. Terrell, R. "Murder With A Blunt Instrument: Hank Aaron."
      Sports Illustrated, 7 (August 12, 1957), 8-11.

1214. "That Home Run." National Review, 26 (April 26, 1974), 471-2.

1215. "U.S. Senate Votes Commendation." Washington Post, (April 10, 1974), p. 18, sec. A.

1216. "Weds Billye Williams On November 12 in Kingston, Jamaica." New York Times, (November 13, 1973), p. 56.

1217. "Willie Mays, Hank Aaron Are Top Vote Getters In First Jet-Seagram Poll." Jet, 43 (November 2, 1972), 51.

1218. Young. D. "Men With A Yen For The Fences." Sports Illustrated, 41 (November 11, 1974), 84+.

DICK ALLEN

1219. Banks, Lacey J. "Richie Allen: I'm My Own Man." Ebony, 25 (July 70), 88-90+.

1220. Kisner, Ronald E. "Dick Allen: Baseball's Big Drawing Card." Jet, 42 (August 3, 1972), 52-56.

1221. "Richie Allen, Pride of the Phillies." Sepia, 13 (September 1964), 52-55.

1222. Robinson, Louie. "The Importance of Being Dick Allen." Ebony, 27 (October 1972), 192-2+.

1223. "Sox Put Allen At Top of The Heap." Jet, 43 (March 15, 1973), 51.

EUGENE BAKER

1224. "It's Good To Be Back In The Majors." Sepia, 12 (August 1963), 63-66.

1225. "Most Important Negro In Baseball." Ebony, 16 (October, 1961) 59-60+.

1226. "Saga of Gene Baker From Player To Manager." Sepia, 10 (October 1961), 75-77.

ERNIE BANKS

1227. "Ageless Ernie Keeper of A Dream." Ebony, 24 (June 1969), 136-140+.

1228. "Banks Demoted To Minors But Still To Be A Cub." Jet, 45 (October 25, 1973), 77.

1229. "Banks Golf Classic Aids Sickle Cell." Jet, 43 (October 5, 1972), 51-53.

1230. "Banks Proves Durocher Wrong." Journal and Sentinel, (April 26, 1970).

1231. "Chicago Baseball Star Ernie Banks Seeks New Role as He Runs For City Council..." Sepia, 12 (March, 1963), 81.

1232. "Ernie Banks Leads 6 to Hall of Fame." Chicago Defender, (August 6, 1977).

1233. "Everybody Likes Ernie Banks." Sepia, 16 (November 1967), 60-64.

1234. "From Banks To Baker To Fame." Ebony, 11 (May 1956), 100-105.

1235. Harrison, Claude. "Mays Aaron and Banks Last of the Old Guard," Philadelphia Tribune, (March 26, 1970).

1236. Naab, Bill. "Ernie Banks: Always A Winner At Bat, A field, But 'Too Nice' For Manager." Black Sports, 4 (March 1975), 38-40.

1237. Simms, Gregory. "Ernie Banks Recalls His Days In The Old Negro' Leagues." Jet, 51 (February 10, 1977), 54-55.

1238. "Small Men, Big Bats: Ernie Banks and Hank Aaron." Ebony, 15 (May 1960), 85-90.

JOE BLACK

1239. Garber, Mary. "Joe Black: Legalize the Spit Ball." Winston-Salem Journal, (March 12, 1972).

1240. "Huckster Joe Black." Sepia, 11 (November 1962), 42-45.

1241. "Joe Black: Brooklyn's Strong Right Arm." Our World, 8 (May 1953), 34-37.

VIDA BLUE

1242. "Baseball's Amazing Vida Blue." Ebony, 27 (September 1971), 94-99.

1243. "Blue Returns To A's For $63,000." Jet, 42 (May 18, 1972), 56-57.

1244. "Guess Who's Coming To Dinner-Vida Blue." Jet, 43 (November 3, 1972), 5.

1245. Kisner, Ronald E. "Vida Blue-Best Pitcher In Baseball." Jet, 4 (July 15, 1971), 52-55.

1246. Kisner, Ronald E. "Vida Chasing The Blues With Goodtime Pitching." Jet, 48 (July 3, 1975), 48-49.

1247. "Vida Blue Is 'Blue' Over Daley In 1972 Contract Negotiations." Jet, 41 (January 27, 1972), 50-51.

1248. "Vida Blue Wins MVP Award-Youngest Named." Jet, 41 (December 2, 1972), 52.

LYMAN BOSTOCK

1249. Young, Andrew S. "Killing of Lyman Bostock." Sepia, 27 (November 1978), 71.

1250. Young, Andrew S. "Baseball's Unspoiled Millionaire." Sepia, 27 (May 1978), 68-72+.

LOU BROCK

1251. "Brock Wins Second Ebony Baseball Prize." Jet, 47 (February 20, 1975), 50.

1252. "Lou Brock: I Would Be A Dam Good Manager." Jet, 52 (September 15, 1977), 52-54.

1253. Simms, Gregory. "Lou Brock Tells Secrets of Easy Base Stealing." Jet, 52 (March 24, 1977), 48-49.

1254. Simms, Gregory. "Lou Brock's Base Steals Are Not Bringing The $$$." Jet, 53 (September 29, 1977), 49.

1255. Wills, Maury. "Why Lou Brock Is A Great Base Stealer." New York Times, (August 7, 1977), p. 2. sec. 5.

1256. Xanthakos, Harry. "Brock Steals Up On 3,000-Hit Mark." Black Sports, 4 (May 1975), 8-9+.

BILL BRUTON

1257. "Bill Bruton: Milwaukee's Golden Boy." Our World, 8 (October 1953), 70-73.

ROY CAMPANELLA

1258. "Baseball's Best Cather; Roy Campanella Acclaimed By Fans As Classiest In Major Leagues." Ebony, 5 (June 1950), 50-54.

1259. "Big Man From Nicetown: Roy Campanella." Time, 66 (August 8, 1955), 50-55.

1260. "Campanella: Dodger's Man of Iron." Our World, 5 (July 1950), 42-45.

1261. "Campanella Named Easter Seals Sports Chairman." Chicago Times, (January 17, 1970).

1262. "Campanella White House Guest." Journal & Guide, (August 21, 1969).

1263. "Campy's Barnstormers." Our World, 9 (February 1954), 75.

1264. "Campy Swings, Dodgers Win." Life, 34 (June 8, 1953), 136-40.

1265. "Can Campanella Come Back." Ebony, 10 (April 1955), 91-92+.

1266. Cousins, N. "His Life Is The Greatest Game Roy Campanella."
Saturday Review, 42 (November 21, 1959), 46-47.

1267. "Does Campy Belong In The Hall of Fame." Sepia, 13
(May 1967), 63-67.

1268. "Everybody's Hero: Roy Campnaella's Heroic Fight To Regain
Control of Body Endears Him To Millions." Ebony, 14
(August 1959), 25-28+.

1269. "Hand That Lost A Pennant." Our World, 10 (May 1955), 14-15.

1270. Hepburn D. "Camp's Valiant Fight To Live." Sepia, 11
(April 1962), 36-39.

1271. Meany, T. "King of the Catcher." Negro Digest, 18
(October 1950), 13-20.

1272. "Out of the Circle: Campanella's Injury." Newsweek,
(February 10, 1958), 81-82.

1273. Roe, E. "Baseball's Greatest Catcher." Our World, 8
(September 1953), 70-73.

1274. "Whatever Happened To Roy Campanella?" Ebony, 72 (March 1972),
154.

1275. Young, Andrew S. "God Made Campanella Great." Sepia, 7
(May 1959), 13-18.

1276. Young, Andrew S. "Saga of Campy." Ebony, 24 (April 1969),
100-102+.

ROD CAREW

1277. Lane, Robert. "Why Don't Twins' Fans Like Rod Carew." Black
Sports, 7 (August 1977), 32-35+.

TOMMY DAVIS

1278. "Tommy Davis." Black Sports, 6 (May 1977), 19-20.

WILLIE DAVIS

1279. "Willie Davis; Baseball Star and Natural Actor." Sepia, 19
(May 1970), 58-59+.

1280. "Dodgers Hope Willie Davis Will Live Up to Potential."
Winston-Salem Journal, (March 8, 1970).

LARRY DOBY

1281. "I'm Not Through." Our World, 7 (March 1952), 56-58.

1282. "Is This Larry Doby's Big Year?" Our World, 5 (August 1950),
43-45.

1283. "Larry Doby's Symbolic Left Hook." Ebony, 12 (September 1957), 51-54.

AL DOWNING

1284. "Al Downing; A Yankee To Watch." Sepia, 13 (June 1964), 52-55.

LUKE EASTER

1285. Goodrich, J. "Luke Easter, King of Swat?" Negro Digest, 8 (August 1950), 3-8.

1286. "Luke Easter." Baseball's New Fence Buster." Our World, 5 (April 1950), 48-50.

1287. Richman, Milton. "Tough Job Ahead." Winston-Salem Journal, (March 11, 1970).

DOCK ELLIS

1288. "Dock Ellis Says Owners Can Afford Big Salaries." Jet, 57 (April 14, 1977), 50.

1289. "Ellis To File Suit After Mace Incident With Stadium Guard." Jet, 42 (May 25, 1972), 49.

CURT FLOOD

1290. Aikens, C. "The Struggle of Curt Flood." Black Scholar, 3 (November 1971), 1-15.

1291. "Flood Returns To States: Wants Baseball Postion." Jet, 51 (October 7, 1976), 50.

1292. Gross, N. "Curt Flood." Ebony, 23 (July 1968), 70-72+.

1293. "Supreme Court Dries Up Flood Case Against Baseball." Jet, 42 (July 13, 1972), 56-57.

1294. Wieck, James. "Curt Flood In Too Deep To Wade Out." Journal & Sentinel, (March 8, 1970).

BOB GIBSON

1295. Angell, R. "Distance." New Yorker, 56 (September 22, 1980), 83-4.

1296. "Bob Gibson; Next 30 Game Winner." Sepia, 17 (November 1968), 78-91.

1297. Kahn, R. "Sports." Esquire, 76 (July 1971), 16+.

1298. "Writers Hang Another Honor On Gibson." Jet, 39 (January 21, 1971), 51.

JOSH GIBSON

1299. "Josh Gibson, Buck Leonard In Baseball's Hall Of Fame." Jet, 42 (August 24, 1972), 51.

1300. "Josh Gibson: Greatest Slugger of Em All." Ebony, 27 (May 1972), 45-59+.

1301. "Josh the Great." New York Amsterdam News, (February 19, 1972).

JUNIOR GILLIAM

1302. Lonesome B. "Junior Gilliam Marries Wealthy St. Louis Socialite." Sepia, 7 (August 1959), 32-35.

KEN GRIFFEY

1303. Holder, Bill. "That Championship Outfield." Black Sports, 5 (April 1976), 18-22.

ELSTON HOWARD

1304. "New Mr. Yankee" Elston Howard." Ebony, 19 (October 1964), 39.

MONTE IRVIN

1305. "I Never Figured It'd Happen, Irvin Says." Jet, 43 (March 1, 1973), 49.

1306. "Monte Irvin, the Red Hot Flop." Our World, 7 (May 1952), 52-54.

REGGIE JACKSON

1307. Barron, Allan P. "That's What The Free Agent Draft Means." Black Sports, 6 (January 1977), 4.

1308. Goss, Clay. "All-New, Better-Than-Ever, Action-Packed, Reggie Jackson Road Show." Encore, 6 (July 5, 1977), 34-55

1309. "Homerun King Reggie Jackson." Ebony, 24 (Octoer 1969), 92-94+.

1310. Langlais, Rudy, "They're Probably Paying Me A Million Too Much." Black Sports, 6 (May 1977), 8-13+.

1311. Libby, Bill. "Truth About Reggie Jackson." Sepia, 27 (November 1978), 33-38.

1312. "New Reggie Defends His Hero Image." Jet, 45 (May 4, 1978), 52-55.

1313. "Reggie Calls Owner A (Bleep); He Wants Out." Jet, 56 (September 6, 1979), 46.

1314. Rhoden, Bill. "Ups and Downs of Reggie Jackson." Ebony, 32 (October 1977), 60-62+.

1315. Scott, Jim. "Say Reggie: A's Ain't Dead." Black Sports, 4
      (June 1975), 12-13+.

1316. "Suspended By Yankees; Reggie, Woman Battle Over Autograph in
      N.Y. Theatre." Jet, 54 (August 3, 1978), 52.

1317. Unger, Norman O. "Humble Reggie Thanks God, Family For Series
      Record." Jet, 53 (November 3, 1977), 54-55.

                        SAM JETHROE

1318. "Baseball's Fastest Player' Hustling Same Jethroe...." Ebony, 5
      (October 1950), 55-56.

1319. Hirshberg, A. "Jethroe And The Sophomore Jinx." Negro Digest, 9
      (August 1951), 34-44.

                        RON LEFLORE

1320. "Leflore Makes Early Bid For New Tigers' Contract." Jet, 56
      (September 13, 1980), 48.

1321. Rhoden, Bill. "Ron Leflore: Stealing Home." Ebony, 30
      (October 1975), 54-56+.

                        BILL LUCAS

1322. "Big and Small Pay Last Respects To Bill Lucas." Jet, 56
      (May 31, 1979), 48-49.

                        WILLIE McCOVEY

1323. Ribowsky, Mark. "Prime of Willie McCovey." Black Sports, 7
      (August 1977), 17-28+.

                        BILL MADDOX

1324. Smith, Sam. "Old Order Changetti: From Dimag and Mick To
      Maddox." Black Sports, 4 (June 1975), 26-29.

                        LEE MAY

1325. Ribowsky, Mark. "May Gives Orioles Edge In A.L. East." Black
      Sports, 5 (August 1975), 48-51.

                        WILLIE MAYS

1326. "A. Daley Comments On Baseball Career of Willie Mays." New York
      Times, (September 25, 1973), p. 52.

1327. "The Amazing Willie Mays." Ebony, 13 (September 1958), 45-52.

1328. "Annual Baseball Roundup: the Last of the Big Bats." Ebony, 26
      (June 1971), 92-4+.

1329. "Background of Trade Rumor." Washington Post, (May 9, 1972), p. 1, sec. D.

1330. Bankhead, T. "What's So Rare As a Willie Mays?" Look, 18 (September 21, 1954), 52+.

1331. Blount, R. "Leading Man: Wondrous Willie." Sports Illustrated, 30 (April 21, 1969), 32-4.

1332. Bonventure, P. "Say Hey and Farewell." Newsweek, 82 (October 1, 1973), 64.

1333. Brody, T. G. "Giant Shot That Forced a Playoff Betwen the Giants and the Dodgers." Sports Illustrated, 17 (October 8, 1962), 18-19.

1334. Brown, J.D. "The Onliest Way I Know: Willie Mays." Sports Illustrated, 10 (April 13, 1959), 130-38.

1335. Cohane, T. "Mystery of Willie Mays." Look, 19 (May 3, 1955), 69-72.

1336. "Comment on New York Mets Preparing A Farewell To Willie Celebration on September 25 honoring Willie Mays." New York Times, (August 31, 1973), p. 21.

1337. "Comment On September 25 Farewell To Willie Mays Night in Shea Stadium, NYC." New York Times, (September 27, 1973), p. 49.

1338. "Court Orders Willie Mays To Pay His Wife Back Alimony." New York Times, (May 24, 1977), p. 28.

1339. "D. Anderson Comments on Baseball Career of Willie Mays Following His Retirement From Game." New York Times, (September 21, 1973), p. 27.

1340. Deford, Frank. "Happy Start For A Happy New Willie." Sports Illustrated, 20 (April 27, 1964), 22-27.

1341. "Duke With Willie." Sports Illustrated, 2 (June 27, 1955), 17.

1342. Dunne, J.G. "It's A Long Way To 714." Saturday Evening Post, 239 (July 30, 1966), 78-81.

1343. "Editorial-Accomplishments Praised." Washington-Post, (May 17, 1972), p. 14, sec. A.

1344. Editorial Noting That Willie Mays Is Retiring From Baseball at End of 73 Season." New York Times, (September 22, 1973), p. 30.

1345. "Editorial on Willie Mays." Washington Post, (January 26, 1979), p. 14, sec. A.

1346. Emstein, C. "Willie Mays: My Story: Excerpts From Willie Mays: My Life In and Out of Baseball." Look, 30 (March 8, 1966), 62-3+, (March 22, 1966), 116-17+, (April 15, 1966), 72-74+.

1347. Flaherty, J. "Love Song To Willie Mays." Saturday Review, 55 (August 26, 1972), 15-16.

1348. "Former Baseball Player, Willie Mays, Currently Touring U.S. as Goodwill Ambassador For Help Young America." New York Times, (November 19, 1974), p. 58.

1349. "Fun and Games With Willie Mays." Ebony, 22 (March 1967), 37-38+.

1350. "Giant." Newsweek, 66 (September 27, 1965), 92.

1351. "Giants Open Up A Lead." Life, 37 (July 12, 1954), 18-19.

1352. Gross, M. "Vist With Willie Mays." Saturday Evening Post, 234 (May 20, 1961), 32-33.

1353. "Hand For Willie." Newsweek, 68 (August 29, 1966), 65.

1354. Harrison,Claude. "Mays, Aaron and Banks Last of the Old Guard." Philadelphia Tribune, (May 26, 1970).

1355. "He Come To Win." Negro History Bulletin, 18 (October, 1954), 13-16.

1356. "He Come To Win." Time, 64 (July 26, 1954), 46-8+.

1357. "I Want to Play More Says Aging (39) Mays." Winston-Salem Journal, (March 18, 1978).

1358. "In Pursuit of Ruth." Newsweek, 67 (May 9, 1966), 88.

1359. "J. Durso Reviews Baseball Career of Willie Mays." New York Times, (September 21, 1973), p. 29.

1360. Johnson, Robert E. "Mays Talks About His Future Career As He Quits Mets." Jet, 44 (October 11, 1973), 12-17.

1361. Kempton, Murray. "Homecoming for Willie Mays (Reprint From September 1972 issue)." Esquire, 80 (October 1973), 284-5+.

1362. Kisner, Ronald E. "A New Willie With A New Team." Jet, 42 (June 22, 1972), 44-48.

1363. "Last Pair of Spiked Baseball Shoes Worn By Willie Mays in His Final Game With New York Mets Will Be Used In Raffle." New York Times, (November 7, 1973), p. 37.

1364. Leggett, William. "How Sweet It Is!" Sports Illustrated, 36 (May 22, 1972), 16-19.

1365. "Letter To The Editor on Baseball Commissioner Bowie Kuhn." Washington Post, (November 16, 1979), p. 20, sec. A.

1366. "Letter To The Editor on Willie Mays." Washington Post, (March 13, 1979), p. 16, sec. A.

1367. Linn, E. Trials of A Negro Idd: Willie Mays." Saturday Evening Post, 236 (June 22, 1963), 70-72.

1368. Linn, E. "Woes of Willie Mays." Saturday Evening Post, 229 (April 13, 1957), 31.

1369. McDermott, J.R. "Willie The Wonder." Life, 56 (May 5, 1964), 50-52.

1370. Mann, J. "They Love Herman and Willie: Juan Marichal and Willie Mays." Sports Illustrated, 23 (September 27, 1965), 24-31.

1371. Mantle, Mickey. "Mantle Fans Mays." Esquire, 70 (August, 1968), 46-7.

1372. "Mays At St. Bernard's: Interview." New Yorker, 49 (June 9, 1973), 25-6.

1373. "Mays Days." Newsweek, 63 (May 4, 1965), 86.

1374. "Mays Fans Mantle." Esquire, 70 (August, 1968), 46-7.

1375. "Mays Halts Career After 23 Years of National League Stardom." Jet, 44 (October 4, 1973), 7.

1376. "Mays in May." Time, 83 (May 22, 1964), 85-6.

1377. Mays, Willie. "What Kids Have Taught Me." Coronet, 38 (May 1955), 91-94.

1378. "Mays Weds M.L. Allen." New York Times, (November 30, 1971), p. 62.

1379. Meany, T. "Senor Mays, Big Hit In San Juan." Colliers, 135 (Jaunary 7, 1955), 48-51.

1380. Meany, T. "Willie's Best Hits Aren't For The Giants." Colliers, 134 (September 3, 1954), 82-5.

1381. Mulvov, M. "Say Hey, No More." Sports Illustrated, 27 (August 7, 1967), 26-9.

1382. "Natural Boy of the Giants." New York Times Magazine, (July 11, 1954), 16+.

1383. "New York Mets Baseball Player Willie Mays...Donates His Spike Shoes To Black-In Between Block Association of Wyckoff Street." New York Times, (October 20, 1973), p. 23.

1384. "New York Mets Reportedly Will Hold Press Conference on September 20 To Announce That Willie Mays Will Retire At End of '73 Season." New York Times, (September 21, 1973), p. 27.

1385. "New York City Police Athletic League on January 13 Names New York
      Mets Baseball Player Willie Mays As 1st Recipient of Superstar
      of the Year Award. New York Times, (January 14, 1973), p. 5,
      sec. 5.

1386. "New Willie." Time, 64 (September 20, 1954), 71.

1387. "People Are Talking About..." Vogue, 124 (August 1, 1954),
      124-5.

1388. "Problems May Face New York Mets." Washington Post, (May 16,
      1972), p. 2, sec. D.

1389. "Profile of Old Baseball Player." Washington Post, (March 15,
      1972), p. 1, sec. D.

1390. "Reaction To Rumors of Trade." Washington Post, (May 7, 1972),
      p. 1, sec. D.

1391. "Return To Paradise." Newsweek, 79 (May 22, 1972), 67.

1392. "Returns To New York City After Trade To Mets." Washington
      Post, (May 12, 1972), p. 1, sec. D.

1393. Robinson, Louie. "Willie May's New Home." Ebony, 18
      (August 1963), 88-92+.

1394. "Rookie of the Year?" Our World, 6 (October, 1951), 66.

1395. "Rumors of Trade To New York Mets." Washington Post,
      (May 6, 1972), p. 1, sec. D.

1396. "Say, Hey," Newsweek, 43 (April 5, 1954), 83-5.

1397. Schrag, P. "Age of Willie Mays." Saturday Review, 54
      (May 8, 1971), 15-17+.

1398. Smith, Red. "May 1st Unanimous Hall of Famer?" Winston-Salem
      Journal, (December 19, 1978).

1399. "Spirit of the Giants." Look, 18 (June 15, 1954), 71-5.

1400. "Teasing Willie: Pepper Game." Life, 36 (March 29, 1954),
      83-4.

1401. "That Boy's So Full of Play." Life, 37 (September 13, 1954),
      133-4+.

1402. "There's Hope For Willie." Ebony, 21 (October 1966), 96+.

1403. "Thumb Out." New Yorker, 30 (July 10, 1954), 15.

1404. "Time Magazine Tells the Willie Mays Story." Negro History
      Bulletin, 18 (October 1954), 13-16.

1405. "Trade's Effect on Giants." Washington Post, (June 16, 1972), p. 1, sec. D.

1406. Unger, Norman O. "Willie H. Mays Stresses Education At Hall of Fame." Jet, 56 (August 23, 1979), 46-47.

1407. "What's Ahead for Willie Mays?" Ebony, 10 (August 1955), 35-40.

1408. "Where the Giants Grow: Willie Mays Moves West." Newsweek, 51. (June 9, 1958), 52-53.

1409. "Which Honor To Choose." Time, 88 (August 26, 1966), 44.

1410. "Willie Forever." Life, 72 (May 26, 1972), 38-39.

1411. "Willie Gets His Gun." Our World, 7 (September 1952), 17-21.

1412. "Willie Mays: Can He Spark A Giant Pennant?" Our World, 9 (May 1954), 80-82.

1413. "Willie Mays Enters Baseball Hall of Fame." Washington Post, (January 24, 1979), p. 1, sec. D.

1414. "Willie Mays Goes West." Look, 22 (April 19, 1958), 106-8+.

1415. "Willie Mays, Hank Aaron Are Top Vote Getters In Jet-Seagram Poll." Jet, 43 (November 2, 1972), 51.

1416. "Willie Mays: He Slugged His Way To A $250,000 Contract." Sepia, 15 (May 1966), 34-38.

1417. "Willie Mays Honeymoons In Acapulco." Ebony, 27 (February 1972), 138-30.

1418. "Willie Mays Leaves Giants To Join Mets." Jet, 42 (May 25, 1972), 51.

1419. "Willie Mays Nobody Knows." Our World, 10 (June 1955), 12-14.

1420. "Willie Mays Pofiled." Washington Post, (July 23, 1977), p. 1, sec. C.

1421. "Willie Mays: The Hottest Thing Since Babe Ruth." Newsweek, 44 (July 19, 1954), 74-6.

1422. "Willie Mays: the $110,000 Baby." Sepia, 12 (May 1963), 73-77.

1423. "Willie Mays - Twilight For Heroes." Washington Post, (July 4, 1971), p. 1, sec. B.

1424. "Willie Takes A Wife." Newsweek, 47 (February 27, 1956), 63.

1425. "Willie The Virtuoso Hurtles On To The Finish." Life, 59 (October 1, 1965), 26-33.

1426. "Willie the Whoop." Newsweek, 38 (September 10, 1951), 63.

1427. "You Can Go Home Again." Newsweek, 59 (June 11, 1962), 91.

1428. Young, Andrew S. "Can Willie Mays Hit 380 This Year?" Sepia, (June 1959), 61-64.

JOE MORGAN

1429. Eugene, David. "Joe Morgan Is A Trouble Maker." Black Sports, 7 (August 1977), 40-45.

1430. Kisner, Ronald E. "Morgan's Clutch Hit Wins Series: Bench Boosts Him For MVP." Jet, 49 (November 6, 1975), 52-54.

1431. Ribowsky, Mark. "Joe Morgan, Pint Sized Pest." Black Sports, 5 (May 1976), 11-13+.

1432. Simms, Gregory. "Why MVP Joe Morgan Doesn't Give A Hoot About Being Most Popular Player." Jet, 52 (June 16, 1977), 50.

1433. Warren, Tim. "Joe Morgan: Nice Guys Can Finish First." Encore, 6 (July 5, 1977), 36-40.

DON NEWCOMBE

1434. "A Big Man Conquers A Big Fear: Don Newcombe Overcomes Fear of Flying." Ebony, 13 (March 1958), 101-2.

1435. "Big Newk In Japan." Ebony, 18 (November 1962), 115-118+.

1436. Creamer, R. "Subject: Don Newcombe." Sports Illustrated, 3 (August 22, 1955), 48.

1437. "Don Newcombe." Ebony, 29 (January 1974), 122.

1438. "Don Newcombe: The Biggest Dodger." Ebony, 10 (October 1955), 108-14.

1439. "It's Good To Be Traded; Don Newcombe, Bill White, Sam Jones." Ebony, 14 (October 1959), 46-48.

1440. "Money Pitcher: Don Newcombe." Newsweek, 45 (June 20, 1955), 86.

1441. Newcombe, Don. "I'm Not A Quitter." Saturday Evening Post, 229 (March 9, 1957), 27.

1442. "Secret of Don Newcombe." Our World, 10 (September 1955), 62-65.

1443. "Team To Beat." Time, 68 (August 20, 1956), 77.

1444. "Will Big Don Win 25?" Our World, 5 (May 1950), 28-32.

1445. Young, Andrew S. "Don Newcombe: Baseball Great Wins Fight Againt Alcoholism." Ebony, 31 (April 1976), 54-56.

AL OLIVER

1446. Ribowsky, Mark. "Bitter Buc." Black Sports, 4 (March 1975),
      24-25+.

SATCHEL PAIGE

1447. "Actor Satch, Ageless Hurler Plays Cavalry Sergeant." Ebony, 15
      (December 1959), 109-110+.

1448. "Black Hall of Famers Get 'Special' Berth, Satchel Paige First
      In." Jet, 4 (July 22, 1971), 48-49.

1449. "Brainiest Man In Baseball; Leroy Satchel Paige Is One of the
      National Games's Smartest Players Both On and Off Field."
      Ebony, 7 (August 1952), 26-28+.

1450. Brosnan, J.P. "Good Pitch Is Better Than A Wild Swing."
      National Review, 12 (June 1962), 446-48.

1451. Brown, George F. "Satchel Paige Tells The World, "You Don't Have
      To Get Old." Sepia, 10 (December 61), 51-54.

1452. Cohane, T. "Ancient Satch." Look, 18 (December 1954), 71.

1453. Donovan, R. "Fabulous Satchel Paige." Colliers, 131
      (May 30, 1953), 62; (June 6, 1953), 20-24; (June 13, 1953),
      54-59.

1454. Fox, W.B. "Conversation With Satchel Paige." Holiday, 38
      (August, 1965), 18.

1455. "The Law Tells Satch Win or Jail." Ebony, 13 (September 1958),
      77-82.

1456. "Lift The Latch For Satchel." Sports Illustrated, 18 (March 11,
      1963), 7.

1457. Lipman, D. "Maybe I'll Pitch Forever: Satchel Paige."
      Saturday Evening Post, 234 (March 11, 1961), 38-39.

1458. "Paige Gets No. 1 Award From Cartoonists Society." Jet, 42
      (April 27, 1972), 56.

1459. "Philosopher's Consolation." Sports Illustrated, 20
      (January 27, 1964), 17.

1460. "Satchel is "Main Event" at Hall of Fame Show." Afro American,
      (August 21, 1971).

1461. "Satchel Paige: Baseball's Methuselah." Our World, 7
      (August 1952), 48-60.

1462. "Satchel Paige Tells of Treatment With Indians, Blast Team For
      His Abuse." Jet, 4 (May 6, 1971), 56.

1463. "Satchel Paige, the Brainiest Man in Baseball." Ebony, 7 (August 1952), 26-38.

1464. "Slow: Satchel Paige." New Yorker, 28 (September 13, 1952), 32-33.

1465. "When Batters Wobble: Satchel Paige." Newsweek, 52 (July 14, 1958), 57-58.

DAVE PARKER

1466. McDonnell, Joe. "World's Greatest Baseball Player." Sepia, 27 (November 1978), 73-77.

1467. Reveron, Derek A. "Dave Parker: Big Man, Big Bat and Baseball's Biggest Salary." Ebony, 34 (October 1979), 84-85+.

1468. Ribowsky, Mark." Dave Parker Is The Closest Thing To Perfection." Black Sports, 7 (May 1978), 44-47.

VADA PINSON

1469. "Vada Pinson of the Cincinnati Reds." Ebony, 15 (September 1960), 86-87.

1470. Terrell, R. "Young Men At Work: Vada Pinson, Willie Tasby." Sports Illustrated, 10 (April 6, 1959), 44-49.

J.R. RICHARDS

1471. Twersky, Marty. "J.R. Richards: So Who Is That." Black Sports, 7 (September 1977), 48-49+.

FRANK ROBINSON

1472. "Angry Robinson Charges Baseball Ignores Blacks." Winston-Salem Journal, (February 8, 1980).

1473. Bilotti, Richard. "Tribe Names Robinson." Winston-Salem Journal, (October 4, 1974).

1474. "Brothers Three of Baseball: Frank Robinson and His Brothers." Ebony, 20 (September 1965), 73-74+.

1475. "Frank Robinson: Hawk Among the Orioles." Ebony, 21 (September 1966), 88-90.

1476. "Frank Robinson: The Challenge of '67." Sepia, 16 (May 1967), 55-59.

1477. "Frank Robinson's Number Retired: Makes Orioles First." Jet, 41 (January 2, 1972), 5.

1478. "Indians Fire Robinson After Two Years." Winston-Salem Journal, (June 20, 1977).

1479. "A Kid and An Old-Timer." Ebony, 12 (June 1957), 41-46.

1480. Lawson, E. "Frank Robinson Comes of Age." Saturday Evening
      Post, 235 (August 25, 1962), 38-42.

1481. Nunn, Bill. "Cycle Achieved in Choice of Frank Robinson."
      The Courier, (October 19, 1974).

1482. "Player of Week: Cincinnati Reds Outfielder Frank Robinson."
      Sports Illustrated, 21 (August 17, 1964), 85.

1483. "Rap With Frank Robinson, Baseball's First Black Manager:
      Interview." Black Sports, 4 (January 1975), 13-14.

1484. "Robinson Becomes First Black Baseball Manager." Jet, 47
      (October 17, 1974), 46-47.

1485. Robinson, Louie. "Frank Robinson Makes Baseball History."
      Ebony, 30 (May 1975), 103-106+.

1486. "Robinson Sparks Opening Day With HR, First Win." Jet, 48
      (April 24, 1975), 52-53.

1487. Sharnik, M. "Moody Tiger of the Reds: Frank Robinson." Sports
      Illustrated, 18 (June 17, 1963), 32-34.

1488. Terrell, R. "Reds At The Cross Road." Sports Illustrated, 7
      (March 10, 1958), 39-42.

1489. Trube, Richard. "Frank Robinson Reveals: What I'll Do As
      Baseball's First Black Manager." Sepia, 24 (May 1975), 37-43.

                          JACKIE ROBINSON

1490. Adderton, Donald. "Ex-Dodger Teammates Recall Jackie's Glory."
      Jet, 52 (May 5, 1977), 52.

1491. Adderton, Donald. "Spirit of Jackie Robinson Pervades All-Star
      Ceremonies." Jet, 52 (August 4, 1977), 52-54+.

1492. "After Ten Years." Newsweek, 48 (December 24, 1956), 49.

1493. "Are They Ganging Up On Jackie?" Our World, 6 (September 1951),
      56-60.

1494. "Attends American Booksellers Convention." Washington Post,
      (June 6, 1972), p. 2, sec. B.

1495. "Attends Stans Testimonial Dinner." Washington Post,
      (February 15, 1972), p. 5, sec. B.

1496. "B. Rickey Denies Rumor Jackie Robinson Will Be Traded."
      New York Times, (August 17, 1950), p. 32.

1497. "Backs Baseball Strike." Washington Post, (April 4, 1972),
      p. 1, sec. D.

1498. "Baseball: Batting At Robinson." Newsweek, 29 (May 1947), 88+.

1499. "Baseball Career Recalled." Washington Post, (October 25, 1972), p. 1, sec. D.

1500. Benjamin, P. "Then and Now: Jackie Robinson." New York Times Magazine, (April 15, 1962), 84.

1501. Bims, H. J. "Black America Says 'Goodbye, Jackie.'" Ebony, 27 (December 1972), 172-2+.

1502. "Biography Film Started." New York Times, (February 26, 1950), p. 5. sec. 2.

1503. Bowen, C. D. "Quarter Century: Its Human Triumphs." Look, 25 (December 5, 1961), 96-8.

1504. "Branch Breaks The Ice: Brooklyn Signed Jack Roosevelt Robinson, Negro Shortstop." Time, 46 (November 5, 1945), 77.

1505. "Branch Rickey Discusses the Negro Baseball." Ebony, 12 (May 1957), 38+.

1506. Brockenbury, L.I. and Bill Libby. "Tale of Two Brothers: Jack and Mack Robinson." Sepia, 11 (October 1962), 66-72.

1507. "Brooklyn Dodgers Sign First Negro To Play for Organized Baseball." Life, 19 (November 26, 1945), 133-4+.

1508. Brown, G.F. "Jackie Robinson: Two Years After Baseball." Sepia, 7 (January 1959), 8-13.

1509. Burbaker, J. "Small Beginning." New Republic, 116 (June 9, 1947), 38.

1510. "Buttoned Lip." Newsweek, 29 (April 21, 1947), 88.

1511. "Can Jackie Make the Hall of Fame?" Negro History Bulletin, 17 (October 1953), 6.

1512. "Daughter Born." New York Times, (January 15, 1950), p. 7, sec. 5.

1513. "Day In The Life of Jackie Robinson." Ebony, 13 (August 1958), 90-92+.

1514. "Does Jackie Robinson Talk Too Much?" Our World, 8 (April 1953), 10+.

1515. "Editorial." Washington Post, (October 25, 1972), p. 22 sec. A.

1516. "Editorial-Integrating Off-Field Baseball." Washington Post, (April 18, 1971), p. 6 sec. C.

1517. Ellis, E.B. "As We Read the Letter: Adam Clayton Powell-Jackie Robinson Controversy," Sepia, 12 (July 1963), 25-27.

1518. "First Negro To Join Organized Baseball." Opportunity, 24 (January 1946), 41.

1519. "4-year Scholarship In Honor of Jackie Robinson Is Established For Black Graduates at Stanford (Conn.) High School by Chesebrough-Pons's Inc." New York Times, (May 12, 1973), p. 67.

1520. "Friends Recall Jackie Robinson." Jet, 43 (November 16, 1972), 51-57.

1521. "From First To Fame: Jackie Robinson." Ebony, 17 (October 1962), 85-86.

1522. "Funeral Services Held." Washington Post, (October 28, 1972), p. 1, sec. E.

1523. "Good Citizens Make Good Communities." Scholastic, 57 (December 13, 1950), 5.

1524. "Hot-Stove League." Time, 55 (February 6, 1950), 69.

1525. "Hurray For Jackie Robinson." Negro History Bulletin, 18 (January 1955), 93.

1526. I Never Had It Made. "Reviewed." Washington Post, (November 13, 1972), p. 1, sec. B.

1527. "If You Can't Beat Him." Time, 68 (December 24, 1956), 43.

1528. "Interview With Jackie Robinson." Black Sports, 7 (August 1977), 8-11+.

1529. "Jack Anderson Column." Washington Post, (July 3, 1972), p. 11, sec. D.

1530. "Jack Roosevelt Robinson." Ebony, 27 (December 1972), 17, 171.

1531. "Jackie Blasts Florida Ball Park Jim Crow." New York Age, (April 2, 1949), 1.

1532. "Jackie Makes Good." Time, 48 (August 26, 1946), 63-4.

1533. "Jackie Robinson." Amsterdam News, (October 28, 1972).

1534. "Jackie Robinson." Crisis, 61 (December 1954), 605-606.

1535. "Jackie Robinson: A Man For All Seasons." Crisis, 79 (December 1972), 345-347.

1536. "Jackie Robinson and Roy Campanella Honored by New York Bible Society For Race Relations Work." New York Times, (December 5, 1949), p. 20.

1537. "Jackie Robinson Balks At Treatment of Blacks After Their Careers End." Jet, 42 (July 6, 1972), 51.

1538. "Jackie Robinson Becomes 1st Negro in Majors to be Named As Most Valuable Player." New York Times, (November 19, 1949), p. 14.

1539. "Jackie Robinson Cited by Catholic War Veterans For Testimony Against Communism." New York Times, (August 31, 1949), p. 26.

1540. "Jackie Robinson's Double Play." Life, 28 (May 8, 1950), 129-32.

1541. "Jackie Robinson Gets Freedoms Foundation Award For July Testimony." New York Times, (November 22, 1949), p. 22.

1542. "Jackie Robinson Goes In Training." Our World, 5 (March 1950), 48-52+.

1543. "Jackie Robinson Honored For Black Excellence By Operation PUSH." Jet, 42 (July 13, 1972), 52-53.

1544. "Jackie Robinson: Mr. Baseball." Our World, 7 (April 1952), 15-18+.

1545. "Jackie Robinson Pitching: Before House Un-American Activities Committee." Newsweek, 34 (August 1, 1949), 15-19.

1546. "Jackie Robinson Scores Big In Business." Sepia, 15 (June 1966), 52-56.

1547. "Jackie Robinson: Show Set." New York Times, (December 9, 1949), p. 54.

1548. "Jackie Robinson Story." Our World, 5 (June 1950), 36-38.

1549. "Jackie Robinson Testifies In Dispute of Robeson Assertion..." New York Times, (July 19, 1949), p. 1.

1550. "Jackie Robinson, Who Broke Color-Barrier in Major League Baseball, Honored As Man of the 25 Years By Sport Magazine." New York Times, (December 5, 1971), p. 5 sec. 5.

1551. Jackie Robinson Wins League's 1940 Batting Champ." New York Times, (December 16, 1949), p. 40.

1552. "Jackie Robinson's Double Play." Life, 28 (May 8, 1950), 129-132+.

1553. "Jackie's Dream Home." Ebony, 12 (March 1957), 83-84+.

1554. Kahn, R. "Sport." Esquire, 76 (November 1971), 24+.

1555. Kahn, R. "Sports." Esquire, 80 (October 1973), 62+.

1556. "Keeping Posted With Jackie." Time, 75 (April 11, 1960), 93.

1557. "Kentucky Colonel Kept Me In Baseball." Look, 19 (February 8, 1955), 82-84+.

1558. Kisner, Ronald and M.C. Thompson. "Jackie Robinson's Courageous Battle Against Blindness." Jet, 43 (October 12, 1972), 52-53.

1559. Kisner, Ronald and M.C. Thompson. "Troubles Cease For Robinson After 53 Years." Jet, 43 (November 9, 1972), 46-48+.

1560. Lardner, John. "Old Emancipator." Newsweek, 47 (April 1956), 85.

1561. Lardner, John. "Reese and Robinson: Team Within A Team." New Times Magazine, (September 18, 1949). 17+.

1562. Lardner, John. Team Within A Team." Negro Digest, 8 (April 1950), 92-97.

1563. "Late Baseball Star Jackie Robinson Is Awarded Posthumously Man of the Year Brotherhood Award by Philadelphia's Congregation Rodelph Shalom." New York Times, (April 29, 1973), p. 4 sec. 5.

1564. "Laurels and Leverage." Time, 54 (November 28, 1949), 40.

1565. "Leading The League." Time, 88 (July 8, 1966), 79.

1566. "Letter On Editorial on Jackie Robinson Testimony on Negroes Stand In Case of War." New York Times, (August 1, 1949), p. 16.

1567. "Letter On Robinson's Statement." New York Times, (July 26, 1949), p. 26.

1568. "Life Goes To Jackie Robinson's Jam Session: $15,000 for Civil Rights." Life, 55 (July 5, 1963), 79-81.

1569. "Making It." Newsweek, 71 (March 18, 1968), 54.

1570. Mann, Arthur W. "The Truth About the Jackie Robinson Case." Saturday Evening Post, 222 (May 13, 1950), 19-21, (May 20, 1950), 36.

1571. Mann, Arthur W. "Say Jack Robinson: Meet the Dodgers' Newest Recruit." Colliers, 117 (March 2, 1946), 67-8.

1572. Meany, T. "Jackies One of the Gang Now." Negro Digest, 8 (May 1950), 8-13.

1573. Morrison, A. "What Jackie Robinson Wants For His Son." Negro Digest, 8 (May 1950), 8-13.

1574. Morse, A.S. "Jackie Wouldn't Have Gotten To First Base Without The Determined Mothering of A Quiet Woman." Better Homes and Gardens, 28 (May 1950), 226+.

1575. "Most Unforgettable Character I've Met." Reader's Digest, 79 (December 1961), 85-90.

1576. "Named To NYS Athletic Commission." New York Times, (May 6, 1971), p. 61.

1577. "Negro Outspoken." Newsweek, 59 (January 29, 1962), 50.

1578. "Negroes Are Americans..." Survey, 85 (August 1949), 410.

1579. "Negroes Are Americans" Excerpts From Statements Before House-Un-American Activities Committee." Life, 27 (August 1, 1949), 22-3.

1580. "New York Post Drops Jackie Robinson Column' Reason Given." Jet, 19 (November 24, 1960), 8.

1581. "No Help Wanted." Time, 54 (November 28, 1949), 40.

1582. "Obituary." Washington Post, (October 25, 1972), p. 1, sec. A.

1583. "On Robinson Testimony." New York Times, (July 20, 1949), p. 24.

1584. Oursler, F. "Rookie of the Year." Reader's Digest, 52 (February 1948), 34-8.

1585. Parrot, Harold and Gil Scott. "Rap With Harold Parrot: Interview." Black Sports, 6 (July 1976), 34-37.

1586. "Plan Stage Debut." New York Times, (October 13, 1947), p. 29.

1587. Pollack, J.H. "Meet A Family Named Robinson." Parents' Magazine, 30 (October 1955), 46-47.

1588. Pye, B. "Jackie Robinson Comes Home To Los Angeles." Sepia, 11 (June 1962), 39-42.

1589. "Race and Big Business." Negro Digest, 13 (November 1963), 19-26.

1590. "Refutes Charges By J. Anderson." Washington Post, (June 29, 1972), p. 9 sec. A.

1591. Reynolds, Quentin. "More Than A Ball Player: Jackie Robinson." Saturday Review, 43 (June 11, 1960), 33.

1592. "Riches For a Rookie." Time, 50 (November 24, 1947), 54.

1593. "Rickey and Robinson." Crisis, 54 (May 1947), 137.

1594. "Robinson For Merit." Newsweek, 30 (September 22, 1947), 80.

1595. Robinson, Mack. "My Brother Jackie." Ebony, 12 (July 1957), 75-76+.

1596. "Robinson Makes Good." Crisis, 53 (October 1946), 277.

1597. "Robinson Replies To Robeson and Others." Christian Century, 66 (August 3, 1949), 908.

1598. Roeder, B. "All-Star Second Baseman; Review of Jackie Robinson." Saturday Review of Literature, 33 (July 15, 1950), 10.

1599. "Rookie." New Republic, 116 (May 19, 1947), 9-10.

1600. "Rookie of the Year." Time, 50 (September 22, 1947), 70-76.

1601. Rosenthal, H. "Are Robby's Rough Days Over?" Negro Digest, 8
      (September 1950), 18-24.

1602. "Royal Robinson." Newsweek, 28 (August 26, 1946), 71.

1603. "Safe at First?" Time, 49 (April 21, 1947), 55.

1604. Slater, Jack. "Jackie Robinson Was A Prince, A Knight." Jet,
      43 (November 9, 1972), 55.

1605. "South Seeks Jackie." Newsweek, 31 (April 19, 1948), 82.

1606. "Speaking Out." Saturday Evening Post, 236 (August 10, 1963),
      10+.

1607. Steiger, G. "Robinson's Rich Rewards." Negro Digest, 8
      (July 1950), 10-12.

1608. "Success; Brooklyn Dodgers Second Baseman As Television-Set
      Salesman." New Yorker, 25 (January 7, 1950), 20.

1609. "To Appear In Motion Picture." New York Times, (October 6, 1947),
      p. 28.

1610. "To Appear On Information Please Radio Program." New York Times,
      (April 17, 1947), p. 38.

1611. "Topic of 2 Letters To The Editor." Washington Post,
      (November 2, 1972), p. 17, sec. A.

1612. "Will Gilliam Top Jackie?" Our World, 8 (August 1953), 64-66.

1613. "Will Jackie Robinson Crack Up?" Ebony, 6 (September 1951),
      23-28.

1614. Williams, F.M. "The Robinson Story A Great Debt." The
      Tennessean, (October 25, 1972).

1615. "Wins Negro History Week Award." New York Times,
      (February 11, 1946), p. 18.

1616. Young, Andrew S. "Black Athlete In The Golden Age of Sports."
      Ebony, 24 (November 1968), 152-54+; (December 1968), 126-28+.

1617. Young, Andrew S. "I Remember Jackie: The Greatest American
      Athlete of Them All." Sepia, 26 (April 1977), 64-72.

1618. Young, Andrew S. "The Jackie Robinson Era." Ebony, 11
      (November 1955), 152-46.

1619. "Your Temper Can Ruin Us! Jackie Robinson." Look, 19
      (February 22, 1955), 78.

GEORGE SCOTT

1620. Ribowsky, Mark. "Keep 'Em Happy George." Black Sports, 7 (September 1977), 17-22.

AL SMITH

1621. "All Smith, White Sox Outfielder." Ebony, 15 (October 1960), 85-88.

WILLIE STARGELL

1622. Anderson, D. "Willie Stargell-Baseball's Peerless Pirate." Reader's Digest, 116 (April 1980), 88-92.

1623. Asinor, E. "Where I Come From, Where I Am Going (Interview)." Sport, 70 (April 1980), 29+.

1624. Cotton, A. "Fine Like Good Wine." Sports Illustrated, 52 (August 20, 1979), 49-50.

1625. "Duke Series Winner Thrilled on Meeting Star Willie Stargell." Jet, 41 (October 28, 1971), 50-51.

1626. Hanks, S. "Willie Stargell: The Making of An MVP." Sport, 70 (January 1980), 12.

1627. Nuwer, H. "Willie Stargell: The Pride of Pittsburgh." Saturday Evening Post, 252 (May-June 1980), 26+.

1628. "Patriarch of the Pirate Family." Sport, 70 (February, 1980), 72.

1629. Sutton, K.F. "Letter From The Publisher." Sports Illustrated, 52 (January 28, 1980), 4.

1630. "Willie Stargell Sets New Monthly Home Run Mark." Jet, 4 (May 13, 1971), 51.

MAURY WILLS

1631. Brody, T.C. "Snake-Sliding Dodger Tries To Steal the Pennant." Sports Illustrated, 17 (October 1, 1962), 22-23.

1632. Leggett, William. "Maury Wills-The Mouse Who Builds The Mountains." Sports Illustrated, 23 (June 12, 1965), 38-42.

1633. "No One Pays $1 For Wills, He Becomes Free Agent." Jet, 43 (November 16, 1972), 5.

1634. "Rap With Maury Wills: Black Athletes and Broadcasting Interview." Black Sports, 5 (April 1976), 24+.

1635. Ribowsky, Mark. "Where There's A Wills, There's A Controversy." Black Sports, 7 (August 1977), 18-19+.

1636. Robinson, Louie. "World's Greatest Diamond Thief: Maury Wills."
      Ebony, 18 (May 1963), 35-36.

1637. "Thief of the Bags." Newsweek, 60 (July 23, 1962), 67.

1638. "Wills To Play In Japan: Salary Is Not Revealed." Jet, 43
      (December 14, 1972), 48.

BASKETBALL

KAREEM ABDUL-JABBAR

1639. "Abdul-Jabbar Suffers Broken Right Hand in Fight With Kent Benson." New York Times, (October 20, 1977), p. 23 sec. 2.

1640. "Alcindor Changes Name To Kareem Abdul Jabbar." New York Times, (September 18, 1971), p. 21.

1641. "Alcindor Makes Pro Debut Today." Winston-Salem Journal, (October 18, 1969).

1642. "Alcindor the Awesome." Ebony, 22 (March 1967), 91-92+.

1643. "ABA Makes $3.25 million Counter Offer; Alcindor Confirms He Will Play With Milwaukee." New York Times, (March 30, 1969), p. 4, sec. 5.

1644. Axthelm, Pete. "Walton Up On High." Newsweek, 89 (May 23, 1977), 75.

1645. "Big Guy Meets The Doctor." Time, 115 (May 19, 1980), 83.

1646. "Big "O" Big Lew, Make Great Team." The New Courier, (December 1970).

1647. Black, S. "I Don't Have Any Hangups About Who I Was." Sport, 70 (June 1980), 23-26.

1648. Carry, P. "Center In A Storm." Sports Illustrated, 38 (February 19, 1973), 16-19.

1649. Carry, P. "Winner Gets To Play Alcindor; Baltimore vs. New York Knicks." Sports Illustrated, 34 (April 26, 1971), 22-4.

1650. "Don't Bring Me Mortals...Bring Me Giants." Black Sports, 6 (January 1977), 35-39.

1651. Farrell, B. "Performer of the Year." Sport, 66 (February 1978), 16-17+.

1652. "Inteview." New York Times, (October 15, 1966), p. 21.

1653. Izenberg, Jerry. "One-On-One Gunfight at Houston's Domed Corral." Sport, 70 (January 1980), 70+.

1654. "Kareem Abdul Jabbar Is Chosen 76-77 Player of Year and Adrian Dantley Rookie of Year in Sporting News Poll of NBA Players." New York Times, (April 6, 1977), p. 7, sec. 2.

1655. "Kareem Abdul Jabbar Voted MVP." New York Times, (May 24, 1977), p. 44.

1656. Langlais, Rudy. "Unlikely Loser: A Joyless Season for Abdul Jabbar." Black Sports, 4 (April 1975), 18-19+.

1657. Lardner, Rex. "Can Basketball Survive Lew Alcindor?" Saturday Evening Post, 240 (January 14, 1967), 70-73.

1658. Looney, Douglas. "Workman Like Lew Alcindor Sticks to His Own "Style." National Observer, (January 25, 1971).

1659. Markus, B. "Who's The Greatest Alcindor, Russell or Chamberlain." Sepia, 2 (November 1971), 32-36+.

1660. McKean, W.J. "High Lew Alcindor: Baskeball's Mt. Everest." Look, 29 (February 9, 1965), 86-90.

1661. Murphy, Frederick F. "Kareem Abdul Jabbar: Exceptional, But Human." Encore, 5 (February 16, 1976), 26-29.

1662. "O-Brien Fines Abdul-Jabbar Record $5,000." New York Times, (October 21, 1977), p. 22.

1663. Papanek, J. "Different Drummer." Sports Illustrated, 52 (March 31, 1980), 54-8+.

1664. Papanek, J. "Tallest Question Mark In L.A." Sports Illustrated, 49 (October 30, 1978), 83-4+.

1665. "Reportedly To Sign Contract With Milwaukee NBA Basketball Team Calling For $1.4 million Salary, Bonus and Other Benefits." New York Times, (March 29, 1969), p. 43.

1666. "Says Alcindor is Unhappy in Milwaukee." The Carolina Times, (March 27, 1971).

1667. Salvo, Patrick William. "Kareem Abdul-Jabbar: Best Man In His Game." Sepia, 27 (March 1978), 47-50.

1668. "Signs 5 Year Contract With Milwaukee Reportedly Calling For Between $1-Million and $1.4 Million; He Comments." New York Times, (April 3, 1969), p. 51.

1669. "Weds J. Brown." New York Times, (May 29, 1971), p. 14.

1670. Wilkes, P. "With Oscar And Lew, Milwaukee is Basketball's Best, But..." Look, 35 (April 6, 1971), 68-70.

1671. "Wilt and Kareem, Basketball's Two Best Big Men." Life, 72 (March 24, 1972), 58-9.

DON BARKSDALE

1672. "Don Barksdale; Baltimore Bullets' Sensational Cager." Our World, 7 (February 1952), 64-66.

1673. "Don Barksdale." Ebony, 5 (December 1949), 31-34.

MARVIN BARNES

1674. "Marvin Barnes Goes From Star To Just Any Inmate." Jet, 57 (June 9, 1977), 48.

1675. Xanthakos, Harry. "Of Fly," Freddie and Marvin The Prodigal." Black Sports, 4 (March 1975), 11.

ELGIN BAYLOR

1676. "Baylor Raps Big Wilt As Head Coach In Pro Ranks." Jet, 45 (October 25, 1973), 80-81.

1677. "Elgin Baylor: Basketball's Mr. Versatility." Sepia, 13 (March 1964), 74-77.

1678. "Elgin Baylor Comes Back." Ebony, 20 (February 1965), 35-36.

1679. Johnson, Al. "Coach of the Jazz." Sepia, 27 (June 1978), 60-64.

1680. Tax, J. "Bunyan Strides Again: Elgin Baylor." Sports Illustrated, 10 (April 6, 1959), 18-19.

DAVE BING

1681. Bing, Dave. "Dave Bing: An Interview." Black Sports, 6 (April 1977), 17-18+.

RON BOONE

1682. Ribowsky, Mark. "Ron Boone Misses The ABA." Black Sports, 6 (May 1977), 30-33.

WILT CHAMBERLAIN

1683. "Article On $1.5 Million Santa Monica, California Mansion Built For Basketball Star Wilt Chamberlain." New York Times, (March 15, 1972), p. 42.

1684. "Big Wilt Signs For Sizeable Increase." Jet, 43 (October 26, 1972), 5.

1685. "Bill vs. Wilt." Life, 51 (December 1, 1961), 51-52.

1686. Breslin, J. "Can Basketball Survive Wilt Chamberlain." Saturday Evening Post, 229 (December 1, 1956), 33.

1687. Brody, T.C. "Meet the New Wilt Chamberlain." Sports Illustrated, 20 (March 2, 1964), 24-5.

1688. Burley, D. "Basketball's Highest Paid Star." Sepia, 7 (January 1959), 70-73.

1689. Burns, B. "They'll Know My Name Again: Interview." Life, 68 (March 13, 1970), 50.

1690. "Cafe Society Rediscovers Harlem." Ebony, 17 (June 1962), 35-36.

1691. Carry P. "High But No Longer Mighty." Sports Illustrated, 39 (October 29, 1973), 44-5+.

1692. "Chamberlain Breaks 20,000 Rebound Mark." Chicago Daily Defender, (January 15, 1971).

1693. "Chamberlain Free Agent? Winston-Salem Journal, (October 15, 1975).

1694. "Chamberlain Wins 9th NBA Rebounding Crown." Philadelphia Tribune, (March 30, 1971).

1695. "DeBusschere Rules on Status." Washington Post, (October 16, 1975), p. 1, sec. B.

1696. Deford, Frank. "Another Big Bluff By Big Wilt Chamberlain," Sports Illustrated, 22 (January 25, 1965), 18-19.

1697. Deford, Frank "On Top, But In Trouble." Sports Illustrated, 30, (August 18, 1969), 10-13.

1698. Deford, Frank. "Waiting Made It Sweeter." Sports Illustrated, 26 (May 1967), 54-56.

1699. Freilicher, L.P. "Wilt the Stilt Chamberlain Not Fall Author For MacMillan." Publisher's Weekly, 203 (May 21, 1973), 34.

1700. "Go West, Tall Man." Newsweek, 72 (July 22, 1968), 50.

1701. "How Do You Stop Him." Time, 81 (January 25, 1963), 40-41.

1702. Izenberg, Jerry. "Day Goliath First Fell." Sport, 70 (March 1980), 45-6+.

1703. Jares, Joe. "Beard Moves Into A New and Ticklish Pad." Sports Illustrated, 29 (October 14, 1968), 76-7.

1704. Lardner, John. "Just Too Much Giant." Life, 62 (April 21, 1967), 82-4+.

1705. "Leap That No One Can Stop." Life, 47 (November 30, 1959), 57-8+.

1706. "Little Man, What Now?" Time, 75 (February 22, 1960), 73.

1707. McGuire, F. "How We Become Champs." Saturday Evening Post, 230 (December 14, 1957), 25.

1708. "Making the Giant Jolly." Time, 87 (April, 1966), 64-5.

1709. "The Man Who May Change Basketball: Wilt Chamberlain." Ebony, 12 (March 1957), 27-30.

1710. Markus, B. "Who's The Greatest Alcindor, Russell or Chamberlain." Sepia, 2 (November 1971), 32-36+.

1711. Masin, H.L. "Greatest of Them All: Wilt Chamberlain." Senior Scholastic, 76 (March 23, 1960), 26.

1712. Masin, H.L. "Run Lakers, Run." Senior Scholastic, 100 (February 14, 1972), 17.

1713. Masin, H.L. "Wilton, The Wonder." Scholastic, 65 (September 15, 1954), 30.

1714. Maule, Tex. "Rescued From Disaster by the Hard To Love Giant." Sports Illutrated, 30 (April 14, 1969), 32-3.

1715. "Nose To Chin Whiskers: Wilt Chamberlain." Time, 89 (January 13, 1967), 51.

1716. "One For The Dipper." Time, 99 (May 22, 1972), 47+.

1717. "Parting Shots." Newsweek, 73 (June 2, 1969), 67.

1718. Robinson, Louie. "All-Time Highest Scorer Is Now Defensive Star: Captain Wilt Leads L.A. Lakers To Best Pro Sports Record Ever." Ebony, 27 (April 1972), 114-121+.

1719. Robinson, Louie. "Big Man, Big Business." Ebony, 19 (August 1964), 57-58.

1720. Robinson, Louie. "High Price of Being Wilt Chamberlain." Ebony, 29 (January 1974), 94-8+.

1721. Ryan, W. "Seven Foot Cage Giant." Color, 10 (November 1955), 19.

1722. Schwartz, Barbara "Just Another High-Priced Rookie." Black Sports, 5 (February 1976), 18-20.

1723. "Seven Foot Man." Newsweek, 48 (December 17, 1956), 96.

1724. "Shoot Wilt." Time, 90 (December 22, 1967), 40.

1725. "Special Dunk." New York Amsterdam News, (February 19, 1972).

1726. "Spirited 76ers." Newsweek, 69 (January 23, 1967), 88.

1727. "Sweet Revenge." Time, 89 (May 5, 1967), 40.

1728. "Taller Than That." Time, 70 (December 23, 1957), 41.

1729. Tax, J. "Chamberlain's Big Mistake." Sports Illustrated, 12 (April 4, 1960), 58-59.

1730. "Tilting With Wilt." Newsweek, 72 (December 30, 1968), 48.

1731. "Unstoppable." Newsweek, 59 (February 5, 1962), 80-1.

1732. "Waiting In Vain For Wilt - Editorial." Black Sports, 5 (December 1975), 12.

1733. "What It Took To Get Wilt." Life, 42 (January 28, 1957), 113-17.

1734. "Wilt and Kareem, Basketball's Two Best Big Men." Life, 72 (March 24, 1972), 58-9.

1735. "Wilt Back In Basketball's New League's Owner-Player." Jet, 57 (October 4, 1979), 50.

1736. "Wilt Chamberlain; House That Wilt Built." Life, 72 (March 24, 1972), 58-63.

1737. "Wilt Talks Back." Time, 87 (February 25, 1966), 76.

1738. "Wilt the Stilt." Time, 66 (December 12, 1955), 61.

1739. "Wilt the Stilt Chamberlain." Look, 21 (February 19, 1957), 118-20.

1740. "Wilt: 'We've Come Too Far To Blow It.'" Winston-Salem Journal, (April 21, 1970).

1741. "Wins TD Club Timmie Award." Washington Post, (January 18, 1976), p. 8 sec. C.

1742. "Womb With A View." Newsweek, 79 (March 13, 1972), 55.

1743. Woodley, R. "Close-Up: He Likes To Keep You Psyched." Life, 66 (May 23, 1969), 69-72+.

1744. Zimmerman, J.G. "Ubiquitous Hands of Mr. C." Sports Illustrated, 16 (February 5, 1962), 28-35.

JIM CHONES

1745. Cheeks, Dwayne. "Odyssey Ends for Travelin' Man Chones." Black Sports, 5 (April 1976), 40-43+.

CHUCK COOPER

1746. "TCB: Dr. Fletcher Johnson." Black Sports, 7 (April, 1978), 27-29.

1747. Young, Jeff C. "Chuck Cooper: The Jackie Robinson of Professional Basketball." Black Collegian, 5 (March-April 1975), 34+.

ADRIAN DANTLEY

1748. "...Andrian Dantley Rookie of Year In Sporting News Poll of NBA Players." New York Times, (April 6, 1977), p. 7, sec. 2.

1749. Ribowsky, Mark. "Travels With Adrian." Black Sports, 7 (February 1978), 23-26+.

DARRYLE DAWKINS

1750. Dowling, Tom. "Of Cool Breezes, Candy Slam, Zandakhan and Panty Snatcher." Black Sports, 7 (May 1978), 18-22+.

WAYNE EMBRY

1751. "Interview With Wayne Embry." Black Sports, 7 (December 1977), 35-37.

JULIUS ERVING

1752. "Basketball Seminar: Dr. J. Tells How To Do It." Black Sports, 5 (April 1976), 10-14.

1753. Bell, M. "Dr. J. Awesome Again!" Sport, 68 (February 1979), 81-3+.

1754. "Big Guy Meets The Doctor." Time, 115 (May 19, 1980), 83.

1755. "Erving Nets Dunk In Aid To Dr. J's Old Prep School." Jet, 50 (April 3, 1976), 53.

1756. Hoening, G. "Doctor J's Toughest Case." New York Times Magazine, (February 13, 1977), 56-61.

1757. "Julius Erving Named Sport Magazine's Performer of Year." New York Times, (January 20, 1977), p. 48.

1758. Kirkpatrick, C. "Hey What's Up With The Doc?" Sports Illustrated, 50 (March 26, 1979), 22-4+.

PHIL FORD

1759. Smith, Janice. "Essencemen: Phil Ford." Essence, 9
(August 1978), 11.

1760. Zucchino, David. "Hey: This Ford Runs Like A Porsche."
Black Sports, 6 (February 1977), 26-8.

WALT FRAZIER

1761. Bailey, Peter. "Walt Frazier: Athlete, Businessman, Man About
Town." Ebony, 29 (March 1974), 46-48+.

1762. Berkow, Ira. "Betrayal of Clyde." Black Sports, 7
(January 1978), 50-54.

1763. Kisner, Ronald E. "Walt Frazier His Sex Image and His
Lifestyle." Jet, 46 (April 4, 1974), 52-56.

1764. Ribowsky, Mark. "Clyde, Pearl and the 'No-Name' Duo." Black
Sports, 5 (January 1976), 32-35+.

1765. Ribowsky, Mark. "Sweet Life of Walt Frazier." Sepia, 25
(January 1976), 62-68.

1766. "Walt Frazier is the Knicks Most Valuable Player." New York
Amsterdam News, (February 19, 1972).

LLOYD FREE

1767. "Lloyd Loses His Job; Scott Takes Pistons." Jet, 43
(November 16, 1972), 48.

ARTIS GILMORE

1768. Hamilton, John Y. "Two Gentle Giants...With Ferocious Talent."
Black Sports, 6 (January 1977), 43+.

HAPPY HAIRSTON

1769. "Los Angeles Lakers Basketball Player Happy Hairston Sues His
Coach B. Sharman on June 15 for $450,000." New York Times,
(June 16, 1973), p. 21.

ELVIN HAYES

1770. Stevens, Joann. "Elvin Hayes: Bullets' Super Star Forward
Finds Community Activity More Demanding Than Basketball."
Black Sports, 6 (August 1976), 16+.

SPENCER HAYWOOD

1771. Evans, Pat. "Jocks On Jazz." Black Sports, 5 (April 1976), 8.

EARVIN "MAGIC" JOHNSON

1772. "Just Another Guy Named Earvin." Sports Illustrated, 48 (January 23, 1978), 48-9.

1773. Keith, L. "He's Gone To The Head of His Class." Sports Illustrated, 49 (November 27, 1978), 48-50+.

1774. Looney, D.S. "And For My Next Trick." Sports Illustrated, 50 (April 10, 1979), 28-38+.

1774. "Magic Johnson Promises Mom I'll Get The Degree." Jet, 56 (August 2, 1979), 49.

1775. Newman, B. "Doing It All For L.A." Sports Illustrated, 51 (November 19, 1979), 30-3.

MARQUES JOHNSON

1776. Ribowsky, Mark. "Marques Johnson Didn't Just Happen To Be Great." Black Sports, 7 (May 1978), 34-39.

JUNIUS KELLOGG

1777. "The Man Who Won't Give Up, Junius Kellogg" Ebony, 12 (April 1957), 17-24.

1778. Reynolds, Quetin. "Nobody's Better Off Dead: Junius Kellogg." Reader's Digest, 72 (March 1958), 160-62.

BOB LANIER

1779. Vecsey, Peter. "Two Gentle Giants...With Ferocious Talent." Black Sports, 6 (January 1977), 42+.

BOB LOVE

1780. Banks, Lacey J. "Cinderellas of the Superstars. B. Love and R. Brown." Ebony, 27 (January 1972), 70-3.

MAURICE LUCAS

1781. Kiersh, Ed. "Cool Hand Luke." Black Sports, 7 (April 1978), 23-26.

JIM MCDANIELS

1782. Ribowsky, Mark." "Jim McDaniels: The Dream That Failed." Black Sports, 7 (April 1978), 44-50.

GEORGE MCGINNIS

1783. "George McGinnis: New Yorker." Black Sports, 5 (August 1975), 5.

1784. Evans, Pat. "Blues Man McGinnis." Black Sports, 5 (June 1976), 41+.

JIMMY MCMILLIAN

1985. Vecsey, Peter. "Goodbye Buffalo, Hello Broadway: Jimmy McMillian Back." Black Sports, 6 (February 1977), 29-32.

MOSES MALONE

1986. "Moses Malone Tops NBA Money List, Over $1-Million." Jet, 56 (August 16, 1979), 50.

1987. "NBA's MVP See Warning In $3-Million Fight Award." Jet, 56 (September 13, 1979), 48.

EARL MONROE

1988. Riley, Clayton. "Earl: The First and Last Word On Guard." Black Sports, 6 (April 1977), 35-39+.

CALVIN MURPHY

1989. "San Diego's Calvin Murphy, Pro Basketball's Tiny Giant." Ebony, 26 (February 1971), 38-4+.

WILLIS REED

1990. "1st Retired Knicks' Jersey Belongs To Ex-Captain Reed." Jet, 51 (October 28, 1976), 48.

1991. "Knicks Fret Over Reed's Knees." Winston-Salem Journal, (March 4, 1970).

1992. Langlais, Rudy. "Can A 6'10" Superstar Who Never Coached A Day In His Life Save The Knicks." Black Sports, 7 (November 1977), 25-29.

1993. Lewis, Glenn. "In The Willis Reed Tradition." Black Sports, 6 (April 1977), 12-14+.

1994. "The New Coosome Twosome: Willis Reed and Kellee Patterson." Jet, 56 (August 23, 1979), 54.

1995. "New York Knicks Basketball Player Willis Reed is Named Winner on July 28 of Maurice Stokes Memorial Award." New York Times, (July 29, 1973), p. 5, sec. 5.

1996. "Reed To Take Over Reins of N.Y. Knicks." Jet, 52 (March 24, 1977), 56.

1997. Willis Reed Named MVP By Players." Winston-Salem Journal, (March 18, 1970).

OSCAR ROBERTSON

1998. "Big O' Big Lew Make Great Team." The New Courier,
(December 1970).

1999. "College Scoring Goes To Cincinnati's Oscar Robertson." Sports
Illustrated, 8 (June 20, 1958), 22.

2000. Deford, Frank. "How K.C. Won an Oscar in the NBA." Sports
Illustrated, 20 (March 16, 1964), 22-23.

2001. "Graceful Giants: Oscar Robertson." Time, 77 (February 17, 1961),
54-56.

2002. Gross, M. "Basketball's Mood Marvel: Oscar Robertson." Saturday
Evening Post, 232 (December 36, 1959), 19.

2003. "In Cincinnati They Call Him The Big O." Life, 48
(January 25, 1964), 69-70.

2004. Leggett, William. "The New Kid On the Block Takes On The Champ."
Sports Illustrated, 13 (November 14, 1960), 24-25.

2005. Masin, H.L. "Wonderful O." Senior Scholastic, 74 (February 6,
1959), 25.

2006. Massaqupi, H. "The Big O." Ebony, 15 (March 1960), 115-21.

2007. "New Look for All-America: Oscar Robertson." Life, 44
(March 10, 1958), 99.

2008. "Oscar Robertson: The Hottest Hands in Basketball." Look, 23
(February 3, 1959), 57-58.

2009. Tax, J. "What Price Glory for Oscar?" Sports Illustrated, 10
(January 26 1959), 18-20.

BILL RUSSELL

2010. "All The Credentials: Bill Russell." Time, 87 (April 19, 1966),
104+.

2011. "Along Came Bill." Time, 67 (January 2, 1956), 36.

2012. "Basketball's Leaning Tower: Bill Russell Leads San Francisco
Dons To National Championship, All-Time Record." Ebony, 11
(April 1956), 50-54.

2013. "Best Big Man On View." Life, 40 (January 16, 1956), 12-14.

2014. "Bill Russell Leaves Seattle After 4 Years as Coach and General
Manager." New York Times, (May 5, 1977), p. 17, sec. 4.

2015. "Bill Russell, The Antenna With Arms." Look, 20
(January 10, 1956), 66-8.

2016. "Bill vs. Wilt." Life, 51 (December 1, 1961), 51-52.

2017. "Can't Miss." Newsweek, 81 (March 12, 1973), 61+.

2018. "Coach Russell." Newsweek, 68 (May 2, 1966), 72-73.

2019. Daley, Arthur. "The Education of A Basketball Rookie: Bill Russell." New York Times Magazine, (February 24, 1957), 22.

2020. "First Part of Profile." Washington Post, (April 25, 1972), p. 3 sec. D.

2021. "For All The Marbles: Bill Russell." Time, 91 February 24, 1967), 57-58.

2022. Huey, Lynda. "Who Is John Briker...And Why Did Bill Russell Do All Those Bad Things To Him?" Black Sports, 6 (April 1977), 50-53.

2023. Lardner, John. "Just Too Much Giant." Life, 62 (April 21, 1967), 82-4.

2024. Linn, E. "I Owe The Public Nothing: Bill Russell." Saturday Evening Post, 238 (January 18, 1964), 60-63.

2025. Markus, B. "Who's The Greatest, Alcindor, Russell or Chamberlain." Sepia, 2 (November 1971), 32-36+.

2026. Masin, H.L. "Russell of Spring." Senior Scholastic, 67 (January 12, 1956), 29.

2027. Masin, H.L. "Nothing But the Best: Bill Russell." Senior Scholastic, 87 (December 9, 1965), 36-37.

2028. Masin, H. L. "Russell of Spring." Senior Shcolastic, 67 (January 12, 1956), 29.

2029. Mrs. R.K. Russell, Wife of Basketball Coach Bill Russell, is Granted Divorce on Sept. 14..." New York Times, (September 16, 1976), p. 11.

2030. "New Role For Bill Russell." Ebony, 22 (January 1967), 60-61+.

2031. "Not A Muscle, Just Russell." Time, 67 (April 2, 1956), 55.

2032. "Ol Massa Russell?" Nation, 200 (March 1, 1956), 211.

2033. Ottum, B. "Panic Is On Again." Sports Illustrated, 21 (November 9, 1964), 18-19.

2034. "Parting Shots." Newsweek, 73 (June 2, 1969), 67.

2035. Plimpton, George. "Reflections In A Diary." Sports Illustrated, 29 (December 23, 1968), 40-4.

2036. Profiled As Rookie Sportscaster." Washington Post, (April 26, 1972), p. 1, sec. C.

2037. Rogin, G. "We Are Grown Men Playing A Child's Game." Sports Illustrated, 19 (November 18, 1963), 74-78.

2038. "Sportsman of the Year." Sports Illustrated, 28 (March 23, 1968), 40-4.

2039. Tax, J. "The Man Who Must Be Different." Sports Illustrated, 8 (February 3, 1958), 29-32.

2040. Tax, J. "Two Big Men in a Tight Pennant Race." Sports Illustrated, 12 (February 22, 1960), 46-47.

CAZZIE RUSSELL

2041. "Cazzie Russell: Sophomore Cage Phenomenon." Ebony, 19 (April 1964), 101-102.

CHARLIE SCOTT

2042. "Teague Award Presented to Scott for 2nd Time." Winston-Salem Journal, (February 28, 1970).

PAUL SILAS

2043. "Interview With Paul Silas." Black Sports, 6 (January 1977), 14-15+.

RANDY SMITH

2044. Weber, Mike. "Randy Smith Only Wants A Rolls Royce, Stocks, A Nice Salary And ..." Black Sports, 6 (February 1977), 33-35+.

MAURICE STOKES

2045. "Boston Celtics General Manager Red Auerbach Announces May 16 $1,000 Scholarship To Jeffrey Richardson of Westinghouse High School, In Memory of Late NBA Star Maurice Stokes." New York Times, (May 17, 1975), p. 21.

2046. "Decade of Pain and Progress." Sports Illustrated, 28 (March 25, 1968), 38-9.

2047. "Dies 36." New York Times, (April 7, 1970), p. 46.

2048. "Film Maurie: D. Anderson Comments." New York Times, (August 4, 1973), p. 15.

2049. Gross, M. "His Brother's Keeper." Readers Digest, 79 (December 1961), 85-90.

2050. "Maurice Stokes Memorial Award." New York Times, (August 10, 1975), p. 3.

2050a."New York Knicks Basketball Player Willis Reed is Named
Winner on July 28 of Maurice Stokes Memorial Award." New York
Times, (July 29, 1973), p. 5, sec. 5.

2051. Paxton, H.T. "I Wake Up Helpless." Saturday Evening Post, 231
(March 14, 1959), 27+.

2052. "Film Maurice, Based On Life of Late Basketball Player Maurice
Stokes." New York Times, (August 2, 1973), p. 31.

2053. Robinson, Louie."Cincinnati's Stricken Giant: Maurice Stokes."
Ebony, 14 (April 1959), 38-42.

2054. "St. Francis College (Loretta, Pa.) To Dedicate Physical Ed.
Center in Stokes Memory." New York Times, (March 10, 1971),
p. 52.

2055. Tax, J. "A Brave Man and A Good Friend: Maurice Stokes." Sports
Illustrated, 12 (February 1, 1960), 10-15.

2056. "Will Bequeaths $91,431 of His $194,862 Estate To St. Francis
College, Loretto, Pennsylvania." New York Times, (August 12,
1970), p. 47.

WES UNSELD

2057. "Scouting Reports: Westley Unseld of the University of
Louisville." Sports Illustrated, 23 (December 6, 1965),
57-58.

KERMIT WASHINGTON

2058. "Interview With Kermit Washington." Black Sports, 7 (May 1978),
40+.

2059. "NBA's MVP See Warning In $3-Million Fight Award." Jet, 56
(September 13, 1979), 48.

JO JO WHITE

2060. Ribowsky, Mark. "Boston Celtics Jo Jo White-Basketball's
Gentle-Hearted Jock." Sepia, 27 (January 1978), 52-55.

2061. Ryan, Bob. "Jo Jo White Superstar (Finally)." Black Sports, 6
(January 1977), 22-25.

SIDNEY WICKS

2062. Ribowsky, Mark."I Don't Really Care Who Likes Me." Black
Sports, 7 (January 1978), 17-20+.

LENNY WILKENS

2063. "Interview With Lenny Wilkens." Black Sports, 7 (April 1978),
16-19+.

2064. Reveron, Derek. "A Cool Coach Who Wins." <u>Ebony</u>, 34 (March, 1979), 94-98+.

JAMAAL WILKES

2065. Russell, Dick. "Raw Silk." <u>Black Sports</u>, 7 (March 1978), 24-26+.

BOXING

MUHAMMAD ALI

2066. "Addresses Senior Class at Harvard." Washington Post,
      (June 5, 1975), p. 1. sec. D.

2067. "After Meeting With Blacks, Ali Cancels S. African Bout." Jet,
      43 (October 19, 1972), 53.

2068. "After Muhammad, Grave Yard." Sports Illustrated, 26 (April
      1967), 28-9.

2069. "Alas, Poor Cassius! Photo-Editorial." Ebony, 20, (July
      1965), 144-145.

2070. Ali, "A Biblical Scholar In Pre-Fight Clowning." Winston-Salem
      Journal, (September 27, 1977).

2071. "Ali Action Overdue." The Afro American, (June 27, 1970).

2072. "Ali Advises Kids To Forget Boxing." St. Louis Sentinel,
      (October 21, 1971).

2073. "Ali Agrees To Fight Foreman." Winston-Salem Journal,
      (February 17, 1978).

2074. Ali Announces May Title Defense." Winston-Salem Journal,
      (April 7, 1977).

2075. "Ali Becomes Critical of U.S. South Africa." Winston-Salem
      Journal, (February 7, 1980).

2076. "Ali...Book Review "Sting Like A Bee." by Jose Torres."
      Washington Post, (October 30, 1971), p. 1, sec. E.

2077. "Ali: Boycott Could Avert War." Winston-Salem Journal, (February 5, 1980).

2078. "Ali Case Reaches The Final Bell." Washington Post, (June 27, 1971), p. 17 sec. A.

2079. "Ali Comes Back But What Lies Ahead in Fight Future." Jet, 45 (February 17, 1974), 52-55.

2080. "Ali Decisions Bugner." Winston-Salem Journal, (July 1, 1975) p. 15.

2081. "Ali Denies He Will Quit." Winston Salem Sentinel, (October 2, 1975).

2082. "Ali Does Roadwork on Freedom Road." Ebony, 34 (October 1979), 102-104+.

2083. Ali Drops Hints He'll Fight Again." Winston-Salem Journal, (November 23, 1976).

2084. "Ali Faces New Round In High Court Fight." Washington Post, (April 18, 1971), p. 17 sec. A.

2085. "Ali Favorite Tonight." Winston-Salem Journal, (September 28, 1976).

2086. "Ali Files Brief With High Court." Washington Post, (February 26, 1971), p. 6, sec. D.

2087. "Ali-Frazier III." Winston-Salem Journal, (September 29, 1975).

2088. "Ali: Gets Wish: White House Visit." Winston-Salem Journal, (December 11, 1974).

2089. "Ali Gives Advice To Man Who Shut His Mouth." Jet, 44 (April, 1973), 46-47.

2090. "Ali Has Plans For Better U.S." Winston-Salem Journal, (April 29, 1976).

2091. "Ali Holds Fireside Chat: Hoping To Bump Norton." Jet, 54 (March 23, 1978), 48-49.

2092. "Ali is Closer To Being Free." Afro-American, (June 27, 1970).

2093. "Ali Jokes, Jabs With Russians." Winston-Salem Journal, (June 14, 1978).

2094. "Ali, King of the Yankee Stadium." Economist, 261 (October 2, 1976), 44.

2095. "Ali Knocks Out Foreman in 8th." Winston-Salem Journal, (October 30, 1974).

2096. "Ali Loses His Punch." Economist, 259 (May 1976), 46.

2097. "Ali, Meets Norton Tuesday." Winston-Salem Journal, (September 27, 1976).

2098. "Ali Plans to Enjoy His Championship For a While." Winston-Salem Journal, (September 17, 1978).

2099. "Ali Puts Blame on Inoki." Winston-Salem Journal, (June 30, 1976).

2100. "Ali Says He Will Box Exhibition For Kids." Afro American, (May 22, 1971).

2101. "Ali Schedules Retirement Party." Winston-Salem Journal, (June 20, 1979).

2102. "Ali Scores TKO Against Lewis In Dublin Bout." Jet, 42 (August 3, 1972), 56.

2103. "Ali Sharp and Trim in Win Over England's Joe Bugner." Jet, 43 (March 1, 1973), 51.

2104. "Ali Shuts Patterson's Eye To Gain TKO." Jet, 43 (October 5, 1972), 54.

2105. "Ali Talks of Retirement." Winston-Salem Sentinel, (September 21, 1975).

2106. "Ali Testifies in $20 Million Suit." Winston-Salem Journal, (June 10, 1980).

2107. "Ali The Gracious." Newsweek, 80 (October 2, 1972), 48.

2108. "Ali, the Pretender?" Newsweek, 81 (October 1, 1973), 54.

2109. "Ali Took His Loss To Frazier Like A Man In Big Soul Fight." Afro American, (March 20, 1971).

2110. "Ali Un Eligible For Military Service." Time, 87 (February 25, 1966), 26.

2111. "Ali Wants To Be 'Biggest Black Man' From The U.S." Jet, 42 (April 27, 1972), 56.

2112. "Ali Wants to Fight Bobick." Winston-Salem Journal, (November 24, 1976).

2113. "Ali Will Ask African Nations To Skip Games." Winston-Salem Journal, (February 1, 1980).

2114. Ali Wins Unanimous Decision. Winston-Salem Journal, (September 29, 1976).

2115. "Ali- You Gotta Believe." Newsweek, 84 (November 11, 1974), 70-1.

2116. "Ali's Army Life." Life, 69 (December 18, 1970), 28-30.

2117. "Ali's Jaw." Newsweek, 81 (April 16, 1973), 52.

2118. "Ali's Next Major Bout: Norton." Winston-Salem Journal,
      (November 19, 1975).

2119. "Ali's Remarks Stun U.S. Officials." Winston-Salem Journal,
      (February 4, 1980).

2120. "Ali's Whipping." Time, 115 (February 18, 1980), 34+.

2121. "Ambassador Ali Meets Brezhnev." Winston-Salem Journal,
      (June 20, 1978).

2122. "Analysis of Fight With Frazier." Washington Post,
      (September 28, 1975), p. 1, sec. C.

2123. "And I'm Already The Greatest!" Newsweek, 63 (March 9, 1964),
      50-1.

2124. "And Then There Was One." Time, 97 (March 22, 1971), 35.

2125. Ander, Dave. "Show Ali A Closeup and He'll Fight Again."
      Winston-Salem Journal, (September 5, 1976).

2126. "Arum: Ali Plan to Fight." Winston-Salem Journal, (December 10,
      1976).

2127. "As the Judge Threw The Book at Muhammad." Sports Illustrated,
      27 (July 3, 1967), 18-19.

2128. "Attends Testimonial For Elijah Muhammad." Washington Post,
      (March 31, 1974), p. 2, sec. A.

2129. "Attends Walter Fauntroy's Birthday Fete." Washington Post,
      (February 24, 1975), p. 1, sec. B.

2130. "Attorney Criticizes WBA For Stripping Ali of Title." Washington
      Post, (June 29, 1971), p. 1, sec. D.

2131. Axthelm, Pete and P. Bonventre. "Ali Born Again." Newsweek, 92
      (September 25, 1978), 68-70.

2132. Axthelm, Pete. "Ali-Frazier Crunch." Vogue, 157 (March 1, 1971),
      115.

2133. Axthelm, Pete. "Say Its So, Ali." Newsweek, 94 (July 9, 1979),
      61.

2134. Axthelm, Pete. "Requiem For a Heavyweight." Newsweek, 96
      (October 13, 1980), 102-3.

2135. Axthelm, Pete. "The Return of the Exiled Champ." Newsweek, 76
      (November 9, 1970), 56-60+.

2136. Banks, Larry J. "Biggest Fight In History." Ebony, 26 (March 1971), 134-6+.

2137. Banks, Larry. "Winner, The Loser, the Crowd." Ebony, 26 (May 1971), 132-4+.

2138. Barron, Allan P. "Some Random Thoughts." On Woody Hayes: On Don King vs. Ali." Black Sports, 7 (January 1978).

2139. "Bell Rings For Cassius- This Time In Court." Sepia, 14 (August 1965), 8-11.

2140. "Benefit To Fight Sickle Cell." Washington Post, (November 25, 1971), p. 1, sec. C.

2141. Berger, P. "Ali's Made For TV Challenger." New York Times Magazine, (January 29, 1978), 30-34+.

2142. Berube, Maurice R. "Defeat of the Great Black Hope." Commonweal, 94 (March 26, 1971), 54-5.

2143. "Big Shrink." Sports Illustrated, 24 (March 21, 1966), 8.

2144. "Billy Graham and Muhammad Ali Meet." Washington Post, (September 21, 1979), p. 19, sec. C.

2145. "Black Muslim Hope." Sports Illustrated, 20 (March 16, 1964), 8.

2146. "Bloody Shame." Newsweek, 68 (May 30, 1966), 83.

2147. Bonventre, P. "Rocky Spinks." Newsweek, 91 (February 27, 1978), 88-89.

2148. "Boxing's Feet of Clay." Saturday Evening Post, 237 (April 18, 1965), 86.

2149. Boyle, R.H. "Champ In the Jug." Sports Illustrated, 26 (April 1967), 30-3.

2150. Boyle R.H. "To Fight or not to Fight." Sports Illustrated, 21 (September 7, 1964), 28-31.

2151. Boyle R.H. "This is What Clay says He Wants." Sports Illustrated, 19 (August 5, 1963), 22-6.

2152. Brennan, M. "Ali and His Educators." Sports Illustrated, 53 (September 22, 1980), 40-57.

2153. Britton, J.H. "Georgia Senator Gets TKOED By His Political Friends'-The Anti-Muhammad Ali Law." Phylon, 32 (Summer 1971), 198-26.

2154. "Brother Says Ali Blessed." Winston-Salem Journal, (September 29, 1975).

2155. Brown, D. "Floyd Fight Like He Slapped Your Mother." Life, 59 (November 19, 1965), 120+.

2156. Buckley, William F. "The Dissenting Champion." National Review, (May 16, 1968), 504.

2257. "Budgeted Beakbusting: Louisville Businessmen Promote Heavyweight Cassius Clay." Business Week, (November 24, 1962), 30-31.

2258. "Bull v. Butterfly: A Clash of Champions." Time, 97 (March 8, 1971), 63+.

2259. Calloway, Earl. "Cassius Clay Slated For Broadway Debut In Bufman's Buck White." Chicago Daily Defender, (November 29, 1969).

2260. "Can History Repeat Itself." Ebony, 33 (December 1977), 104-106+.

2261. "Cassius Clay Did It Again." Sepia, 12 (August 1963), 67.

2262. "Cassius Clay Stage Beckons." National Observer, (October 20, 1969).

2263. "Cassius Clay: Weak on Test, Strong on Finances." U.S. News and World Report, 56 (March 30, 1964), 10.

2264. "Cassius Lives It Up." Newsweek, 56 (September 19, 1960), 75-6.

2265. "C. Marcellus Clay, Esq." Sports Illustrated, 18 (June 10, 1963), 18-25.

2266. "Cassius-Still Champ!" Sepia, 15 (January 1966), 80-81.

2267. "Cassius (Muhammad Ali) Clay Wins Again." Sepia, 19 (December 1970), 71-73.

2268. "Cassius X." Newsweek, 63 (March 16, 1964), 74.

2269. "Cassius X." Time, 83 (March 13, 1964), 78.

2270. "CBS Cashes in on Ratings From Muhammad Ali-Leon Spinks Fight." Washington Post, (February 1978), p. 1, sec. D.

2271. "Celebrities Attending Fight." Washington Post, (May 1, 1976), p. 4, sec. A.

2272. "Challenge Shortage." Newsweek, 68 (November 28, 1966), 65.

2273. "Champ Is No Chump, Ali Resigns WBA Title." Winston-Salem Journal, (June 27, 1979).

2274. "Championship Fight." Sepia, 13 (April 1964), 79-82.

2275. "Champs African Love Affair." Ebony, 19 (September 1964)
85-86.

2276. "Clay Appeal Conviction To U.S. Supreme Court." New York Times,
(July 7, 1968), p. 6.

2277. "Clay Begins 10-day Jail Sentence For Old Traffic Violation,
Dade County, Fla." New York Times, (December 17, 1968), p. 2.

2278. "Clay Calls For Racial Separation." Winston-Salem Journal,
(September 19, 1969).

2279. "Clay Career Highlights." New York Times, (June 29, 1971),
p. 24.

2280. "Cassius Clay." Sepia, 11 (August 1962), 35-38.

2281. "Clay Case Discussed Among Others On Which Court Will Rule."
New York Times, (June 28, 1971), p. 1.

2282. "Clay Draft Evasion Case Reviewed." New York Times, (July 4,
1971), p. 3, sec. 4.

2283. "Clay Hails Decision." New York Times, (January 12, 1971), p. 40.

2284. "Clay In Chicago Gets News of Court Decision, Reaction Is Calm."
New York Times, (June 29, 1971), p. 24.

2285. "Clay Is At The Top...What Now?" Sepia, 16 (April 1967), 22-25.

2286. "Clay Notes Possible Decisions That U.S. Supreme Court May Hand
Down." New York Times, (June 23, 1971), p. 33.

2287. "Clay Personality Sketch." New York Times, (March 7, 1971),
p. 24, sec. 4.

2288. "Clay Reportedly Will Visit Saudi Arabia." New York Times,
(February 21, 1971), p. 2.

2289. "Clay To Play Lead Role in Musical." Winston-Salem Journal
 & Sentinel, (October 30, 1969).

2290. "Clay Turns To Teaching." Sacramento Observer, (May 1, 1969).

2291. "Clay Visits Mecca." New York Times, (December 31, 1971), p. 17.

2292. "Clay vs. Draft." Senior Scholastic, 90 (May 12, 1967), 19-20.

2293. "Clay vs. Marciano: The Super Fight." Life, 68
(January 30, 1970), 42-3.

2294. "Clay Watches Muhammad in Ring and Loves Him." The Afro-
American, (January 24, 1970).

2295. "Clay Wins Again." Sepia, 16 (January 1967), 67-71.

2296. "Closed Circuit Telecasts." Washington Post, (October 30, 1974), p. 1, sec. E.

2297. Cobb, V. and Gregory Simms. "Muhammad Ali 'Ends' His Wondrous Boxing Career." Jet, 55 (October 5, 1978), 52-55.

2298. "Cohen Column on Muhammad Ali." Washington Post, (February 19, 1978), p. 1, sec. B.

2299. "Comment on U.S. Supreme Court Decision To Review His Conviction For Refusal To Submit To Military Induction." New York Times, (January 17, 1971), p. 3. sec. 4.

2300. "Coments On Frazier-Foreman Fight." Washington Post, (January 23, 1973), p. 1 sec. D.

2301. "Comments On Foreman Bout." Washington Post, (October 31, 1974), p. 1, sec. D.

2302. "Confessions of FBI." Newsweek, 73 (June 16, 1969), 29-30.

2303. "Cooper, Ralph. "Clay Better Off Without Sugar Ray." The Voice of Hope, (March 14, 1970).

2304. Cope, Myron. "Muslim Champ." Saturday Evening Post, 237 (November 14, 1964), 32-34.

2305. Corduso, B. "Final Daze." Crawdaddy, (May 1978), 50-54.

2306. "Anderson Discusses Clay's Reaction To Supreme Court Decision." New York Times, (June 29, 1971), p. 24.

2307. "Reeves Comments On Relationship Between Clay and Negroes." New York Times, (May 17, 1971), p. 35.

2308. Das, K. "Ali's Mouth: Mightier Than The Fist [Malaysia]." Far Eastern Review, 89 (July 11, 1975), 14.

2309. "Daughter Born." New York Times, (June 20, 1968), p. 61.

2310. "Decison for Allah; Supreme Court Ruling On Draft Exemption." Newsweek, 78 (July 12, 1971), 61+.

2311. "Defeats Joe Frazier." Washington Post, (October 1, 1975), p. 1, sec. E.

2312. "Delinger Column on Muhammad Ali." Washington Post, (May 5, 1977), p. 1, sec. C.

2313. "Delinger Column on Muhammad Ali." Washington Post, (March 13, 1978), p. 13 sec. D.

2314. "Delinger Column-Muhammad Ali-Leon Spinks Fight." Washington Post, (February 17, 1978), p. 1, sec. C.

2315. Demaret, K. "Muhammad Ali, His Days Numbered As Lord of the Ring Has A Mean Act To Follow." People, 10 (October 30, 1978), 24-9.

2316. "Destination Unkown." Newsweek, 67 (March 14, 1966), 93.

2317. Diaz, John. "Muhammad Ali Sets up training in Miami." Pittsburgh Courier, (January 23, 1971).

2318. "Dissent Champion." Nation Review, 19 (May 16, 1967), 504-6.

2319. "Don't Call Me Champ; "Supreme Court Decision," Nation, 213 (July 19, 1971), 104-5.

2320. "Dream." Time, 81 (March 22, 1963), 78-81.

2321. Dundee, Angelo and Tex Maule. "Ali Takes A Crown And A Cause." Sports Illustrated, 27 (August 21, 1967), 36-40.

2322. Dundee, Angelo and Tex Maule. "He Could Go To Jail And Still Be Champ." Sports Illustrated, 27 (August 28, 1967), 32-34.

2323. Dundee, Angelo and Tex Maule. "Life In A Hot Corner." Sports Illustrated, 27 (August 14, 1967), 64-72.

2324. "Dundee Would Never Tell Ali When to Quit Ring." Winston-Salem Journal, (October 30, 1977), 14.

2325. "Early End for Early Bird." Newsweek, 68 (August 15, 1966), 79.

2326. "Earns 40¢ a Week As Trusty In Jail's Kitchen." New York Times, (December 21, 1968), p. 53.

2327. "Editorial-Ali To Make A Long Story Longer." Washington Post, (March 10, 1971), p. 18, sec. A.

2328. "Editorial-Muhammad Ali- A Bad Rap Overturned." Washington Post, (July 2, 1971), p. 24 sec. A.

2329. "Editorial on Muhammad Ali." Washington Post, (February 17, 1978), p. 16, sec. A.

2330. "Edwards, C.W. "Muhammad Ali On Campus." Catholic World, 210 (November 1969), 69-73.

2331. Egerton, J. "Heritage of a Heavyweight." New York Times Magazine, (September 28, 1980), 54-6.

2332. Easkin, L. "Young Cassius Clay, The Bonus Boy of Boxing." Negro Digest, 11 (December 1961), 31-34.

2333. "Excerpts From Foreign Editorials on Muhammad Ali's Defeat." Washington Post, (March 3, 1978), p. 22, sec. A.

2334. "Eyes Career." Washington Post, (Parade Magazine), (May 2, 1976), p. 28.

2335. "Fans Continued Support on Muhammad Ali Viewed." Washington Post, (February 17, 1978), p. 3, sec. B.

2336. Faust, I. "What If Muhammad Ali Reviewed Jose Torres Book, Sting Like A Bee?" Esquire, 77 (May 1972), 120-1+.

2337. "Feats of Clay: Clay-London Fight." Time, 88 (August 12, 1966), 54.

2338. "Featured." Washington Post, (April 25, 1976), p. 19, sec. Potomac Magazine.

2339. Fentress, C. "Champ." New Times, 10 (March 20, 1978), 80.

2340. "Fight." New Yorker, 47 (March 20, 1971), 32-5.

2341. Fight Boycott Threat Eases, Meeting Is Set." Washington Post, (January 17, 1971), p. 3, sec. D.

2342. "Fight: Fan's Opinions." New Yorker, 46 (December 26, 1970), 16-17.

2343. "Fight of the Century, Joe Louis vs. Cassius Clay." Sepia, 16 (September 1967), 70-74.

2344. "Figure of Clay In Madame Tussaud's Wax Museum, London." New York Times, (July 28, 1971), p. 23.

2345. "1st In Series From Sheed Biography." Washington Post, (September 21, 1975), p. 1, sec. D.

2346. "5th Excerpt From Sheed Biography." Washington Post, (September 25, 1975), p. 1, sec. C.

2347. "$500,000 Workout." Newsweek, 78 (August 9, 1971), 75.

2348. "Fix That Wasn't." Sports Illustrated, 20 (April 3, 1964), 17.

2349. Flaherty, J. "Kid Never Had A Chance." Macleans, 91 (September 25, 1978), 38-40.

2350. "Zora Folley Ranks Muhammad Ali As No. 1." Sports Illustrated, 26 (April 10, 1967), 32.

2351. "For The Road, Muhammad Ali Wants To Win The Title A Third (And Final) Time." Jet, 54 (September 14, 1978), 47-48.

2352. "Foreman-Ali Title Bout Promoted." Washington Post, (March 2, 1973), p. 1, sec. D.

2353. "Foreman Bout Viewed." Washington Post, (October 30, 1974), p. 1, sec. F.

2354. "Former World Heavyweight Boxing Champ Muhammad Ali and Wife Sue IRS To Recover $97,048.68 In Income Taxes..." New York Times, (May 11, 1972), p. 54.

2355. "Former World Heavyweight Boxing Champ Muhammad Ali Becomes Father of Boy." New York Times. (May 16, 1972), p. 39.

2356. "Former Heavyweight Boxing Champ Cassius Clay Discloses That He Will Visit Communist China During Summer." New York Times, (January 28, 1972), p. 69.

2357. "Former World Heavyweight Boxing Champ Muhammad Ali Is Trying To Sell His Cherry Hill, N.J. Home for $250,000. New York Times, (December 14, 1972), p. 100.

2358. "Former World Heavyweight Boxing Champ Muhammad Ali Issued Warrant..." New York Times, (March 3, 1972), p. 25.

2359. "Former World Heavyweight Boxing Champ Muhammad Ali Purges Self of Contempt of Court Charges..." New York Times, (March 8, 1972), p. 37.

2360. "400 Blows." Newsweek, 66 (December 6, 1965), 64.

2361. "4th Excerpt From Sheed Biography." Washington Post, (September 24, 1975), p. 1, sec. F.

2362. "Frazier Awarded Decision As Ali Goes Down In 15th." Washington Post, (March 9, 1971), p. 1, sec. A.

2363. Frazier, Joe. "Cassius Who?" Ebony, 27 (May 1972), 68-72+.

2364. Furlong, W.B. "Wind that Blew in Chicago." Sports Illustrated, 24 (March 7, 1966), 26-7.

2365. "Gaseous Cassius." Time, 89 (May 5, 1967), 23-4.

2366. "Gets Hickok Athletic Award." Washington Post, (January 15, 1975), p. 1, sec. D.

2367. Gordon, Candy. "Two Women Look At Ali-Norton, Before And After." Black Sports, 6 (January 1977), 27-30+.

2368. "Governments Round." Newsweek, 70 (July 3, 1967), 2+.

2369. "Government Says Clay Claimed Draft Exemption as Black Muslim Min. In Last-Ditch Effort To Avoid Induction." New York Times, (January 19, 1968), p. 21.

2370. "Greatest Is Gone." Time, 111 (February 27, 1978), 72-75+.

2371. "The Greatest" Muhammad Ali Reviewed." Washington Post, (May 21, 1977), p. 1, sec. C.

2372. "Greatest, Not the Smartest." Economist, 274 (February 9, 1980), 34.

2373. Gross, M. "I Want To Destroy Clay." Sports Illustrated, 21 (October 19, 1964), 42-44.

2374. "Grr, Gate, Great!" Sports Illustrated. 39 (December 24, 1973), 32-3.

2375. Hamill, Pete. "Disintegration Of A Folk Hero." Harpers Bazaar, 104 (May 1971), 104-5.

2376. Hamill, Pete. "Gaudy Tragedy of A Black Champ." Life, 65 (October 25, 1968), 66A-66B+.

2377. Hamil, Pete. "Muhammad Ali: This Is About Me!" Life, 65 (October 25, 1968), 66.

2378. "Hands of Clay." Newsweek, 68 (September 19, 1966), 68.

2379. "Hare Was No Rabbit." Life, 58 (February 12, 1965), 97-8.

2380. Harrison, Claude. "Ali Racing Against Time in Bid to Regain Heavyweight Title." Philadelphia Tribune, (November 24, 1970).

2381. "Hate & Love Clay-Terrell Fight." Time, 89 (February 17, 1962), 55.

2382. Haveman, E. "Fighter At the Cross Roads." Sports Illustrated, 39 (December 24, 1973), 93.

2383. "Head For Figures." Newsweek, 67 (January 24, 1966), 79.

2384. "Heavyweight In A Larger Ring." [Interview By H. Quinn]. Macleans, 93 (July 7, 1980), 10-11.

2385. "How About that Whozis Clay-Mildenberger Fight." Time, 88 (September 16, 1966), 70.

2386. "How Cassius Clay Lost His Cool." Sepia, 15 (June 1966), 16-21.

2387. "I'll Chop that Big Monkey To Pieces." Life, 54 (February 15, 1963), 62a.

2388. "I'm A Little Special." Sport Illustrated, 20 (February 24, 1964), 14-15.

2389. "I'm Sorry But I'm Through Fighting Now." Esquire, 73 (May 1970), 120-2.

2390. "I'm The Greatest." Life, 54 (February 15, 1963), 62-63.

2391. "In Clay Corner." Christian Century, 84 (May 3, 1967), 580.

2392. "Integration: As Negro Champ Views It." U.S. News and World Report, 56 (March 16, 1964), 20.

2393. "Interviewed About Joe Frazier." Washington Post, (January 28, 1974), p. 1, sec. D.

2394. "Into The Fiery Furnace." Newsweek, 69 (May 8, 1967), 72.

2395. "It Happened Again." Sepia, 14 (July 1965), 79.

2396. "It Takes A Heap of Salongo." Newsweek, 84 (September 23, 1974), 72-3.

2397. Izenberg, Jerry. "Ali Is Still The Champion." Black Sports, 6 (January 1977), 26-30+.

2398. Izenberg, Jerry. "Angry Man In Search of Ali." Sport, 71 (July 1980), 40-3.

2399. Izenberg, Jerry. "Bee Stings the Bear." Sport, 70 (February 1980), 83-4.

2400. "Joe Frazier & Muhammad Ali." Winston-Salem Journal, (March 9, 1971).

2402. John, Ralph. "Muhammad Ali Kayos Rocky In Eighth." Carolina Peacemaker, (January 31, 1970).

2403. Jones, L. "In the Ring: Cassius Clay." Nation, 198 (June 19, 1964), 661-62.

2404. "Jose Torres Book, Sting Like A Bee, Reviewed." New York Times, (October 22, 1971), p. 36.

2405. "Justice Stewart Seems To Back Ali's Pacifism." Washington Post, (April 20, 1971), p. 8, sec. A.

2406. "K.O. for Cassius." Time, 89 (June 30, 1967), 20.

2407. Kane, M. "Art of Ali." Sports Illustrated, 30 (May 5, 1969), 48-57.

2408. Kane, M. "Greatest Meets The Grimmest." Sports Illustrated, 23 (November 15, 1965), 36-8.

2409. Kane M. "Massacre." Sports Illustrated, 25 (November 21, 1966) 22-5.

2410. Kane, M. "Muslim Ministers to a South Paw." Sports Illustrated, 25 (September 19, 1966), 34-35.

2411. Kane, M. "Welcome Back Ali!" Sports Illustrated, 33 (September 14, 1970), 20-3.

2412. Kane, M. "You Watch Out Ali." Sports Illustrated, 25 (November 14, 1966), 26-9.

2413. Kempton, Murry. "I Whipped Him And I'm Still Pretty." New Republic, 150 (March 7, 1964), 9-10.

2414. Kidd, James. "Yes Sir, Mr. Ali." Christian Century, 85 (October 30, 1968), 1383-5.

2415. "Kindred Column on Muhammad Ali and Jimmy Ellis." Washington Post, (September 29, 1977), p. 1, sec. B.

2416. "Kindred Column on Ali Black Muslims & Predicted Win Over Spinks." Washington Post, (February 14, 1978), p. 1., sec. D.

2417. Kisner, Ronald E. "Ali Charts New Horizons After Victory." Jet, 51 (October 14, 1976), 12-13+.

2418. Kisner, Ronald E. "Ali Looks Ahead After Regaining His Boxing Title." Jet, 47 (November 21, 1974), 52-57.

2419. Kisner, Ronald E. "Can Ali Keep His Title From Ken Norton." Jet, 51 (September 23, 1976), 52-56.

2420. Kisner, Ronald E.. "Foreman and Ali Stage Africa's Biggest Fight." Jet, 47 (September 26, 1974), 50-53.

2421. Kisner, Ronald E. "Has Success Spoiled Ali." Jet, 49 (October 16, 1975), 54-58.

2422. Kisner, Ronald E. "Is Their Marriage on the Rocks?" Ebony, (December 1975), 176.

2423. Kisner, Ronald E. "Muhammad Ali Era Ignited Black Sports Revolution." Jet, 51 (November 11, 1976), 94-97.

2424. Kisner, Ronald E. "New Look At Muhammad Ali." Jet, 50 (April 22, 1976), 52-55.

2425. Kisner, Ronald E. "Where Can Ali Go Now." Jet, 4 (April 15, 1971), 52-55.

2426. Kisner, Ronald E. "Zaire Postscript: Ali Out Duels For Crown." Jet, 47 (November 14, 1974), 52-54.

2427. Kornbluth, Jesse. "Muhammad Goes To The Mountain." New Times, (September 6, 1974), 48.

2428. Kram, Mark. "Ali In A World of His Own." Sports Illustrated, 38 (February 26, 1973), 56+.

2429. Kram, Mark. "At The Bell..." Sports Illustrated, 34 (March 8, 1971), 18-21.

2430. Kram, Mark. "Battered Face of A Winner, Ali-Frazier Fight." Sports Illustrated, 34 (March 15, 1971), 16-21.

2431. Kram, Mark. "Crafty Win For Muhammad." Sports Illustrated, 40 (February 4, 1974), 16-19.

2432. Kram, Mark. "Fight's Lone Arranger." Sports Illustrated, 41 (September 2, 1974), 30-4.

2433. Kram, Mark. "He Moves Like Silk, Hits Like A Ton." Sports Illustrated, 33 (October 26, 1970), 16-19.

2434. Kram, Mark. "Introducing In The Back Room, the Man With A Package." Sports Illustrated, 40 (January 28, 1974), 34-5+.

2435. Kram, Mark. "Jawful Test On The Mountain." Sports Illustrated, 39 (September 3, 1973), 42-3.

2436. Kram, Mark. "Just Call Him Shubert Ali." Sports Illustrated, 37 (October 2, 1972), 24-5.

2437. Kram, Mark. "Senario of Pride and Decline." Sports Illustrated, 40 (January 21, 1974), 22-4+.

2438. Kram, Mark. "Smashing Return of the Old Ali." Sports Illustrated, 33 (November 2, 1970), 18-19.

2439. "L. Kippett On Widespread Misconception About Scope and Content of U.S. Supreme Court Decision." New York Times, (July 9, 1971), p. 21.

2440. "Legality of Clay Wiretap Remains Open." New Courier, (July 21, 1969).

2441. "Leon Spinks Defeats Muhammad Ali For World's Heavyweight Crown." Washington Post, (February 16, 1978), p. 1, sec. D.

2442. "Leon Spinks: The 'Boy' Did A Man's Job On Muhammad Ali." Ebony, 33 (May 1978), 130-131+.

2443. Leonian, Phillip. "The Art of Ali." Sports Illustrated, (May 5, 1969).

2444. "Letter To The Editor on Muhammad Ali." Washinton Post, (October 1, 1978), p. 6, sec. C.

2445. "Letter To The Editor on References To Muhammad Ali's Age." Washington Post, (February 25, 1978), p. 14, sec. A.

2446. Levin, D. "Bury His Heart A Wounded Jaw." Sports Illustrated, 38 (April 9, 1973), 28-9.

2447. Lewis, Ida. "Pele and Ali: A Look At Two Champions-Editorial." Encore, 6 (October 10, 1977), 9.

2448. Lewis, Shawn D. "Wives of Ali and Spinks Talk About Their Husbands." Jet, 55 (October 5, 1978), 16+.

2449. Lewis, W.S. "Word To The Wise or Ali." Encore, 9 (May 1980), 52.

2450. Liebling, A.J. "Poet & Pedagogue." New Yorker, 8 (March 3, 1962), 104.

2451. Liebling, A.J. "Reporter at Large." New Yorker, 38 (March 3, 1962), 104+.

2452. Liebling, A.J. "Sporting Scene." New Yorker, 39 (March 30, 1963), 122.

2453. Lipsyte, Robert. "Cassius Clay, Cassius X, Muhammad Ali." New York Times Magazine, (October 25, 1964), 29.

2454. Lipsyte, Robert. "I Don't Have To Be What You Want Me To Be, Says Muhammad Ali." New York Times Magazine, (March 7, 1971), 24-5.

2455. Lipsyte, Robert. "I'm Free To Be Who I Want." New York Times Magazine, (May 28, 1967), 29.

2456. "Louisville Lip." Time, 80 (November 23, 1962), 37-8.

2457. Lovesey, J. "If Cassius Can't Punch the London Isn't Down." Sports Illustrated, 25 (August 15, 1966), 16-19.

2458. "Low Blows Tax Blows." Newsweek, 67 (April 11, 1966), 64.

2459. "Lunch For A Lion." Time, 86 (December 3, 1965), 73.

2460. "McCarthy Column on Boxing." Washington Post, (April 29, 1976), p. 1, sec. E.

2461. "McCarthy Column on Muhammad Ali's Appeal to Intellectuals." Washington Post, (September 22, 1978), p. 17, sec. A.

2462. McDermott, J.R. "Liston Turned on the Evileye Clay Didn't Notice." Life, 56 (March 6, 1964), 34-9.

2463. McEwen, Tom. "Boxing Wants Cassius Out." Winston-Salem Journal & Sentinel, (December 14, 1969).

2464. McWilliams, C. "Muhammad Ali For Congress." Nation, 227 (July 22, 1978), 69-70.

2465. MacGregor, R. "Sting Like Butterfly, Float Like A Bee - A Sad Epitaph For Muhammad Ali." Mcleans, 91 (March 6, 1978), 57.

2466. Mailer, Norman. "Ali-Frazier Fight With Editorial Comment." Life, 70 (March 19, 1971), 3, 18-19+.

2467. "Man, the Rabbit & the Boy." Time, 82 (August 2, 1963), 52.

2468. "Mann Column - Heavyweight Fight In The Wire Room." Washington Post, (March 3, 1971), p. 18, sec. A.

2469. Martin, Louis. "Muhammad Ali Matches Words With Deeds." Chicago Daily Defender, (November 6, 1970).

2470. Massaquoi, H.J. "Private World of Muhammad Ali." Ebony, 27
      (September 1972), 144-8+.

2471. Massaquoi, H.J. "Unconquerable Muhammad Ali." Ebony, 24 (April
      1969), 168-170+.

2472. Maule, Tex. "Agony and Ecstasy." Sports Illustrated, 37 (July
      10, 1972), 16-17.

2473. Maule, Tex. "Cassius To Win A Thriller." Sports Illustrated, 22
      (May 24, 1965), 22-5.

2474. Maule, Tex. "Cruel Ali With All the Skills." Sports Illustrated,
      26 (February 13, 1967), 18-21.

2475. Maule, Tex. "End of A Beautiful Friendship; Muhammad Ali-J.
      Ellis Fight." Sports Illustrated, 35 (August 2, 1971), 10-11.

2476. Maule, Tex. "For Ali, A Time To Preach." Sports Illustrated, 28
      (February 19, 1968), 26-8+.

2477. Maule, Tex. "Got To Look Good To Allah." Sports Illustrated,
      35 (November 29, 1971), 28-9.

2478. Maule, Tex. "He Has Heavy Things On His Mind." Sports
      Illustrated, 35 (July 26, 1971), 24-6.

2479. Maule, Tex. "I'm Not Worried About Ali." Sports Illustrated,
      26 (June 19, 1967), 18-21.

2480. Maule, Tex. "Left That Was." Sports Illustrated, 26 (February
      6, 1967), 14-17.

2481. Maule, Tex. "Liston's Edge." Sports Illustrated, 20 (February
      24, 1964), 18-21.

2482. Maule, Tex. "Mouth That Nearly Roared." Sports Illustrated, 38
      (April 23, 1973), 28-30+.

2483. Maule, Tex. "A Quick, Hard Right and Needless Storm of Protest."
      Clay-Liston Fight." Sports Illustrated, 22 (June 7, 1965), 22-24.

2484. Maule, Tex. "Showdown With a Punching Bag." Sports Illustrated,
      24 (March 28, 1966), 34-7.

2485. Maule, Tex. "Sting of the Louisville Lip." Sports Illustrated,
      22 (February 17, 1964), 50-51.

2486. Maule, Tex. "Sudden Rush of Heavies." Sports Illustrated, 24
      (February 21, 1966), 14-17.

2487. Maule, Tex. "Yes, It Was Good and Honest." Sports Illustrated,
      (March 9, 1964), 20-25.

2488. Maule, Tex and Bill Russell. "I Am Not Worried About Ali."
      Sports Illustrated, 26 (June 1967), 18-21.

2489. Maule, Tex and M. Sharnik. It's Gonna Be The Champ and the Tramp." Sports Illustrated, 34 (February 1, 1971), 14-17.

2490. "Mike Wallace Compares Ali-Frazier Training Methods." St. Louis Metro Sentinel, (February 27, 1971).

2491. "Mismatch of the Century." Ebony, 23 (May 1968), 58-60.

2492. Moore, Marianne. "I'm The Greatest." Album Notes, Columbia Records, C58893.

2493. Morgenstern, Joseph. "Knock-Out, Put-On." Newsweek, 74 (December 8, 1969), 122+.

2494. Moses, D. "Ride on, You Lip of Louisville." Life, 54 (February 15, 1963), 66.

2495. "Most Subdued Cassius." Life, 57 (November 27, 1964), 81-82.

2496. "Mouth: Incident With Ernie Terrell." Time, 89 (January 6, 1967), 73.

2497. "Muhammad Ali and Joe Frazier Feature." Washington Post, (March 4, 1979), p. 6, sec. Parade Magazine.

2498. "Muhammad Ali Arrive For May 16 Title Defense at Capital Centre." Washington Post. (May 6, 1977), p. 1, sec. C.

2499. "Muhammad Ali Arrives For May 16 Title Defense at Capital Centre." Washington Post. (May 6, 1977), p. 1, sec. C.

2500. "Muhammad Ali-Ex-Champ is Already a Legend." St. Louis Sentinel, (February 20, 1971).

2501. "Muhammad Ali Helps Launch National Dental Care Campaign in D.C." Washington Post, (December 23, 1979), p. 25, sec. A.

2502. "Muhammad Ali Hits Broadway." Carolina Peacemaker, (November 15, 1969).

2503. "Muhammad Ali in Africa." Sports Illustrated, 20 (June 1, 1964), 20-25.

2504. "Muhammad Ali Interviewed." Washington Post, (May 4, 1978), p. 1, sec. B.

2505. "Muhammad Ali Marries Veronica Porch." Washington Post, (June 20, 1977), p. 4, sec. B.

2506. "Muhammad Ali Meets His Match." Economist, 266 (February 18, 1978), 50.

2507. "Muhammad Ali Meets Leonid Brezhnev In Moscow." Washington Post, (June 20, 1978), p. 1, sec. A.

2508. "Muhammad Ali Pledges $100,000; How About You?" Crisis, 83 (November, 1976), 306.

2509. "Muhammad Ali Retains Boxing Title In Win Over Ernie Shavers." Washington Post. (September 30, 1977), p. 1, sec. D.

2510. "Muhammad Ali Sees Liston Cut Up Wepner." Philadelphia Tribune, (July 4, 1970).

2511. "Muhammad Ali Speaks At National Press Club Luncheon." Washington Post, (August 28, 1976), p. 3, sec. E.

2512. "Muhammad Ali Spends $200,000 on Gift Tickets To Fight." Washington Post, (May 16, 1977), p. 1, sec. D.

2513. "Muhammad Ali Tries to Wrestle With Antonio Inoki." Winston-Salem Journal, (June 30, 1976).

2514. "Muhammad Ali (Cassius Clay) Visits Africa." Sepia, 13 (November 1964), 8-13.

2515. "Muhammad Ali Visits Soviet Union." Washington Post, (June 14, 1978), p. 1, sec. D.

2516. "Muhammad Ali Visits Vietnamese Refugess in Hong Kong." Washington Post, (December 23, 1979), p. 25, sec. A.

2517. "Muhammad Ali Wins Back Heavyweight Championship." Washington Post, (June 16, 1978), p. 1, sec. A.

2518. "Muhammad Ali's Finances A Puzzle To News Media." Jet, 54 (April 13, 1978), 53.

2519. "Muhammad Ali's Loss Ends An Era of Color, Style and Class." Jet, 53 (March 9, 1978), 52-53.

2520. "Muhammad Ali's Personal Cook, Lana Shabazz, Interviewed." Washington Post, (May 15, 1977), p. 4, sec. C.

2521. "Muhammad in Action." The New Courier, (September 12, 1970).

2522. "Muhammad On The Mountaintop." Time, 104 (November 11, 1974), 84-7.

2523. "Muhammad To Visit Soviet Union." Washington Post, (February 28, 1978), p. 1, sec. D.

2524. Murray, J. "No Phanton Punch With Account by J. Murray." Sports Illustrated, 22 (June 7, 1965), 48-53.

2525. Nakashima, L. "Not Only Foster Got Stung." Sports Illustrated, 36 (April 10, 1972), 80+.

2526. "Named AP Athlete of 1970's." Washington Post, (January 14, 1980), p. 7c, sec. D.

2527. Neiman, L. "He's the Smartest and Fastest Man That There is with Brushstroke or Footwork." Esquire, 68 (September 1967), 136-137.

2528. Neiman, L. "Muhammad is a Whiz." Esquire, 68 (September 1967), 136-137.

2529. "New York Athletic Commission Assesses Fine." Washington Post, (January 26, 1974), p. 1 sec. D.

2530. "New York State Athletic Commission Chairman E.B. Dooley Gratified by Supreme Court Decision." New York Times, (June 29, 1971), p. 24.

2531. "Newspaper Course: Popular Culture 10-Athletes." Washington Post, (March 30, 1978), p. 7, sec. DC.

2532. Nipson, Herb. "How Good Is Cassius Clay." Ebony, 19 (April 1964), 77-80.

2533. "No More Boasting, Just the Fight." Life, 69 (October 23, 1970), 44-49.

2534. "Norton Wins Split Decision In California." Washington Post, (April 1, 1973), p. 1, sec. D.

2535. "Now There Is One Champion." Newsweek, 77 (March 22, 1971), 72-76.

2536. "Odd Couple Plays Zaire." Sport, 69 (October 1979), 91-92.

2537. Olsen, J. "Case of Conscience." Sports Illustrated, (May 9, 1966), 34-36.

2538. "$100 Misunderstanding." Newsweek, 63 (February 24, 1964), 58.

2539. O'Neil, Mildred. "Afro Visits Muhammad Ali In His Home." Afro-American, (April 3, 1971).

2540. Nunn, Bill. "Ali, Ali, Ali, Was Betitting, Chant in Malaysia." The Courier, (July 12, 1975).

2541. "Ottaway Eyes News Coverage of Bout." Washington Post, (September 28, 1974), p. 18, sec. A.

2542. Parks, Gordon. "Redemption of the Champion." Life, 61 (September 9, 1966), 76-7.

2543. Patterson, Floyd and G. Talese. "In Defense of Cassius Clay." Esquire, 66 (August 1966), 55-58.

2544. Patterson, Floyd. "Cassius Clay Must Be Beaten; With Editorial Comment." Sports Illustrated, 23 (October 11, 1965), 19, 78-80.

2545. Patterson, Floyd. "I Want To Destroy Clay." Sports Illustrated, 21 (October 19, 1964), 42-44.

2546. "Picking Foreman's Foe." Time, 103 (January 28, 1974), 59.

2547. Phillips, B.J. and P. Ainslie. "Requiem For A Heavyweight." Time, 116 (October 13, 1980), 78.

2548. "Playing Grown Ups." Time, 84 (November 13, 1964), 104-105.

2549. Plimpton, George. "Breaking A Date For The Dance." Sports Illustrated, 41 (November 11, 1974), 22-29.

2550. Plimpton, George. " Miami Notebook: Cassius Clay and Malcolm X." Harper Magazine, 25 (June 1964), 54-61.

2551. Plimpton, George. "No Requiem For A Heavyweight." Sports Illustrated, 34 (April 5, 1971) 84-86+.

2552. Plimpton, George. "Notes From The Battle of New Orleans." Rolling Stone, (November 2, 1978), 52-6.

2553. Plimpton, George. "Sportsman of the Year." Sports Illustrated, 41 (December 23, 1974), 84-9+.

2554. Plimpton, George. "They'll Be Swinging In The Rain." Sports Illustrated, 41 (September 30, 1974), 36-8+.

2555. Plimpton, George. "Watching the Man In the Mirror." Sports Illustrated, 33 (November 23, 1970(, 30-3+.

2556. Plimpton, George. "World Champion Is Refused A Meal." Sports Illustrated, 22 (May 17, 1965), 24-7.

2557. Poinsett, A. "Look At Cassius Clay: Biggest Mouth In Boxing." Ebony, 18 (March, 1963), 35-36.

2558. "Portable Pulpit." Sports Illustrated, 25 (September 5, 1966), 8.

2559. "Povich Analyzes Upcoming Fight." Washington Post, (February 13, 1973), p. 1, sec. D.

2560. "Povich Previews Frazier Fight." Washington Post, (January 28, 1974), p. 1 sec. D.

2561. "Povich Views Reaction To Title Bout." Washington Post, (January 26, 1973) p. 1, sec. E.

2562. "Praised For Aid To Africa." Washington Post, (April 24, 1976), p. 4, sec. B.

2563. "Preparations For Frazier Fight." Washington Post, (September 12, 1975), p. 1, sec. D.

2564. "The Price Muhammad Ali Paid For Being Black." Jet, 4 (July 22, 1971), 52-55.

2565. "Profiled." Washington Post, (April 18, 1976), p. 1, sec. C.

2566. "Promoter Hits Ali With $10 Million Racial Slander Suit." Winston-Salem Journal, (September 20, 1978).

2567. "Promoters Spar For Ali's Next Bout." Business Week, (December 12, 1970), 21.

2568. "Prophet's Margin: Clay." Newsweek, 61 (March 25, 1963), 96.

2569. "Publicity For Public Relations Geo County Eyed." Washington Post, (April 29, 1976), p. 1, sec. C.

2570. "Punching Brag." Newsweek, 61 (March 8, 1963), 93.

2571. Putnam, P. "Better Not Sell The Old Man Short." Sports Illustrated, 53 (September 29, 1980), 20-25.

2572. Putnam, P. "Doom In The Desert." Sports Illustrated, 53 (October 13, 1980), 34-40.

2573. Putnam, P. "He's The Greatest, I'm The Best." Sports Illustrated, 48 (February 27, 1978), 14-19.

2574. Putnam, P. "Latest From The Greatest." Sports Illustrated, 52 (April 14, 1980), 16-20.

2575. Putnam, P. "Old Lion Eyes Leon." Sports Illustrated, 49 (September 11, 1978), 20-25.

2576. Putnam, P. "One More Time To The Top." Sports Illustrated, 49 (September 25, 1978), 16-19+.

2577. Quinn, H. "Rolling With the Last Con." Macleans, 93 (October 13, 1980), 38-39.

2578. "R. Lipsyte Comment On Court Expected Ruling." New York Times, (June 28, 1971), p. 41.

2579. "R. Lipsyte On U.S. Supreme Court Decision Clearing Clay of Draft Violation Charges." New York Times, (July 1, 1971), p. 65.

2580. "Reader's Opinion Poll Pick Their Favorite In Ali-Spinks Title Fight." Jet, 54 (September 14, 1978), 46+.

2581. "Reflecting on Ali." Winston-Salem Journal, (February 17, 1978).

2582. "Retains Heavyweight Boxing Title." Washington Post, (May 17, 1975), p. 1, sec. C.

2583. "Retirement Premature: Ali Won't Quit Now." Jet, 51 (October 21, 1976), 46-48.

2584. "Return of the Ringmaster." _Time_, 96 (November 9, 1970), 35.

2585. "Return To The Ring." _Newsweek_, 76 (September 14, 1970), 123-4.

2586. "Revenge Not Sought by Ali." _Philadelphia Tribune_, (July 13, 1971).

2587. Richardson, Jack. "Ali On Peachtree." _Harper_, 242 (January 1971), 46-9+.

2588. Rodda, J. "Tight-Lipped." _New Statesman_, 94 (August 12, 1977), 221-22.

2589. Rogin, G. "Battle of the Lionhearted." _Sports Illustrated_, 24 (April 11, 1966), 32-4.

2590. Rogin, G. "Campaign Is Ended for an Ancient Warrior: Archie Moore-Cassius Clay Fight." _Sports Illustrated_, 17 (November 26, 1962), 18-21.

2591. Rogin, G. "Cautious Comes of Age." _Sports Illustrated_, 15 (October 16, 1961), 22.

2592. Rogin, G. "Champion As Long As He Wants: Cassius Clay." _Sports Illustrated_, 23 (November 29, 1965), 20-25.

2593. Rogin, G. "Giant They Love To Hate With Account." _Sports Illustrated_, 23 (December 6, 1965), 40-5+.

2594. Rogin, G. "Man in the Champ's Corner: Cassius Clay." _Sports Illustrated_, 22 (May 24, 1965), 32-36.

2595. Rogin, G. "Rabbit Hunt In Vegas." _Sports Illustrated_, 23 (November 22, 1965), 34-9.

2596. Rogin, G. "Still Hurt and Lost." _Sports Illustrated_, (November 16, 1964), 22-7.

2597. "Rookie and the Vet." _Ebony_, 20 (January 1965), 56-58.

2598. "Run, Cassius Run." _New Yorker_, 40 (March 7, 1964), 43-44.

2599. Sanders, Charles L. "Muhammad Ali Challenges Black Men." _Ebony_, 30 (January 1975) 120-2+.

2600. "Say Muhammad Lost His Fight At Party With Friends." _Jet_, 44 (April, 1973), 46.

2601. "Says Its Eavesdropped On Several of Clay's Phone Conversations..." _New York Times_, (August 31, 1968), 21.

2602. Schaap, Dick. "Happiest Heavyweight." _Saturday Evening Post_, 234 (March 25, 1962), 36+.

2603. Schecter, Leonard. "Fall and Rise of Muhammad Ali." _Look_, 35 (March 9, 1971), 62-66.

2604. Schecter, Leonard. "The Passion of Muhammad Ali." Esquire, 69 (April, 1968), 128-31+.

2605. Schulberg, B. "Chinese Boxes of Muhammad Ali; Excerpt From Loser and Still Champion:Muhammad Ali." Saturday Review, 55 (February 26. 1972), 21-6.

2606. Schulberg, B. "Loser." Saturday Evening Post, 243 (Fall 1971), 57+.

2607. Schuyler, Ed. "Shavers Has Chance But Ali Finesse Will Win." Winston-Salem Journal, (September 28, 1977), p. 38.

2608. "2nd Excerpt From Sheed Biography." Washington Post, (September 22, 1975), p. 1, sec. D.

2609. "Secret Honeymoon of the Champ." Ebony, 23 (November 1967), 144-146+.

2610. "Senator Johnson Moves In On Ali-Frazier Bout." Jet, 39 (January 7, 1971), 54.

2611. "Senator Says Ali is Hero." Winston-Salem Journal, (October 10, 1975).

2612. Shrake, Edward. "Blood at the Arsenal." Sports Illustrated, 24 (May 30, 1966), 20-23.

2613. Shrake, Edward. "It Was The Mouth By A Whisker." Sports Illustrated, 39 (September 17, 1973), 42-3.

2614. Shrake, Edward. "Live! Booze! Girls! Ali! This Is Fighting?" Sports Illustrated, 37 (December 4, 1972), 30-2+.

2615. Shrake, Edward. "Bundini: Svengali In Ali's Corner." Sports Illustrated, 34 (February 15, 1971), 32-36.

2616. Shrake Edward. "Ready for the Bloodletting." Sports Illustrated, 24 (May 23, 1966), 74.

2617. Shrake, Edward. "Taps For the Champ." Sports Illustrated, 26 (May 8, 1957), 11, 19-25.

2618. Shaw, I. "Muhammad Ali and the Little People." Esquire, 72 (November 1969), 121-5+.

2619. "Sickening Spectacle In A Ring." Life, 59 (December 3, 1965), 42-42A.

2620. Simms, Gregory. "Ali Finds The Right Combination: Films, Fights and Religion." Jet, 51 (February 17, 1977), 46-50+.

2621. Simms, Gergory. "Ali Reveals New Goals: Two $4 Million Fights, Retirement and Organizer." Jet, 53 (November 3, 1977), 50.

2622. Simms, Gregory. "Ali Tells Why He Puts God Ahead of Women and Money." Jet, 54 (July 27, 1978), 44-47.

2623. Simms, Gregory. "Ali's New Family." Jet, 52 (May 5, 1977), 28-31.

2624. Simms, Gregory. "Can Old Man Ali Accomplish the Impossible." Ebony, 33 (September 1978), 114+.

2625. Simms, Gregory. "Foreman: When I Told Ali About God, Do You Know What He Said." Jet, 53 (October 13, 1977), 54-55.

2626. Simms, Gregory. "Herbert Muhammad No Longer 'Owns' Ali In Revised Legal Contract." Jet, 54 (June 22, 1978), 13-14.

2627. Simms, Gregory. "Hollywood-Black and White-Digs Its New Hero: The Greatest, Muhammad Ali." Jet, 51 (January 20, 1977), 12-16.

2628. Simms, Gregory. "Marriage For Muhammad, Khalihah Ali End in Divorce and Respect." Jet, 51 (January 20, 1977)), 12-16.

2629. Simms, Gregory. "Muhammad Ali Takes A Beautiful Bride." Jet, 52 (July 7, 1977), 14-16.

2630. Simms, Gregory. "Muhammad, Khalilah Ali Share Sunday Dinner." Jet, 53 (December 15, 1977), 14-16.

2631. Simms, Gregory and Vandell Cobb. "Muhammad Ali Ends His Wondrous Boxing Career." Jet, 55 (October 5, 1978), 52-55.

2632. Simpson, Coreen. "Two Women Look At Ali-Norton, Before and After." Black Sports, 6 (January 1977), 27-30+.

2633. "Since Clay Became 1-A." U.S. News and World Report, 62 (May 1, 1967), 18.

2634. "Picket Boxing Writers Assn. Dinner, NYC to Protest Lifting of Clay's Heavyweight Title." New York Times, (January 15, 1968), p. 37.

2635. "Skinning the Cat." Time, 88 (November 25, 1966), 64.

2636. Slater, Jack. "Loneliness of the Man At The Top." Ebony, 35 (July 1980), 33-6+.

2637. "Smith Column-Ali's Latest Victory His Biggest Rematch." Washington Post, (June 29, 1971), p. 5, sec. D.

2638. "South Africa Offers Clay $300,000 for 10-Lecture Tour This Winter." New York Times, (July 29, 1971), p. 25.

2639. "Speaking of Indignities." Time, 87 (April 8, 1966), 75.

2640. "Speaks To 2 Groups on Children." Washington Post, (March 18, 1976), p. 3, sec. D.

2641. "Split Decision For Diplomat, Ali." U.S. News and World Report, 88 (February 18, 1980), 6.

2642. Stephens, J.M. "With Ali Freed, Court Also Gives Legal Okay To Black Muslim Religion." Jet, 4 (July 15, 1971), 6-7.

2643. Stevens, Joann. "Act Three: Ali-Norton." Black Sports, 6 (September 1976), 10-13.

2644. Strasser, S. "Muhammad Ali." U.S. News and World, 88 (February 18, 1980), 6.

2645. "Struggles of a Champ." Sepia, 15 (November 1966), 79-81.

2646. "Subdued Ali Visits USSR." Winston-Salem Journal, (June 13, 1978).

2647. "Subject of Micheal Getter Column." Washington Post, (May 30, 1976) p. 7, sec. B.

2648. "Subject of Sally Quinn Column." Washington Post, (April 10, 1976), p. 1, sec. B.

2649. "Superfight." Time, 95 (January 19, 1970), 59.

2650. "Supreme Court Decision Set." New York Times, (June 27, 1971), p. 1, sec. 5.

2651. "Supreme Court, 8-0 With Justice Marshall Abstaining Overturns Clay Conviction For Refusing Induction." New York Times, (June 29, 1971), p. 1.

2652. "Suspends Trainer, Drew Brown." Washington Post, (January 25, 1973), p. 4, sec. F.

2653. Sutton, I. "Intimate Look At The Champ." Ebony, 22 (November 1966), 148-58.

2654. Sutton, I. "Quiet Family Life of Muhammad Ali." Ebony, 26 (January 1971), 118-22.

2655. "Sylvester Stallone Article on Muhammad Ali & Boxing." Washington Post, (May 15, 1977), p. 1, sec. C.

2656. "Taxes Effect on Giveaway Plan." Washington Post, (February 23, 1975), p. 2, sec. D.

2657. "22 Grid Stars, Muhammad Ali Thrill 600 at All-American Fete." The New Courier, (January 23, 1971), p. 15.

2658. "Theater of Cruelty, Clay-Terrell Fight." Newsweek, 69 (February 20, 1967), 87.

2659. "Theater of the Absurd." Time, 85 (June 4, 1965), 68-9.

2660. "3rd Excerpt From Sheed Biography." Washington Post, (September 23, 1975), p. 1, sec. D.

2661. Thompson, H.S. "Last Tango In Vegas." Rolling Stone, (May 4, 1978), 40-46; (May 18, 1978), 62-69+.

2662. Thompson, T. "Battled of the Undefeated Giants." Life, 70 (March 5, 1971), 3, 40-9.

2663. "Top of Life." Washington Post, (February 22, 1975), p. 11, sec. A.

2664. Torres, Jose. "Sting Like A Bee." (Review), Saturday Review, 54 (November 6, 1971), 46-7.

2665. Townsend, W.H. "Rage of the Aged Lion." American Heritage, 11 (June, 1960), 34-7.

2666. "Training Program Viewed." Washington Post, (April 25, 1976), p. 1, sec. D.

2667. Tuckner, Howard. "Man, It's Great To Be Great." New York Times Magazine, (December 9, 1962), 47-8+.

2668. "Two Documentary Films Reviewed." Washington Post, (September 2, 1975), p. 5, sec. B.

2669. "Two Down, One To Go." Time, 96 (December 21, 1970), 48.

2670. Unger, Norman. "Battered Ali Satisfied With Victory." New Courier, (December 19, 1970).

2671. "U.S. Appeals Court, New Orleans Upholds Clay Conviction. New York Times, (May 7, 1968), p. 9.

2672. "U.S. Appeals Court New Orleans Upholds Clay Conviction." New York Times, (May 7, 1968), p. 9.

2673. "U.S. Justice Department Urges Court Reject Appeal." New York Times, (August 7, 1968), p. 34.

2674. "U.S. Supreme Court Agrees To Decide Whether Cassius Clay Is Entitled To Draft Deferment as Conscientious Objector." New York Times, (January 12, 1971), p. 40.

2675. "U.S. Supreme Court To Hear Clay's Appeal From Draft Evasion Conviction Within Week." New York Times, (April 18, 1971), p. 4, sec. 5.

2676. "U.S. Tells Court Muhammad Ali Failed To Object To All Wars." Washington Post, (April 7, 1971), p. 3, sec. A.

2677. "Upcoming Earnie Shavers-Muhammad Ali Bout Discussed." Washington Post, (September 25, 1977), p. 1, sec. B.

2678. "Variety Show Reviewed." Washington Post, (September 13, 1975), p. 4, sec. C.

2679. "Vint Lawrence Cartoon on Muhammad Ali." Washington Post, (May 22, 1977), p. 8, sec. F.

2680. "Violent Coronation In Kinshasa." Time, 104 (September 23, 1974), 100-102.

2681. "Visits Skyline Elementary In Md." Washington Post, (April 23, 1976), p. 1, sec. B.

2682. Wallace, Robert. "Spoken Like A True Clay." Life, 53 (November 30, 1962), 88-9.

2683. "Weary Butterfly." Newsweek, 76 (December 21, 1970), 68+.

2684. "What Miffs Ali? Ask His Sparring Partner." Jet, 57 (June 9, 1977), 50.

2685. "What Next?" Newsweek, 69 (April 3, 1967), 56.

2686. "While Ali Babbled." Newsweek, 65 (February 15, 1965), 60.

2687. "Will Ali Fight Again." Newsweek, 73 (April 7, 1969), 52+.

2688. "Winner If Not Champ." Time, 98 (July 12, 1971), 53.

2689. "Winning With Honors." Encore American & Worldwide News, (January 20, 1975).

2690. "Wins Decision Over Jimmy Young." Washington Post, (May 1, 1976), p. 1, sec. A.

2691. "Wins TD Club Timmie Award." Washington Post, (January 18, 1976), p. 8, sec. C.

2692. "Wins 12 Round Bout With Bugner." Washington Post, (February 15, 1973), p. 1, sec. H.

2693. "With Mouth & Magic." Time, 83 (March 6, 1964), 66.

2694. Wolfe, Tom. "Marvelous Mouth." Esquire, 60 (October 1963), 146.

2695. Woods, P. "Return of Muhammad Ali Alias Cassius Marcellus Clay Jr." New York Times Magazine, (November 30, 1969), 32-3+.

2696. "World's Greatest." New York Amsterdam News, (January 18, 1972).

2697. Young, Andrew S. "Cassius Clay and The Black Muslims." Sepia, 13 (May, 1964), 62.

2698. Young, Andrew S. "Clay Needs Boxing; Boxing Needs Him." The Michigan Chronical, (September 17, 1970).

2699. Young, Andrew S. "How Muhammad Ali Lost His Title." Sepia, 27 (April 1978), 60-67.

2700. Young, Andrew S. "Is Muhammad Ali All Washed Up?" Ebony, 28 (July 1973), 83-84+.

2701. Young Andrew S. "Man Who Shut Muhammad's Mouth." Sepia, 221 (August 1973), 16-20.

2702. Young, Andrew S. "Why Ali Can Never Beat Frazier." Sepia, 2 (July 1971), 28-33.

2703. "Young Once Again At 36." Time, 112 (September 25, 1978), 103.

2704. Zeitlin, Arnold. "Ali Has Become Status Symbol to Third World." Winston-Salem Journal, (September 21, 1975).

2705. Ziegel, Vic. "Ali Goes For Broke." New York, 13 (April 7, 1980), 46-8.

2706. Ziegel, Vic. "Ali, Spinks and The Battle of New Orleans." New York, 11 (October 2, 1978), 91-2+.

2707. Ziegel, Vic. "Once More With Feeling." New York, 13 (September 29, 1980), 63-5.

HENRY ARMSTRONG

2708. "Armstrong Accepts Ambers Bout." New York Times, (March 8, 1939), p. 25.

2709. "Armstrong Bout With L. Feldman Planned." New York Times, (February 26, 1939), p. 5, sec. 5.

2710. "Armstrong Defeats Ross For Title." New York Times, (June 1, 1938), p. 26.

2711. "Armstrong Plans." New York Times, (June 2, 1938), p. 28.

2712. "Armstrong Treated By Doctor: Plans Long Vacation." New York Times, (August 19, 1938), p. 23.

2713. "Armstrong Wins, Clinches Claim To Title." New York Times, (October 30, 1937), p. 15.

2714. "B. Ross-Henry Armstrong Bout: Armstrong Trains." New York Times, (May 6, 1938), p. 31.

2715. "Henry Armstrong-L. Ambers Bout Planned." New York Times, (November 27, 1938), p. 10, sec. 5.

2716. "Henry Armstrong Signed To Fight B. Ross For Title." New York Times, (March 9, 1938), p. 27.

2717. "L. Ambers-Henry Armstrong Bout-Armstrong Wins." New York Times, (August 18, 1938), p. 24.

2718. "New York State Athletic Commission Approves Proposed P. Sarron-H. Armstrong Bout." New York Times, (August 11, 1937), p. 18.

2719. "Reverend Henry Armstrong: Triple Titled Ex-Boxer Is St. Louis Minister Fighting Sin." Black Sports, 5 (April 1976), 36-37+.

2720. "Sarron-Armstrong Plans." New York Times, (October 19, 1937), p. 33.

2721. "Sarron-Armstrong-Training Ends." New York Times, (October 28, 1937), p. 35.

HOGAN BASSEY

2722. Kane, M. "Springfield Rifle Takes The Title: Davey Moore Defeats Hogan Bassey." Sports Illustrated, 10 (March 30, 1959), 34-39.

2723. "The Gentle Champion: Hogan Bassey." Ebony, (December 1958), 66-68.

JIMMIE CARTER

2724. "Boss of the Lightweights; Jimmie Carter." Our World, 9 (February 1954), 14-15.

EZZARD CHARLES

2725. "All of A Sudden: Ezzard Charles." Time, 56 (December 18, 1950), 69-70.

2726. "Champ Ezzard Charles vs. Joe Louis: Pabst Brewing Co. Pays $125,000 For TV-Radio Rights." New York Times, (September 11, 1950), p. 44.

2727. "Champion Is a Feeling: Ezzard Charles." Newsweek, 37 (January 22, 1951), 18.

2728. "Charles Seeks New York State Recognition." New York Times, (October 16, 1949), 10, sec. 5.

2729. "Charles-Walcott Chicago Bout Set." New York Times, (March 24, 1949), 39: (March 27, 1949), p. 8, sec. 5.

2730. "Charles and Walcott Signed." New York Times, (March 3, 1949), p. 34.

2731. "Ezzard Charles Cleared In Death of S. Baround: After Feb. 20 Bout." New York Times, (March 7, 1948), p. 2, sec. 5.

2732. "Ezzard Charles Defeats Joe Walcott for NBA Title." New York Times, (June 23, 1949), p. 35.

2733. "Ezzard Charles Defeats P. Valentino." New York Times, (October 15, 1949), p. 19.

2734. "Ezzard Charles Found To Have Heart Ailment; Must Take Rest." New York Times, (May 5, 1950), p. 27.

2735. "Ezzard Charles Knocks Out G. Lesnevich in 7th Round to Retain NBA Title." New York Times, (August 11, 1949), p. 16.

2736. "Ezzard Charles vs. Joe Louis: A. Daley Comment on Louis." New York Times, (September 17, 1950), p. 2, sec. 5.

2737. "E. Charles vs. J. Louis; Boxers Compared." New York Times, (September 24, 1950), p. 7, sec. 5.

2738. "Ezzard Charles: Winner and New Champion!" Time, 58 (July 30, 1957), 66.

2739. "Ezzard Charles: Winner and Old Champion." Life, 31 (July 30, 1951), 66-67.

2740. "Heavyweight Champ Ezzard Charles Contract Sold To J. Mintz and T. Tannas." New York Times, (December 7, 1949), p. 46.

2741. Heinz, W.C. "Strange Case of Ezzard Charles." Saturday Evening Post, 224 (June 7, 1952), 34.

2742. Lardner, John. "Bloodshel Overdue: Ezzard Charles." Newsweek, 43 (June 14, 1954), 64.

2743. Liebling, A.J. "Reporter At Large: Charles Marciano Fight." New Yorker, 30 (July 10, 1954), 44.

2744. Liebling, A.J. "Reporter At Large: Charles Marciano Fight." New Yorker, 30 (October 2, 1954), 75-82.

2745. "Old Folks: Charles-Walcott Fight." Newsweek, 38 (July 30, 1951), 45.

2746. "Portrait: Ezzard Charles." Newsweek, 37 (April 2, 1951), 59.

2747. "Portrait: Ezzard Charles." Time, 51 (October 16, 1950), 42.

2748. "Ring '49 Ratings: Ezzard Charles Named Boxer of Year." New York Times, (December 25, 1949), p. 30.

2749. Schulberg, B. "Charles vs. Marciano." Sports Illustrated, 1 (September 13, 1954), 62-63.

2750. Schulberg, B. "Rematch Is No Match." Sports Illustrated, 1 (September 27, 1954), 58-60.

2751. "This is What Charles Took From Marciano." Life, 36 (June 28, 1954), 16-17.

2752. "Twice is Once Too Often: Second Marciano-Charles Fight." Life, 27 (September 27, 1954), 32.

2753. "Virginia State Athletic Commission Denies Charles Championship Recognition." New York Times, (August 12, 1949), 21.

KID CHOCOLATE

2754. "Kid Chocolate, the Boxer Who Listened to Mother." Ebony, 12 (April 1957), 49-52.

CURTIS COKES

2755. Preece, H. "Curtis Cokes Discovers A New Career." Sepia, 21 (February 1972), 60-64+.

2756. "Welterweight Champion of the World Voted Texas Professional Athlete of the Year." Sepia, 18 (March 1969), 70.

HOWARD DAVIS

2757. Ribowsky, Mark. "The Kid's A Walking Goldmine." Black Sports, 7 (January 1978), 38-44.

GEORGE FOREMAN

2758. Carter, Ulish. "Foreman Decks Norton 3 Times Wins by TKO." The Courier, (April 6, 1974).

2759. Cooper, Ralph. "George Foreman on the Rise." The Voice of Hope, (January 24, 1970).

2760. "Foreman Fires Sadler: Will Manage Himself." Jet, 44 (July 19, 1973), 48.

2761. "Foreman Wants To Fight Soon." Winston Salem Journal, (June 17, 1976).

2762. Frazier Retires After Foreman Wins TKO In 5." Winston-Salem Journal, (June 16, 1976).

2763. "George Foreman Born Again, May End His Boxing Career." Jet, 52 (May 5, 1977), 56-57.

2764. "George Foreman Marries 1972 Miss Black Teenage America." Jet, 53 (September 8, 1977), 28-29.

2765. Horton, Joseph. "Glad To Be Back Heavyweight Champion George Foreman Speaks His Mind On Racial Issues." Sepia, 23 (September 1974), 45-48.

2766. Kisner, Ronald E. "Foreman and Ali Stage Africa's Biggest Fight." Jet, 47 (September 26, 1974), 50-54.

2767. Kisner, Ronald E. "It Was Just My Night Foreman Says of His Win." Jet, 43 (February 8, 1973), 58-59.

2768. Norman, Shirley. "How I'll Be Champ Again...George Foreman." Sepia, 25 (June 1976), 58-62.

2769. Simms, Gregory. "Foreman Quits For God and Mom: Heavyweights Sorry To See Him Go." Jet, 52 (May 26, 1977), 52-53.

2770. Simms, Gregory. "Foreman: When I Told Ali About God, Do You Know What He Said." Jet, 5 (October 13, 1977), 54-56.

2771. Simms, Gregory. "George Foreman Says He Sins No More." Jet, 52 (September 8, 1977), 28-29.

2772. Simms, Gregory. "Young Predicts KO Over Strong Foreman." Jet, 51 (March 10, 1977), 48+.

2773. Wolf, David. "In Search of George Foreman." Black Sports, 6 (February 1977), 36-42+.

BOB FOSTER

2774. "Light Heavyweight Champ Bob Foster Has His Day: $12,000 Raised For Youths." Jet, 42 (September 14, 1972), 46-47.

JOE FRAZIER

2775. "Analysis of Fight With Frazier." Washington Post, (September 28, 1975), p. 1, sec. C.

2776. "Bad Joe Frazier KOs Bob Foster." Pittsburgh Courier, (November 28, 1970).

2777. Browder, Jim. "Explosive Fists of Joe Frazier." Sepia, 18 (February 1969), 76-78.

2778. "Comments On Frazier-Foreman Fight." Washington Post, (January 23, 1973), p. 1, sec. D.

2779. "Defeats Joe Frazier." Washington Post, (October 1, 1975), p. 1, sec. E.

2780. "Ellis All Smiles Frazier Frowns." Winston-Salem Journal, (February 12, 1970).

2781. "Frazier Is Named 'Fighter of Year': Manager Durham Also Recieves Top Honors." Jet, 42 (April 27, 1972), 57.

2782. "Frazier, Quarry Fight Grows Hot." The Sacramento Observer, (May 21, 70).

2783. "Frazier Retires After Foreman Wins TKO in 5." Winston-Salem Journal, (June 16, 1976).

2784. "Frazier's KO Mark Tops Champs." Guide & Journal, (December 26, 1970).

2785. "Heavyweight Joe Frazier A Stockholder's Dream." Ebony, 23 (November 1967), 136-142.

2786. "Joe Frazier Thinks About Retirement." Winston-Salem Journal, (January 15, 1970).

2787. "Joe Frazier Wins Neil Award." Winston-Salem Journal, (January 16, 1970).

2788. Kisner, Ronald E. "Joe Frazier: Is His Boxing Title Doomed?" Jet, 43 (January 1973), 46-48.

2789. Langlais, Rudy. "Rap With Joe Frazier: Interview." Black Sports, 5 (October 1975), 22-23+.

2790. "Pick Frazier Top KO Heavyweight Puncher." Daily Defender, (November 6, 1970).

2791. "Requiem For A Heavyweight." Black Sports, 6 (July 1976), 4.

2792. Richman, Milton. "It's Over For Frazier." Sentinel, (June 16, 1976).

2793. Simms, Gregory. "Joe Frazier Is Ready For Ring Return, Against His Manager's Wishes." Jet, 53 (January 19, 1978), 54-55.

2794. Stewart, Ted. "Joe Frazier Buys A Plantation For 'Mama'." Sepia, 221 (February 1973), 38-46.

2795. "The Smoking Joe Frazier Revue." Winston-Salem Journal, (November 23, 1976).

2796. Thompson, C.S. "Joe Frazier Proves That He Is The Greatest." Jet, 39 (March 25, 1971), 52-59.

2797. Ziegel, Vic. "I Got To Prove Joe Frazier Is Still The Guy He Was." Black Sports, 7 (February 1978), 56-60.

KID GAVILAN

2798. "Kid Gavilan, Boxing's Happiest Champ." Ebony, 8 (October 1953), 22-27.

2799. "Kid Gavilan Called In Boxing Commission Probe of L. Fenton Bout." New York Times, (November 3, 1949), 44.

LARRY HOLMES

2800. Antone, Roane. "How Larry Holmes Upset Ken Norton." Sepia, 27 (August 1978), 60-67.

2801. "Holmes Accepts Pay Cut TV Loss, To Fight Weaver." Jet, 56 (June 7, 1979), 48.

2802. "Holmes Gambles WBC Belt vs. Shavers In Las Vegas." Jet, 56 (September 6, 1979), 50.

2803. Kiersh, Ed. "I Feel Like The Lone Ranger." Black Sports, 7 (May 1978), 50+.

2804. Kisner, Ronald E. "New Champ Likes Simple Life, Popeye, Gong Show." Jet, 54 (June 29, 1978), 52-54.

2805. "WBC Champ Holmes May Return To Spar With Ali." Jet, 54 (August 3, 1978), 52.

JACK JOHNSON

2806. "Accused By "John Bull" of Framing Up Fraudulent Contract." Times, (July 15, 1914), p. 7.

2807. "Agrees On Welch As Referee for Bout With Willard." New York Times, (March 26, 1915), p. 11.

2808. "American Bettors Warned Against Proposed Fight With Moran." New York Times, (June 7, 1914), p. 4, sec. 4.

2809. "Answers Auto Speeding Charge, Municipal Court, Chicago; Demands Jury Trial With At Least 2 Negro Jurors." New York Times, (April 2, 1910), p. 9.

2810. "Appeal From $100 Fine Denied." New York Times, (April 7, 1911), p. 6.

2811. "Appeal Granted." New York Times, (June 24, 1913), p. 2.

2812. "Applies For Passports, May Return Here." New York Times, (April 8, 1915), p. 11.

2813. "Arranges For His Surrender." New York, (April 6, 1920), p. 17.

2814. "Arrest Warrant Issued on Traffic Violation Charge. New York Times, (January 23, 1908), p. 25.

2815. "Arrested and Fined For Auto Speeding, Woodstock, Ont." New York Times, (August 7, 1909), p. 4.

2816. "Arrested As His Dog Lacerates Detroit Citizen's Arm." New York Times, (February 9, 1910), p. 9.

2817. "Arrested at Mexican Border." New York Times, (July 21, 1920), p. 16.

2818. "Arrested For Assaulting, White Burlesque Actress H. Cooper, NYC." New York Times, (November 26, 1910), p. 2.

2819. "Arrested For Reckless Driving, NYC." New York Times, (July 20, 1910), p. 3.

2820. "Arrested For Speeding, San Francisco." New York Times, (June 23, 1910), p. 9.

2821. "Arrested In London For Using Foul Language." New York Times, (September 24, 1914), p. 7.

2822. "Arrives In London, Says That He Will Appear In Music Halls.
      New York Times, (August 25, 1913), p. 3.

2823. "Arrested, NYC For Driving Car With Chicago License." New York
      Times, (May 16, 1911), p. 11.

2824. Arrives in New York City; Receives Enthusiastic Welcome From
      Negro Admirers." New York Times, (March 30, 1909), p. 10.

2825. "Asks Early Trial For Smuggling." New York Times, (March 11,
      1913), p. 17.

2826. "Assault Case Comes Up For Trial General Sessions Court, NYC."
      New York Times, (October 26, 1910), p. 5.

2827. "At Havana." New York Times, (February 22, 1915), p. 7.

2828. "Bail Forfeited, Government Has No Chance To Collect." New York
      Times, (October 6, 1914), p. 7.

2829. "Bail To Be Forfeited." New York Times, (July 3, 1913), p. 18.

2830. "Barely Saved From Knockout By Jim Johnson." New York Times,
      (December 20, 1913), p. 1.

2831. "Barred From All Detroit Hotels." New York Times, (February 6,
      1910), p. 3, sec. 4.

2832. "Barred From Hotel Because He Is A Negro, Salt Lake City." New
      York Times, (August 18, 1909), p. 7.

2833. "Barred From O'Connell's Gymnasium." New York Times, (January
      10, 1913), p. 12; (January 12, 1913), p. 2, sec. 4.

2834. "Becomes Naturalized Citizen of France." New York Times,
      (October 13, 1913), p. 3.

2835. "Books Passage For U.S." New York Times, (February 6, 1920),
      p. 15.

2836. "Boxes in Leavenworth Prison." New York Times, (September 22,
      1920), p. 11.

2837. "Bribery Charges Against Officials Reported To Have Aided His
      Flight Are Dismissed." New York Times, (February 12, 1914), p.
      18.

2838. "Burns And Johnson Prepare For World's Heavyweight Championship
      in Sydney, Australia." New York Times, (December 21, 1908), p. 7.

2839. "Burns Defeat Blang of Australia, Melbourne; To fight Johnson For
      World's Heavyweight Champ." New York Times, (September 3, 1908),
      p. 5.

2840. "Burns Favored Over Johnson." New York Times, (December 25,
      1908), p. 5.

2841. "Burns To Fight Johnson for World's Heavyweight Championship."
      New York Times, (September 3, 1908), p. 5.

2842. "Buys Home For Mother In Galveston." New York Times, (June 13,
      1909), p. 18.

2843. "Buys New Car; Escapes Serious Injury In Accident, New Jersey."
      New York Times, (May 24, 1909), p. 5.

2844. "C.L. Gardner Tells U.S. Com. How Carranzistas Soldiers Forced
      American Proprietors To Apologize To Him Following Restaurant
      Refusal of Waitress To Serve Him and How He Heads Jack Johnson
      Land Co. in Mexico City which is Conducting Propoganda To Bring
      Negroes Away From the U.S." New York Times, (January 18, 1920),
      p. 2.

2845. "Cables Friends He Is To Fight Bull." New York Times, (June 20,
      1916), p. 12.

2846. "California Supreme Court Refuses To Revise 25-Day Jail Term."
      New York Times, (April 2, 1911), p. 6, sec. 3.

2847. "Cartoon On Him Being In London For Coronation." New York Times,
      (June 18, 1911), p. 16, sec. 5.

2848. "Cartoon On His Fame." New York Times, (July 30, 1911), p. 2,
      sec.3.

2849. "Case To Be Called To The Bar In Chicago, Bond Will Be Forfeited."
      New York Times, (October 12, 1913), p. 5, sec. 5.

2850. "Celebrates 1st Anniversary of His Accession to Title of World
      Heavyweight Champ At His Mother's Home." New York Times,
      (December 27, 1909), p. 8.

2851. "Charges Dropped When Pinder Fails To Appear." New York Times,
      (October 27, 1910), p. 2.

2852. "Chicago Authorities Will Refuse Him Bail." New York Times,
      (July 2, 1920), p. 4.

2853. "Comment on Former Champ J. Johnson Career." New York Times,
      (June 11, 1946), p. 1.

2854. "Comments on Louis-Sharkey Prospects." New York Times, (August 9,
      1936), p. 7, sec. 5.

2855. "Compared With Willard, His Record." New York Times, (April 4,
      1915), p. 1, sec. 4.

2856. "A Concession To Prejudice, Editorial." New York Times,
      (March 29, 1915), p. 8.

2857. "Convicted of Violating White Slave Law; Motion For New Trial
      Filed." New York Times, (May 14, 1913), p. 1.

2858. "Court Orders Him To Pay $1,100 To Sculptor C. Sciarrino For Bust Modeled For Him." New York Times, (May 17, 1911), p. 3.

2859. "Critically Ill." New York Times, (February 25, 1913), p. 20.

2860. "Cuban Minister Protest Bout." New York Times, (March 30, 1915), p. 12.

2861. Daley, A. "Johnson, Jack: Greatest Craftsman of Them All." Negro Digest, 11 (May 10, 1962), 7-9.

2862. "Defeats German Urbach in Wrestling Match." New York Times, (November 26, 1913), p. 1.

2863. "Denies He Has Taken Out French Naturalization Papers, Asks For U.S. Passport To Russia." New York Times, (September 19, 1914), p. 6.

2864. "Denies Report He Is Negotiating To Buy Behr Mansion, Brooklyn." New York Times, (August 6, 1910), p. 4.

2865. "District Attorney of Chicago Will Enter Into Negotiations With Him On His Return To Chicago, Will Serve Sentence for Violating the Mann Act and Then Challenge Jack Dempsey for the Heavyweight Title." New York Times, (February 5, 1920), p. 2.

2866. "Drops Appeal From Sentence; Prepares To Leave For Leavenworth Prison." New York Times, (September 21, 1920), p. 16.

2867. "Early Trial Indicated." New York Times, (March 15, 1910), p. 6.

2868. "Editorial." New York Times, (January 22, 1910), p. 8.

2869. "Editorial." New York Times, (March 27, 1915), p. 10.

2870. "Editorial." New York Times, (April 17, 1915), p. 10.

2871. "Editorial." New York Times, (June 28, 1914), p. 14, sec. 2.

2872. "Editorial." New York Times, (August 27, 1913), p. 6.

2873. "Editorial On Appearance In Opera." New York Times, (October 4, 1936), p. 8, sec. 4.

2874. "Editorial On Decision To Invest Fight Winnings In Government Bonds." New York Times, (July 13, 1910), p. 6.

2875. "Editorial On Johnson Description of Self in Court As Actor." New York Times, (July 22, 1910), p. 6.

2876. "Encounters Racial Discrimination at Vancouver Hotels." New York Times, (March 11, 1909), p. 7.

2877. "Engagements May Be Canceled By Manager of Music Halls." New York Times, (August 22, 1913), p. 4.

2878. "Engagements Postposed; Appears In Music Hall Boxes, Is Defended by Lord Queensberry." New York Times, (August 26, 1913), p. 3.

2879. "Entire Amount of Bond Signed by Mrs. J. Ritter In White Slavery Case Must Be Paid To The Government." New York Times, (September 8, 1915), p. 13.

2880. "Fails To Appear In Court On Charge." New York Times, (June 24, 1910), p. 10.

2881. "Fails To Win Release From Jail." New York Times, (April 3, 1911), p. 7.

2882. "Federal Attorney Investigating Alleged Laxity of Jailer." New York Times, (September 4, 1920), p. 7.

2883. "Fight Postponed Till April 5, on Protest of American Minister To Cuba." New York Times, (March 28, 1915), p. 11, sec. 2.

2884. "Fined." New York Times, (July 21, 1910), p. 2.

2885. "Fined As Auto Speeder." New York Times, (January 24, 1930), p. 21.

2886. "Fined By London Magistrate For Obstructing Street With Auto." New York Times, (October 29, 1914), p. 8.

2887. "Fined For Running Automobile With Muffler Open." New York Times, (May 30, 1913), p. 4.

2888. "Fined For Smuggling." New York Times, (April 24, 1913), p. 1.

2889. "Fined For Speeding." New York Times, (March 29, 1936), p. 17.

2890. "Fined For Speeding, Cleveland." New York Times, (August 19, 1910), p. 7.

2891. "Forfeiture of Bond Ordered." New York Times, (October 14, 1913), p. 10.

2892. "Funeral"-Jack Johnson. New York Times, (June 12, 1946), p. 27.

2893. "Galveston, Texas Reception Committee May Cancel Welcome for Him After Misunderstanding About His White Wife." New York Times, (March 16, 1909), p. 7.

2894. "Gets Jail Term For Speeding, San Francisco." New York Times, (March 26, 1911), p. 6.

2895. "Gets Suspended Sentence For Overtime Parking." New York Times, (February 17, 1937), p. 11.

2896. Gilmore, Al Tony. "Jack Johnson and White Women: The National Impact." Journal of Negro History, 58 (January, 1973), 18-38.

2897. Gilmore, Al-Tony. "Toward An Understanding of Jack Johnson Confession." Negro History Bulletin, 36 (May 1973), 108-109.

2898. "Goes To Maine For Rest After Nervous Breakdown." New York Times, (November 19, 1910), p. 13.

2899. "Goes To Victoria, British Columbia." New York Times, (March 10, 1909), p. 5.

2900. "Goods Seized By Brewing Company." New York Times, (January 11, 1913), p. 12.

2901. "Governor of Lower California Will Prohibit Bout with Norton." New York Times, (July 4, 1920), p. 16.

2902. "Grand Jury, Gets Case." New York Times, (January 29, 1910), p. 5.

2903. "Has 3 Bouts in Leavenworth Prison Ring." Times, (September 22, 1920), p. 11.

2904. "Havana Police Are Investigating Johnson's "Fake" Story." New Times, (March 15, 1919), p. 12.

2905. "Heavyweight Championship Title Recognized by French Boxing Federation." New York Times, (May 7, 1914), p. 9.

2906. "Heavyweight Match Between Jack Johnson and Burns Called Off." New York Times, (March 8, 1908), p. 1, sec. 4.

2907. "Heavyweight Title Not Recognized By French Federation of Boxing Clubs." New York Times, (October 29, 1913), p. 9.

2908. "Held In Bail For Grand Jury On Charge of Felonious Assault." New York Times, (January 24, 1910), p. 3.

2909. "His Auto Hit By Another While He Was Driving Friends Around Cobe Cup Race Course, Crown Pt. Ind." New York Times, (July 17, 1909), p. 2.

2910. "His Scheduled Pittsburgh Parade Prevented by Police Department." New York Times, (April 20, 1909), p. 7.

2911. "Hostile Demonstrations Prevent Wrestling Matches In Sweden." New York Times, (January 1, 1940), p. 31; (January 2, 1940), p. 21.

2912. "Ill." New York Times, (January 1, 1940), p. 31; (January 2, 1940), p. 21.

2913. "Illustration in London." New York Times, (July 9, 1910) p. 7, sec. 3.

2914. "In London." New York Times, (July 13, 1913), p. 2, sec. 3.

2915. "In Paris; Says He Will Return To America When Wanted."
New York Times, (July 11, 1913), p. 3.

2916. "Is In Canada, Plans To Sail For Europe, But Will Not Forfeit
Bond." New Times, (June 27, 1913), p. 3.

2917. "Is On Way To Tia Juana." New York Times, (March 15, 1920), p.
19.

2918. "Is Negotiating For Estate In Rutherford, N.J." New York Times,
(April 18, 1913), p. 1.

2919. "Is Seized In Attempt To Leave Chicago." New York Times,
(January 15, 1913), p. 6.

2920. "Is Warned To Stay In Chicago." New York Times, (January 16,
1913), p. 18.

2921. "Issues Statement From Cal. Jail." New York Times, (July 22,
1920), p. 13.

2922. "Jack Johnson Claims He Allowed Willard To Win Title At Havana
and Demand A Return Match." New York Times, (March 14, 1919),
p. 10.

2923. "Jack Johnson Forfeits $25 Bond For Speeding." Broad Ax,
(November 15, 1924), 1.

2924. "Jack Johnson Has A Boxing Academy In Spain." New York Times,
(June 1, 1916), p. 12.

2925. "Jack Johnson Is Barred From Nebraska: Former Heavyweight Champ
Will Not Be Permitted To Fight at Scottsbluff." Broad Ax,
(August 19, 1922), 2.

2926. "Jack Johnson, Some Man." Encore, 4 (August 18, 1975), 9.

2927. "Jack Johnson Starts Work For Match With Wills." Broad Ax,
(July 19, 1924), 2.

2928. "Jailed For Thrashing N. Pinder in Saloon Brawl, NYC." New
York Times, (January 21, 1910), p. 18.

2929. "Johnson Indicted." New York Times, (February 2, 1910), p. 5.

2930. "Joe Louis Comment on Jack Johnson." New York Times, (June 11,
1946), p. 46.

2931. "Johnson Returns To NYC." New York Times, (March 23, 1910),
p. 12.

2932. "Johnson Says He Never Doubted Outcome of Fight." New York
Times, (December 27, 1908), p. 3, sec. 4.

2933. "Johnson Wins Bout." New York Times, (December 26, 1908),
p. 8.

2934. "Judge Carpenter Denies Report That Bail Is Forfeited." New York Times, (July 4, 1973), p. 3.

2935. "Jury Finds Him Not Guilty." New York Times, (Apil 6, 1910), p. 9.

2936. "Kitchel's Dream of Glory." Sports Illustrated, 1 (October 18, 1954), 80-81.

2937. "Killed In Auto Accident: Biography." New York Times, (June 11, 1946), p. 1.

2938. "Knocks Out Wrestler." New York Times, (November 30, 1913) p. 3, sec. 4.

2939. "Lands at Tampico For Fight With Willard." New York Times, (February 19, 1915), p. 10.

2940. Lardner, John. "Jack Johnson Era of Boxing." Negro Digest, 8 (November 1949), 24-34.

2941. "Leaves Montreal For Europe, Will Be Arrested If He Stops At Quebec." New York Times, (June 30, 1913), p. 16.

2942. "Letter Asking N.Y. Times to Protest Against Bout." New York Times, (March 26, 1915), p. 12.

2943. "May Be Arrested On Old White Slavery Charge." New York Times, (April 6, 1915), p. 8.

2944. "May Be Pardoned in Time To See Dempsey-Carpenter Bout." New York Times, (June 24, 1921), p. 4.

2945. "Meets Ex-King Manuel II." New York Times, (August 25, 1911), p. 4.

2946. "Motion Picture of Bouts Will Not Be Shown." New York Times, (December 16, 1920), p. 23.

2947. "Motor From Scranton to NYC." New York Times, (October 17, 1910), p. 11.

2948. "Moving Pictures of Fight Barred From This Country, Customs Men Warned By Treasury Dept." New York Times, (April 16, 1915), p. 8.

2949. "Must Pay Damages To Woman Hit By His Punching Bag." New York Times, (June 22, 1913), p. 10, sec. 2.

2950. "Must Serve Sentence." New York Times, (June 29, 1921), p. 11.

2951. "Negro Attorney Goes To Washington to Ask For His Pardon." New York Times, (November 20, 1920), p. 6.

2952. "New Trial Granted." New York Times, (May 13, 1914), p. 9.

2953. "Offered $55,000 To Meet Wills." New York Times, (June 18, 1921), p. 11.

2954. "Offers To Surrender If Accorded Certain Privileges, Is Under Indictment for Violation of Mann White Slave Act." New York Times, (July 10, 1920), p. 15.

2955. "Ordered To Leave Mexico by Gov. of Lower California; U.S. Dept. of Justice Agents Wait At Border To Seize Him." New York Times, (June 16, 1920), p. 23.

2956. "Outside Film Concerns Obtain Copyright in Cuba." New York Times, (April 15, 1915), p. 11.

2957. "Passes Through Canada On Way To France; Cannot Be Deported Under Canadian Law; Sec. Bryan Asks That He Be Held." New York Times, (June 28, 1913), p. 2.

2958. "Passport To Be Denied Him, Motion-Picture Injunction Suit Postponed." New York Times, (April 10, 1915), p. 9.

2959. "Plans Return To U.S." New York Times, (January 30, 1920), p. 16.

2960. "Plea For Bail Refused." New York Times, (July 27, 1920), p. 5.

2961. "Pleads Guilty To Speeding Charge." New York Times, (December 2, 1936), p. 32.

2962. "Practically Penniless in Spain." New York Times, (February 17, 1919), p. 3.

2963. "Practice Army 'Bomb' Hits Car." New York Times, (October 21, 1941), p. 25.

2964. "President Menocal and Cabinet To Witness Fight With Willard." New York Times, (April 2, 1915), p. 12.

2965. "Promoter H. McIntosh Offers Former Champ J.J. Jeffries $50,000 to Fight Johnson In Australia." New York Times, (December 28, 1908), p. 5.

2966. "Proposal To Deprive Him of His Title Rejected By International Boxing Union." New York Times, (December 13, 1913), p. 11.

2967. "Put In Cell For 5 hrs. While Friends Raise $1,500 Bail." New York Times, (March 24, 1910), p. 18.

2968. "R.J. Mitchell Killed by B. Buffington Who Was Trying To Kill Johnson, Pittsburgh." New York Times, (December 22, 1910), p. 2.

2969. "Reaches Mexican Border." New York Times, (March 31, 1920), p. 12.

2970. "Registers Jewels With U.S. Customs Prior To Getting Abroad." New York Times, (June 6, 1911), p. 18.

2971. "Re-Indicted." New York Times, (May 1, 1913), p. 5.

2972. "Released On Bail; Returns Chicago." New York Times, (March 25, 1910), p. 5.

2973. "Released On $1,500 Bail." New York Times, (February 3, 1910), p. 2.

2974. "Removed To Geneva Jail." New York Times, (July 29, 1920), p. 28.

2975. "Repeats Charge, Says Sol. Lewisohn Was Go-Between." New York Times, (February 8, 1914), p. 5, sec. 3.

2976. "Reported Killed In Crash, China." New York Times, (January 1, 1939), p. 19.

2977. "Reports That He Is To Appear In Finish Fight In Mexico." New York Times, (April 2, 1920), p. 18.

2978. "Retains Championship Against Frank Moran, Description of Fight." New York Times, (June 28, 1914), p. 1, sec. 2.

2979. "Returns To NYC." New York Times, (December 22, 1911), p. 15.

2980. "Ring Records." New York Times, (April 5, 1915), p. 12.

2981. "Sails For Europe With Wife." New York Times, (June 7, 1911), p. 20.

2982. "Sails For Spain Intends To Open Gymnasium in Havana." New York Times, (April 21, 1915), p. 10.

2983. "Sentenced." New York Times, (September 15, 1920), p. 17.

2984. "Sentenced To Imprisonment and Fined For White Slave Crime." New York Times, (June 5, 1913), p. 1.

2985. "Sheriff Denies He Receives Liberties." New York Times, (September 5, 1920), p. 23, sec. 8.

2986. "Smuggled Diamond Neglace Belonging To Former Wife Sold At Auction." New York Times, (July 13, 1913), p. 5, sec. 2.

2987. "Speedy Trial Promised." New York Times, (February 4, 1910), p. 5.

2988. "Spends $4,956 of $5,100 Purse Won In Recent Fight With J. O'Brien To Settle Debts." New York Times, (May 23, 1909), p. 3.

2989. "States That He Paid Federal Officials To Escape From Chicago, Charges Denied." New York Times, (January 25, 1914), p. 6, sec. 2.

2990. "Sudden Stardom For James Earl Jones, as Jack Johnson." Sepia, 18 (June 1969), 56-59.

2991. "Summoned On Complaint of A. Sachs For Failure To Carry Out Restaurant Concession Agreement." New York Times, (April 13, 1937), p. 52.

2992. "Taken To Joliet Jail." New York Times, (July 26, 1920), p. 11.

2993. "Threatened With Arrest in Mexico." New York Times, (February 23, 1915), p. 11.

2994. "Title To Heavyweight Boxing Championship Declared Vacant By International Boxing Union." New York Times, (November 6, 1913), p. 9.

2995. "To Appear In Opera." New York Times, (September 30, 1936), p. 27.

2996. "To Be Extradicted and Returned To Chicago For Violation of Mann Act." New York Times, (February, 17, 1915), p. 8.

2997. "To Be Tried Before Judge Carpenter On Charge of Smuggling." New York Times, (April 22, 1913), p. 6.

2998. "To Leave Sydney, Australia For Vancouver, BC To Begin Tour." New York Times, (February 5, 1909), p. 8.

2999. "Trains In Rain; President Menocal Denies Placing Wager On Fight." New York Times, (April 3, 1915), p. 10.

3000. "Trial Begins; "Yank" Kenny Will Be Witness." New York Times, (May 8, 1913), p. 20.

3001. "Trial Postposed By Illness. New York Times, (February 26, 1913), p. 9.

3002. "Trial Put Off Despite Johnson Attorney Objections." New York Times, (February 9, 1910), p. 4.

3003. "Two Creditors File Claim Against Him In Paris." New York Times, (July 1, 1914) p. 1.

3004. "Vaudeville Artists In London May Prevent His Appearance There." New York Times, (August 20, 1913), p. 1.

3005. "Was Jack Johnson's Boxing's Greatest Champ?" Ebony, 18 (January 1963), 67-70.

3006. Wiggins, W.H. "Jack Johnson As Bad Nigger, The Folklore of His Life." Black Scholar, 2 (January 1971), 35-46.

3007. "Will Be Boycotted by London Music Hall Artists." New York Times, (August 22, 1913), p. 1.

3008. "Will Be Deported From Mexico." New York Times, (July 19, 1919), p. 27.

3009. "Will Engage in Out In Lower Cal." New York Times, (April 8, 1920), p. 12.

3010. "Will Not Be Permitted To Box On Eve of His Release From Prison." New York Times, (June 30, 1921), p. 13.

3011. "Will Not Be Released On Bail Until September." New York Times, (July 28, 1920), p. 16.

3012. "Will Live In Paris Suburb, 'Plans' Sanitorium." New York Times, (July 19, 1913), p. 4.

3013. "Will Visit New York For Talk With J. Jeffries." New York Times, (March 17, 1909), p. 7.

3014. "Will Return To Chicago When His Appeal From Conviction Under Mann White Slave Act Is To Be Heard." New York Times, (September 16, 1913), p. 7.

3015. "Will Visit NY for Talk with J. Jeffries." New York Times, (March 17, 1909), p. 7.

3016. "Willard Wins In 26th Round, Johnson To Retire." New York Times, (April 6, 1915), p. 1.

3017. "Willard's Victory, Editorial." New York Times, (April 6, 1915), p. 10.

3018. "Wins 2 Bouts In Leavenworth Penitentiary." New York Times, (May 29, 1921), p. 20.

3019. "Wins 2 Bouts in Leavenworth Prison." New York Times, (November 26, 1920), p. 19.

3020. "Wins World Heavyweight Boxing Championship in Bout With T. Burns Sydney, Australia." New York Times, (December 26, 1908), p. 8.

JOHN LESTER JOHNSTON

3021. "John Lester Johnston: The Man Who Broke Jack Dempsey's Ribs." Ebony, 15 (January 1960), 80-85.

TIGER JONES

3022. Leggett, William. "An Angry Tiger Jumps On Joey." Sports Illustrated, 23 (November 1, 1965), 20-21.

3023. "Television Most Successful Slugger; Tiger Jones Has Current Record of 42 TV Bouts." Ebony, 15 (September 1960), 55-56.

3024. "Tiger Jones: TV's Most Successful Slugger." Ebony, 15 (September 1960), 55-59.

SAM LANGFORD

3025. "Amazing Careers of Sam Langford, Boxer." Ebony, 11 (April 1956), p. 97-105.

3026. "Orbituary: Sam Langford." Newsweek, 47 (January 23, 1956), 71.

3027. "Sam Langford: In Boxing's Golden Age He Was The Man With the Golden Gloves and Arch Nemisis of Jack Johnson." Black Sports, 6 (October 1976), 56-57.

SUGAR RAY LEONARD

3028. Axthelm, Pete. "America's Fighter." Newsweek, 94 (December 10, 1979), 133.

3029. Axthelm, Pete. "Big Brawl In Montreal." Newsweek, 95 (June 30, 1980), 40-41.

3030. Axthelm, Pete. "Matador and The Bull." Newsweek, 95 (June 23, 1980), 48-52.

3031. "Battle of Montreal." Time, 115 (June 30, 1980), 61.

3032. Berber, P. "Boxing's His Business." New York Times Magazine, (June 24, 1979), 14-16+.

3033. "Brothers Hands Were Nice." Black Sports, 9 (November 1976), 39-43.

3034. "Comment." New York Times, (January 21, 1980), p. 2, sec. p.

3035. "Comments On Leonard Victory." New York Times, (December 2, 1979), p. 3, sec. 5.

3036. "Dave Anderson Interview With Leonard..." New York Times, (June 18, 1980), p. 25.

3037. "Don King Says He Offered Leonard $2.5 Million To Meet Duran." New York Times, (February 7, 1980), p. 9.

3038. Langdon, D. "Jocks." People, 12 (December 3, 1979), 119-20.

3039. "Leonard Earns Largest Payday In Sports History ($10 million)." New York Times, (June 21, 1980), p. 15.

3040. "Leonard Plans To Turn Pro." Winston-Salem Journal, (November 17, 1976).

3041. "Leonard To Defend Title Against Roberto Duran." New York Times, (April 16, 1980), p. 11, sec. 2.

3042. "Marries Juanita Wilkinson." New York Times, (January 20, 1980), p. 7, sec. 5.

3043. Nack, W. "On Top Of The World." Sports Illustrated, 52 (December 10, 1979), 26-9.

3044. Nack, W. "Right On For Roberto." Sports Illustrated, 53 (June 30, 1980), 14-21.

3045. Nack, W. "Sugar Sure Is Sweet." Sports Illustrated, 51 (November 26, 1979), 92-6+.

3046. "Phil Berger on Career of Sugar Ray Leonard." New York Times, (June 24, 1979), p. 14, sec. 6.

3047. Putnam, P. "Day the Gold Turned Green." Sports Illustrated, 46 (February 14, 1977), 18-19.

3048. Quinn, H. "Lord of the Ring." Macleans, 93 (June 30, 1980), 36.

3049. "Red Smith on Leonard and His Relationship With Juanita Wilkinson, Who He Plans To Marry on June 28." New York Times, (December 1, 1979), p. 17.

3050. Schruers, F. "Sugar Ray Leonard Inc." Rolling Stone, (June 26, 1980), 40-43+.

3051. "Sugar Ray Leonard and Roberto Duran Sign For Bout." New York Times, (May 10, 1980), p. 16.

3052. "Sugar Ray Leonard Retains His World Boxing Council Championship With 4th-Round KO of Davey Green." New York Times, (April 1, 1980), p. 13, sec. 2.

3053. "Sugar Ray Leonard Scores 1st Round KO Over Daniel Gonzales." New York Times, (March 25, 1979), p. 5, sec. 5.

3054. "Sugar Ray Leonard Wins World Boxing Council's Championship with 15th Round KO of Wilfredo Benitez." New York Times, (December 1, 1979), p. 15.

3055. "Sweet Prince of the Welterweights." Sport, 70 (February 1980), 71.

3056. "Top Rank Inc. President Bob Arum Says He Has Offered Roberto Duran $1 million To Fight Sugar Ray Leonard for World Boxing Council's Welterweight Championship." New York Times, (February 5, 1980), p. 22, sec. 3.

3057. Unger, Norman O. "Savoring the Sweet Smell of Success." Ebony, 35 (March 1980), 66-7+.

3058. Unger, Norman O. "Sugar Ray Leonard, New Boxing Kingpin, Puts Family First." Jet, 57 (December 20, 1979), 46-49.

3059. Warren, T. "Sweet Taste of Sugar's Success." Encore, 7 (March 6, 1978), 20-2+.

3060. "World Boxing Council Champion Sugar Ray Leonard Dismisses His Trainer Dave Jacobs In Pay Dispute." New York Times, (February 3, 1980), p. 11.

3061. "World Boxing Council Warns Sugar Ray Leonard That He Faces Possibility of Losing His Title Unless He Defends It Against Roberto Duran." New York Times, (March 26, 1980), p. 8, sec. 2.

3062. Ziegel, Vic. "Sugar Ray Leonard: How Sweet He Is." New York, 13 (June 23, 1980), 32-3.

                              SONNY LISTON

3063. Astor, G. "Sonny Liston: King of The Beasts." Look, 28 (February 25, 1964), p. 67-68.

3064. Boyle, Robert H. "Sonny Stands Alone." Sports Illustrated, 19 (July 29, 1963), 12-15.

3065. Boyle, Robert H. "Taking Stock on Sonny Liston." Sports Illustrated, 20 (April 6, 1964) 24-27.

3066. Boyle, Robert H. and M. Sharnik. "Heavyweight Muddle." Sports Illustrated, 181 (March 25, 1963), 12-15.

3067. Breslin, J. "Be A Champ, Act A Champ." Saturday Evening Post, (September 22, 1962), 62-63.

3068. Barnes, R.L. "Heavyweight With A Past: Sonny Liston." Saturday Evening Post, 230 (August 13, 1960), 28.

3069. "Depends on How You Look At It: Foreign Press Reports on Sonny Liston." Sports Illustrated, 19 (August 5, 1963), 9.

3070. "I Come to Fight Not Make Love was Motto of Liston." Philadephia Tribune, (January 12, 1971).

3071. Kisner, Ronald E. "Death Voids Court Trial For Ex-Heavyweight Champ Sonny Liston." Jet, 39 (January 21, 1970, 52-55.

3072. Lafontaine, B. "He's Just Got That Look: Sonny Liston." Sports Ilustrated, 22 (April 26, 1965), 32-34.

3073. Liebling, A.J. "Sporting Scene: Patterson Vs. Liston Return Fight." New Yorker, 39 (August 10, 1963), 62.

3074. Liebling, A.J. "Sporting Scene: Sonny Liston." New Yorker, 38 (July 7, 1962), 78 (October 6, 1962), 103-10.

3075. Liston, Sonny. "Famous Last Words: Interview." Esquire, 58 (October 1962), 104-107.

3076. McDermott, J.R. "Liston Turned on the Evil Eye." Life, 56 (March 6, 1964), 34-39.

3077. McKinneny, J. "Sonny Liston: A Smell of Rain and Victory."
Sports Illustrated, 17 (August 27, 1962), 50.

3078. "Man With A Sock: Sonny Liston." Time, 74 (August 17, 1959), 46.

3079. Maule, Tex. "Liston's Edge: A Lethal Left." Sports Illustrated,
20 (February 24, 1964), 18-21.

3080. Maule, Tex. "Yes, It Was Good and Honest." Sports Illustrated,
(March 9, 1964), 20-25.

3081. Morrison, Alan. "Sonny Liston: Boxing's Angry Man." Ebony, 17
(August 1962), 46-48.

3082. Murphy, J. "Champ Behind the Mask." New York Times Magazine,
(July 21, 1963), 18.

3083. Patterson, Floyd. "I Live With Myself: Patterson Liston Fight."
Sports Illustrated, 19 (August 5, 1963), 27.

3084. Rogin, G. "Facts About The Big Fight: Liston-Patterson Fight."
Sports Illustrated, 17 (October 8, 1962), 20-27.

3085. Rogin, G. "Heavyweight In Waiting: Liston KO's Zora Foley."
Sports Illustrated, 13 (August 1, 1960), 49-50.

3086. Rogin, G. and M. Sharnik. "Can't A Fellow Make A Mistake?"
Sports Illustrated, 15 (July 17, 1961), 22-24.

3087. Skeleton, B. "Sparing Partner Looks Them Over." Sports
Illustrated, 17 (September 24, 1962), 26.

3088. "Symposium: Opinions on Liston's Right to Fight." Sports
Illustrated, 16 (February 12, 1962), 10-11.

3089. Watson, E. "Really A Hug Fest: Liston-Machen Fight." Sports
Illustrated, 13 (September 19, 1960), 111-12.

3090. "Who Can Beat Him?" Newsweek, 62 (August 5, 1963), 68-69.

JOE LOUIS

3091. "A. Daley On Louis Career." New York Times, (June 20, 1948),
p. 16, sec. 6.

3092. "Adamant Champ." Newsweek, 19 (May 5, 1947), 83.

3093. Adams, C. "Introducing the New Joe Louis." Saturday Evening
Post, 213 (May 10, 1941), 26-7+.

3094. "Admitted to Denver Psychiatric Hospital on Court Order; No
Reason for Action Given." New York Times, (May 2, 1970), p. 20.

3095. Axthelm, Pete. "Brown Bomber by B. Schulberg: Review." Newsweek,
79 (May 22, 1972), 68.

3096. "Benefit Show, Salute To The Champ, Joe Louis Set." New York Times, (August 2, 1970), p. 2.

3097. "Bethune-Cookman College on May 22 Cites Boxer Joe Louis For His Efforts To Help Blacks Achieve Equality In World of Sports." New York Times, (May 23, 1973), p. 55.

3098. "Bible Reading Louis." Newsweek, 6 (July 6, 1935), 22.

3099. "Big Joe vs Jersey Joe." Newsweek, 30 (August 11, 1947), 81.

3100. "Biography By Gerald Astor Reviewed." Washington Post, (February 27, 1975) p. 10, sec. 2.

3101. "Black Moses." Time, 38 (September 29, 1941), 60+.

3102. Bliven, B. Jr. "Humpty Dumpty Had A Great Fall." New Republic, 99 (July 12, 1939), 277.

3103. "Blow That KO'd Joe Louis." U.S. News & World Report, 42 (January 25, 1957), 63-4+.

3104. "Bomber's Salute Here Wednesday." Michigan Chronicle, (August 15, 1970).

3105. Bourne-Vanneck, V.P. "Why Was Joe Louis Snubbed?" New York Age, (March 19, 1949), p. 1.

3106. "Boxer Tax Troubles." U.S. News and World Report, 41 (December 28, 1956), 8.

3107. "Braddock and Louis To Sign." New York Times, (June 6, 1937), p. 12, sec. 5.

3108. "Braddock-Louis Train." New York Times, (June 6, 1937), p. 12, sec. 5.

3109. "Braddock-Louis Title Bout Proposed." New York Times, (February 1, 1937), p. 23.

3110. "Braddock Says Louis Has Reached Peak of Trainings." New York Times, (January 27, 1936), p. 24.

3111. Bromberg, L. "Can Joe Louis Last As A Boxing Promoter?" Negro Digest, 8 (November 1949), 47-49.

3112. Bromberg, L. "How Joe Louis Punch Feels." Negro Digest, 8 (April 1950), 11-14.

3113. Brown, E. "Joe Louis the Champion, Idol of His Race, Sets A Good Example of Conduct." Life, 8 (June 17, 1940), 48-50+.

3114. Brown, H. "Louis and Lewis." Nation, 144 (February 6, 1937), 156.

3115. Burley, D. "Love Life of Joe Louis: Romances of Most Eligible
      Negro Bachelor Have Involved Beautiful Women Around Nation."
      Ebony, 6 (July 1951), 22-26.

3116. Byoir, C. "Joe Louis Named the War; Poem." Collier's, 109
      (May 16, 1942), 14.

3117. Carroll, Ted. "Huge Bankroll Is Joe's Ace: Louis Has Right
      Kind of Financial Backing." New York Age, (March 12, 1949),
      p. 16-17.

3118. "Celebrities Honor Joe Louis in Las Vegas." Pittsburgh Courier,
      (May 29, 1971).

3119. "Champions's Crown Totters: Louis and Walcott." Life, 23
      (December 15, 1947), 36-7.

3120. "City Pays Tribute to Champ of Champs." Michigan Chronicle,
      (August 22, 1970).

3121. "Comment on Louis-Charles Bout." New York Times, (October 1,
      1950), p. 2, sec. 4.

3122. "Comments On Louis-Sharkey Prospects." New York Times, (August
      9, 1936), p. 7, sec. 5.

3123. "Condition Noted." New York Times, (November 10, 1977), p. 10,
      sec. 4.

3124. "Court Medical Exam for Louis Canceled by Agreement of Attorneys;
      He Will Be Transferred to VA Hospital." New York Times, (May
      13, 1970), p. 7.

3125. "D. Anderson Comments on B. Nagler's Book on Former World
      Heavyweight Boxing Champ Joe Louis, His Boxing Career and His
      Alleged Use of Drugs." New York Times, (June 3, 1972), p. 23.

3126. "Decides To Return To Ring." New York Times, (October 15, 1950),
      p. 4, sec. 5.

3127. "Detroit Council Joins Joe Louis Salute, Renames Washington Blvd.
      In His Honor." The Pittsburgh Courier, (August 15, 1970).

3128. "Dusky Meteor." Literary Digest, 121 (June 13, 1936), 36.

3129. "Editorial On Louis." New York Times, (October 1, 1941), p. 20.

3130. "Establishment Let Joe Louis Down." The Michigan Chronicle,
      (August 29, 1970).

3131. "Exhibition Tour of Camps and Forts in 2nd Corps Area Planned."
      New York Times, (May, 16, 1942), p. 19.

3132. "Ex-Wife Weds Dr. A.L. Spaulding." New York Times, (May 21,
      1950), p. 47.

3133. "Farr and Louis Meet At Signing For Bout." New York Times, (July 28, 1937), p. 26.

3134. Fay, B. "Why Did Joe Louis Change His Mind About Retiring." Collier's, 122 (November 20, 1948), 74.

3135. "Federal Government Files $58, 938 Income Tax Lien for Unpaid '47 Tax, Chicago." New York Times, (May 20, 1950), p. 72.

3136. Ferrell, J.T. "Fall of Joe Louis." Nation, 142 (June 27, 1936), 834-836.

3137. "Fidel and The U.S. Negro." Time, 75 (June 6, 1960), 36.

3138. "Fighter Joe Louis Signs Up To Fight for the U.S." Life, 12 (January 26, 1942), 24.

3139. "Foe For Joe." Time, 52 (December 28, 1948), 75.

3140. "Former Champion Joe Louis To Be Honored." The Carolina Times, (August 15, 1970).

3141. "From One Champ to Another." Winston-Salem Journal & Sentinel, (February 1, 1970).

3142. "Furlough Sought For J. Louis to Permit Him to Defend Title." New York Times, (February 5, 1942), p. 28.

3143. "Galento and Louis Train." New York Times, (June 8, 1939), p. 35.

3144. Gallico, P. "Citizen Barrow." Readers Digest, 40 (June, 1942), 21-5.

3145. Garvey, Marcus. "The World As It Is: Joe Louis and The Germans." The Black Man, 4, (February 1939), 19-20.

3146. Garvey, Marcus. "The World As It Is: Joe Louis." The Black Man, 2, (July-August, 1936), 19-20.

3147. "Gentlemen's Agreement." Time, 53 (March 14, 1949), 82.

3148. "George J. Friedman Letter Holds Roger Wilkins Misquoted Joe Louis On His Famous Statement About Winning WW II in His Nov. 13 Article on Reggie Jackson." New York Times, (November 27, 1977), p. 2, sec. 5.

3149. Hannagan, S. "Black Gold." Saturday Evening Post, 208 (June 20, 1936), 14+.

3150. "Heavyweights' Come To Joe Louis On His 65th Birthday." Jet, 56 (June 7, 1979), 30-31.

3151. Heinz, W.C. "What Happended To Joe Louis' $4,000,000." Negro Digest, 9 (March 1951), 87-94.

3152. Higgins, C. "Salute To Joe." Ebony, 25 (October, 1970), 158-62.

3153. "Honored At Testimonial Dinner N.Y.C." New York Times, (May 22, 1942), p. 31.

3154. "How Joe Louis Lost 43 Pounds." Ebony, 13 (May 1958), 55-57.

3155. "I Didn't Raise My Boy To Be A Fighter." Negro Digest, 9 (February 1951), 3-6.

3156. "I'd Do It All Over Again Says Joe Louis." Ebony, 11 (November 1955), 65-70.

3157. "Illustration With Wife Leaving Hospital." New York Times, (October 17, 1980), p. 36.

3158. "In Stable Condition After Being Operated On By Heart Specialist Dr. Michael E. Debakey." New York Times, (November 4, 1977), p. 26.

3159. "J. Blackburn Predicts Louis' Undefeated Retirement." New York Times, (November 12, 1939), p. 12, sec. 5.

3160. "J. DaGrosa Plans To Bar Louis Bouts." New York Times, (December 11, 1950), p. 33.

3161. "T. Galento's Promoters Seek Bout With Louis." New York Times, (October 12, 1935), p. 22.

3162. "Jersey Journal Says It "Owns" A Bit of Joe Louis Too." New York Age, (March 12, 1949), p. 11.

3163. "J. Louis- B. Baer." New York Times, (January 1, 1942), p. 40.

3164. Joe Louis Benefit Exhibition Bout Planned For Polo Grounds All-Sports Carnival." New York Times, (May 26, 1942), p. 28.

3165. "J. Louis-Billy Conn Bout, Louis Training Plans." New York Times, (January 1, 1946), p. 30.

3166. "J. Louis: Camp Upton." New York Times, (June 20, 1942), p. 18.

3167. "J. Louis Exhibition Bouts, Ft. Hamilton Arena Brooklyn." New York Times, (June 6, 1942), p. 19.

3168. "J. Louis Gets E.J. Neil Memorial Plague." New York Times, (January 1942), p. 21.

3169. "J. Louis Plans Central and South America Exhibition Tour." New York Times, (December 23, 1946), p. 26.

3170. "J. Louis to Box Exhibition Bout Honululu." New York Times, (October 24, 1946), p. 38.

3171. "J. Louis to Start Training." New York Times, (May 23, 1942), p. 18.

3172. "Joe Louis and Jesse Owens." Crisis, 42 (August 1935), 241.

3173. "Joe Louis and The Negro Press." Crisis, 43 (August 1936), 241.

3174. "J. Louis Arrives, Los Angeles for Furlough: Comments." New York Times, (October 14, 1942), p. 30.

3175. "Joe Louis Asks New York State Athletic Commission Championship Recognition." New York Times, (July 29, 1949), p. 16.

3176. "Joe Louis-B. Conn Bout." New York Times, (June 3, 1946), p. 31.

3177. "Joe Louis-B. Conn Bout: Louis Wins By Knockout in 8th Round." New York Times, (June 20, 1946), p. 1.

3178. "Joe Louis-B. Conn Exhibition Bout Approved, Chicago." New York Times, (November 9, 1948), p. 37.

3179. "Louis-Burman Bout: Louis Retains Title." New York Times, (September 28, 1938), p. 34.

3180. "Joe Louis-C. Burman Bout: Louis Retains Title." New York Times, (January 22, 1941), p. 25.

3181. "Joe Louis-C. Burman Bout: Men To Stop." New York Times, (January 22, 1941), p. 25.

3182. "Joe Louis-C. Sheppard Bout Proposed for Baltimore Next Spring." New York Times, (November 16, 1946), p. 12.

3183. "Joe Louis Cancels Plans To Retire, To Defend Title, June '49." New York Times, (October 20, 1948), 41.

3184. "Joe Louis-Charles Bout Set; Louis To Get 35% of Net." New York Times, (August 18, 1950), p. 25.

3185. "Joe Louis Decides On Comeback." New York Times, (July 25, 1950), p. 34.

3186. "Joe Louis Denies Plan To Box Lesnevich; Insists His Retirement Is Definite." New York Times, (July 21, 1948), p. 32.

3187. "J. Louis Denies Rept. of Quitting Ring; Tells M. Jacobs Statement Misunderstood, Assoc. Press Quotes Louis on Original Rept." New York Times, (October 13, 1942), p. 27.

3188. "Joe Louis Exhibition, Manila." New York Times, (May 6, 1949), p. 35.

3189. "Joe Louis Exhibition Salt Lake City." New York Times, (January 26, 1950), p. 32.

3190. "Joe Louis Exhibition St. Petersburg, Fla." New York Times, (February 8, 1950), p. 37.

3191. "Joe Louis Exhibition Tour, Boston." New York Times, (November 15, 1949), p. 34.

3192. "Joe Louis Exhibition Tour, Dallas." New York Times, (March 20, 1949), p. 2, sec. 5.

3193. "Joe Louis Exhibition, Newark." New York Times, (November 23, 1949), p. 39.

3194. "Joe Louis Exhibitions; Mich. State Comm. Scores Detroit Show." New York Times, (December 16, 1949), p. 39.

3195. "Joe Louis Gets B'rith Sholom Award." New York Times, (October 6, 1949), p. 45.

3196. "J. Louis Gets E.J. Neil Memorial Plague." New York Times, (January 22, 1942), p. 21.

3197. "Joe Louis-H. Thomas Bout Comment." New York Times, (April 3, 1938), p. 6, sec. 5.

3198. "Joe Louis-H. Thomas Bout-Louis Wins." New York Times, (April 2, 1938), p. 10.

3199. "Joe Louis-H. Thomas Preview." New York Times, (April 1, 1938), p. 18.

3200. "Joe Louis Honored at Caesar's Palace." Washington Post, (November 1978), p. 1., sec. F.

3201. "Joe Louis Officially Retires." New York Times, (March 2, 1949), p. 1.

3202. "Joe Louis Philosophy: Ex-Champ's Most Notable Quotations Are As Treasured As His Phenomenal Boxing Record." Ebony, 11 (September 1956), 52-54.

3203. "J. Louis Plans to Retire From Ring Comment Career." New York Times, (October 12, 1942), p. 1.

3204. "Joe Louis Plans to Visit Hall Named in His Honor." Winston-Salem Journal, (July 15, 1980).

3205. "Joe Louis Postpones Retirement." New York Times, (September 18, 1948), p. 13.

3206. "Joe Louis, Promoter." Life, 26 (March 14, 1949), 32.

3207. "Joe Louis Rejects Ezzard Charles Challenge." New York Times, (January 22, 1950), p. 2, sec. 5.

3208. "Joe Louis Ring Record." New York Times, (March 2, 1949), p. 35.

3209. "Joe Louis-T. Maunello Bout: Training Plans." New York Times, (August 7, 1946), p. 24.

3210. "Joe Louis To Announce Official Retirement Soon." New York Times, (August 21, 1948), p. 13.

3211. "Joe Louis To Continue Comeback." New York Times, (December 1, 1950), p. 35.

3212. "Joe Louis Tour, Nassau." New York Times, (March 2, 1949), p. 35.

3213. "Joe Louis Uncertain About Retirement." New York Times, (Septembe 15, 1948), p. 44.

3214. "Joe Louis Unchallenged Champion of The People." Michigan Chronicle, (August 22, 1970).

3215. "Joe Louis Undecided On Retirement.' New York Times, (October 3, 1950), p. 38.

3216. "Joe Louis vs. B. Benneh." New York Times, (April 23, 1935), p. 29.

3217. "Joe Louis vs. G. Stanton." New York Times, (May 8, 1935), p. 26.

3218. "Joe Louis vs. H. Birkie." New York Times, (January 12, 1935), p. 20.

3219. "Joe Louis vs. L. Ramage." New York Times, (February 22, 1935), p. 31.

3220. "Joe Louis vs. N. Brown." New York Times, (March 30, 1945), p. 20.

3221. "Joe Louis vs. O. Barry." New York Times, (March 9, 1935),,), p. 11.

3222. "Joe Louis vs. R. Lazar." New York Times, (April 13, 1935), p. 18.

3223. "Joe Louis vs. R. Toles." New York Times, (April 26, 1935), 26.

3224. "Joe Louis vs. W. Davis." New York Times, (May 4, 1935), p. 8.

3225. "Joe Takes A Wife." Ebony, 11 (March 1956), 45-46+.

3226. "Joe vs. Joe, Who Won?" Newsweek, 30 (December 15, 1947), 77.

3227. "Joe Wins One For Uncle Sam." Ebony, 12 (January 1957), 42+.

3228. "Joe's Last Fight." Time, 52 (July 5, 1948), 40.

3229. "June Bout With Louis Planned." New York Times, (September 4, 1937), p. 7.

3230. Kieran, John. "A Champion All The Way: Joe Louis." Opportunity, 20 (February, 1942), 48-49.

3231. "L. Firpo Seeks A Cestac-Joe Louis Bout." New York Times, (January 3, 1948), p. 19.

3232. Lardner, John. "Final (it better be) Curtain." Newsweek, 32 (July 5, 1948), 65.

3233. Lardner, John. "Great Louis Mystery." Newsweek, 32 (June 21, 1948), 84.

3234. Lardner, John. "How History Is Made." Newsweek, 49 (April 29, 1957), 66.

3235. Lardner, John. "Pathos of Taxes." Newsweek, 47 (January 16, 1956), 66.

3236. "Last Week." Time, 47 (June 17, 1946), 61-62.

3237. "Letter Discounting Louis Record." New York Times, (June 17, 1939), p. 21.

3238. "Letter On Gov. Murphy's Greeting To Louis." New York Times, (June 24, 1938), p. 18.

3239. "Letter Praising Louis." New York Times, (September 30, 1939), p. 14.

3240. "Letters On Louis Bout." New York Times, (July 2, 1938), p. 9.

3241. "Letters On Sports Writers' Estimate of Joe Louis." New York Times, (February 4, 1939), 9; (February 11, 1939), p. 11.

3242. Linn, E. "Joe Louis: Oh Where Did My Money Go?" Saturday Evening Post, 228 (January 7, 1956), 22-3+.

3243. "Little Joe Louis, Joe Brown." Ebony, 13, (July 1958), 88-91.

3244. "Louis-Agodoy Bout Planned." New York Times, (November 14, 1939), p. 28.

3245. "Louis-A. Simon Bout: Joe Louis To Train at Ft. Dix." New York Times, (March 3, 1942), p. 19.

3246. "Louis-A.Simon Bout Plans." New York Times, (April 6, 1941), p. 2, sec. 5.

3247. "Louis-A. Simon Bout: Training." New York Times, (March 16, 1941), p. 4, sec. 5.

3248. "Louis Again Says He Will Retire." New York Times, (June 29, 1948), p. 28.

3249. "Louis and Braddock Sign, Madison Square Garden Cord Threatens Action." New York Times, (February 20, 1937), p. 11.

3250. "Louis and Braddock To Sign." New York Times, (February 18, 1937), p. 25.

3251. "Louis and Farr Training." New York Times, (August 8, 1937), p. 6.

3252. "Louis and Schmeling Plan Other Bouts Before Title Fights."
      New York Times, (December 16, 1937), p. 41.

3253. "Louis and Thomas Practice." New York Times, (March 16,
      1938), 30; (March 27, 1938), p. 8, sec. 5.

3254. "Louis-B. Baer Bout Plans." New York Times, (April 18, 1941),
      p. 28.

3255. "Louis-B. Baer Bout Plans." New York Times, (November 13, 1941),
      39; (November 18, 1941), p. 37.

3256. "Louis-B. Baer Bout Plans." New York Times, (December 9, 1941),
      p. 50.

3257. "Louis-B. Baer Contract Signed." New York Times, (December 17,
      1941), p. 41.

3258. "Louis-B. Baer Bout: Louis and Baer Train." New York Times,
      (December 23, 1941), p. 31.

3259. "Louis-Baer Bout: Louis Wins, Decision Contested." New York
      Times, (May 24, 1941), p. 19.

3260. "Louis-Baer: Letter." New York Times, (May 10, 1941), p. 12.

3261. "Louis Comments." New York Times, (May 11, 1949), p. 42.

3262. "Louis Comments On Future Bouts." New York Times, (July 13,
      1938), p. 25.

3263. "Louis Comments On Rivals." New York Times, (November 20, 1941),
      p. 41.

3264. "Louis Confident of Victory." New York Times, (March 26, 1935),
      p. 26.

3265. "Louis-Conn Bout: Formal Articles Signed." New York Times,
      (June 4, 1941), p. 30.

3266. "Louis-Conn Bout: Louis To Open Pompton Lakes, N.J. Training
      Site." New York Times, (May 1, 1946), p. 34.

3267. "Louis-Conn Bout Planned." New York Times, (May 2, 1941), p. 31.

3268. "Louis Conn Bout: Louis Wins." New York Times, (June 19, 1941),
      p. 1.

3269. "Louis-Conn Promoter Jacobs Drops Plans for $100 Ring Side Seats
      Applicants From 40 States and 3 Foreign Countries Seek Tickets."
      New York Times, (February 1, 1946), p. 26.

3270. "Louis Denies Reports He Will Retire After Conn Bout." New York
      Times, (April 13, 1946), p. 21.

3271. "Louis Denies Reports of Retirement." New York Times, (June 25, 1938), p. 9.

3272. "Louis Earned Over $4 Million In Ring." Michigan Chronicle, (May 16, 1970).

3273. "Louis-Farr Result Voted Biggest Surprise of Year in AP Poll." New York Times, (December 18, 1937), p. 14.

3274. Louis-G. Dorazio Bout: Louis Signs." New York Times, (February 4, 1941), p. 25.

3275. "Louis 5-13 Favorite." New York Times, (June 23, 1948), p. 35.

3276. "Louis Found Fit; Comments." New York Times, (June 16, 1948), 39.

3277. "Louis-Galento Bout Planned." New York Times, (February 28, 1939), p. 23.

3278. "Louis-Galento Return Bout Planned." New York Times, (September 17, 1949), p. 4, sec. 5.

3279. "Louis Interviewed By Moscow Pravda Reporter." New York Times, (June 16, 1946), p. 5, sec. 3.

3280. "Louis-J. Roper Bout Planned." New York Times, (February 8, 1939), p. 26.

3281. "Louis Leads in Ring Magazine Rankings." New York Times, (December 27, 1937), p. 18.

3282. "Louis-Lewis Contract Signed." New York Times, (December 17, 1938), p. 19.

3283. "Louis May Box Schmeling For Crown If Braddock is Unable to Defend Title." New York Times, (August 20, 1936), p. 17.

3284. "Louis May Defend Title in London Bout With J. Doyle or L. Harvey." New York Times, (June 25, 1937), p. 28.

3285. "Louis May Make Exhibition Tour." New York Times, (January 28, 1939), p. 9.

3286. "Louis May Meet A. Lovell." New York Times, (December 13, 1939), p. 37.

3287. "Louis-Musto Bout: Banned, Cleveland." New York Times, (March 11, 1949), p. 12.

3288. "Louis-Musto Bout: Louis Wins." New York Times, (April 9, 1941), p. 34.

3289. "Louis-Musto Bout: Training." New York Times, (April 6, 1941), p. 2, sec. 5.

3290. "Louis 1942 Plans." New York Times, (December 7, 1941), p. 1, sec. 5.

3291. "Louis-Nova Bout: Detroit Makes Bid." New York Times, (July 4, 1941), p. 10.

3292. "Louis-Nova Bout: Louis Interviewed." New York Times, (July 5, 1941), p. 19.

3293. "Louis-Nova Bout; Louis Wins." New York Times, (September 30, 1941), p. 1.

3294. "Louis-Nova Bout: Plans." New York Times, (September 3, 1941), p. 29.

3295. "Louis Objects To Plan To Keep Conn Out of Ring Till Last Minute." New York Times, (June 6, 1941), p. 28.

3296. "Louis On Tour: Sergeant Joe Starts 100-day Boxing Swing Around Nation's Army Posts." Life, 15 (September 13, 1943), 34-5.

3297. "Louis Opens War Against Self-Service Elevator Apts." New York Age, (March 19, 1949), 1, 9.

3298. "Louis-Pastor Bout-Louis Retains Title." New York Times, (September 21, 1939), p. 27.

3299. "Louis Pastor Bout: Preview." New York Times, (September 20, 1939), p. 35.

3300. "Louis-Pastor Bout: Training." New York Times, (September 14, 1939), p. 29.

3301. "Louis Picks French Lick Training Site." New York Times, (January 30, 1946), p. 21.

3302. "Louis Plans Another Title Bout." New York Times, (January 7, 1942), p. 27.

3303. "Louis Praised-Editorial." New York Times, (June 24, 1948), p. 8, sec. 4.

3304. "Louis Reiterates Plans To Retire After Bout." New York Times, (February 25, 1948), 30; (February 26, 1948), p. 29.

3305. "Louis Reiterates Intention To Retire." New York Times, (June 26, 1948), p. 11.

3306. "Louis Reported Anxious To Meet Nova." New York Times, (July 31, 1941), 21.

3307. "Louis Reported Considering Political Career." New York Times, (June 27, 1948), p. 1, sec. 5.

3308. "Louis Reported in Good Condition." New York Times, (June 2, 1948), p. 41.

3309. "Louis-Roper Bout-Louis Retain Title." New York Times, (April 18, 1939), p. 30.

3310. "Louis-Roper Bout Plans." New York Times, (April 16, 1939), p. 10, sec. 5.

3311. "Louis-Roper Bout-Preview." New York Times, (April 17, 1939), p. 21.

3312. "Louis Says He Must Knock out Conn to Win." New York Times, 19 (January 12, 1946), p. 19.

3313. "Louis-Schmeling Bout-Both Sign." New York Times, (May 12, 1938), p. 31.

3314. "Louis-Schmeling Bout: Both Train." New York Times, (May 30, 1938), p. 15.

3315. "Louis-Schmeling Bout: Both Train." New York Times, (May 31, 1938), p. 27.

3316. "Louis-Schmeling Bout: Louis Comment." New York Times, (June 23, 1938), p. 14.

3317. "Louis-Schmeling Bout-Louis Wins By Knockout In 1st Round." New York Times, (June 23, 1938), p. 1.

3318. "Louis-Schmeling Bout-Preview." New York Times, (June 22, 1938), p. 28.

3319. "Louis-Schmeling Bout To Be Held on June 22." New York Times, (March 19, 1938), p. 18.

3320. "Louis-Schemling Bout: Training." New York Times, (June 1, 1938), p. 26.

3321. "Louis-Schmeling Bout: Training." New York Times, (June 2, 1938), p. 28.

3322. "Louis Scores Da Grosa Action." New York Times, (December 12, 1950), p. 48.

3323. "Louis Signed For June Bout; To Get 40% of Net Gate." New York Times, (January 9, 1948), p. 29.

3324. "Louis Signs 5-yr. Contract With M. Jacobs; Wants 4 Fights Per Yr; Financial Rept; German Press Comment." New York Times, (June 24, 1937), p. 32.

3325. "Louis Signs For H. Thomas Bout in Chicago." New York Times, (February 25, 1938), p. 23.

3326. "Louis Signs for Bout With A Simon." New York Times, (February 26, 1942), p. 24.

3327. "Louis Signs For Sept. 18 Bout With Marriella." New York Times, (July 11, 1946), p. 15.

3328. "Louis-Simon Bout: Louis Wins." New York Times, (March 22, 1944), p. 10.

3329. "Louis Starts Training." New York Times, (August 1, 1937), p. 4.

3330. "Louis Starts Training For J. Roper Bout." New York Times, (March 9, 1939), p. 27.

3331. "Louis To Box L. Nova." New York Times, (June 22, 1941), p. 1, sec. 5.

3332. "Louis to Fight Abroad in Summer." New York Times, (June 27, 1937), p. 3.

3333. "Louis To Meet J.H. Lewis, Challenger." New York Times, (November 3, 1938), p. 29.

3334. "Louis to Rest for 2 to 6 Months." New York Times, (September 2, 1937), p. 28.

3335. "Louis To Rest Till September." New York Times, (June 20, 1941), p. 25.

3336. "Louis Training Plans." New York Times, (January 1, 1946), p. 30.

3337. "Louis Trains." New York Times, (September 21, 1935), p. 9.

3338. "Louis Trains For Roper Bout." New York Times, (March 29, 1939), p. 27.

3339. "Louis Undergoes Physical Exam." New York Times, (September 11, 1946), p. 10.

3340. "Louis Wins." New York Times, (January 26, 1939), p. 24.

3341. "Louis Wins." New York Times, (June 23, 1937), p. 1.

3342. "Louis Wins By Decisions." New York Times, (August 31, 1937), p. 1.

3343. "Louis Wins; Comments." New York Times, (January 10, 1942), p. 19.

3344. "Louis Wins $47,000 and Puts His Camp on the Wagon." Newsweek, 6 (August 17, 1935), 24.

3345. "Louis Wins, Retires." Life, 25 (July 5, 1948), 57-8+.

3346. "Louis's Condition." New York Times, (June 11, 1937), p. 28.

3347. "Loves of Joe Louis." Ebony, 34 (November 1978), 43-46+.

3348. Lucas, Bob. "The Truth About Joe Louis." Sepia, 2 (December 1971), 14+.

3349. Lucas, Bob and Isaac Sutton. "Joe Louis Fights To Walk Again." Jet, 54 (June 22, 1978), 44-58.

3350. Maley, R. "Joe Louis Greatest Fight." Newsweek, 38 (November 12, 1951), 116.

3351. Miller, M. and P. Stong. "And Still Champion: Review of Joe Louis, American." Saturday Review of Literature, 28 (December 8, 1945), p. 28+.

3352. Mitchell, J. "Joe Louis Never Smiles." New Republic, 84 (October 9, 1935), 239-40.

3353. "Money Ain't Everything." Time, 49 (March 3, 1947), 52.

3354. Murray, Jim. "The One and Only Joe Louis." The Michigan Chronicle, (August 15, 1970).

3355. Nagler, B. "How Joe Louis Got 'Hooked' On Cocaine." Sepia, 21 (Septemeber 1972), 22-24+.

3356. "NBA Grudgingly Places Louis at Head of Rankings." New York Times, (September 14, 1937), p. 28.

3357. "New Joe Louis." Life, 24 (June 21, 1948), 61.

3358. "NY Boxing Assn. to Honor J. Louis With Scrolls at Polo Grounds All Sports Carnival for Contributions at Army & Navy Relief Funds." New York Times, (June 9, 1942), p. 32.

3359. "N.Y. Nixes Out Louis Title Go: Promoter Joe Draws Frowns of Col. Eagan." New York Age, (March 12, 1949), p. 1.

3360. "New York State Athletic Commission Approves Louis-Galento Bout." New York Times, (April 1, 1939), p. 13.

3361. "Offer Made for Title Bout Between Louis And Winner of Gustanga-Thomas Fight." New York Times, (July 12, 1937), p. 24.

3362. "Offer Made To Louis For Philadelphia Bout With T. Galento." New York Times, (July 6, 1938), p. 62.

3363. "On The Ropes." Time, 52 (November 1, 1948), 44.

3364. "Pageant Salutes Louis." Negro History Bulletin, 16 (June 1953), 201.

3365. "Paradoxical Louis: Brown Bomber Has Prize Ring Scribes All Upset Again." Literary Digest, 122 (August 26, 1936), 34.

3366. Parker, D. "Champ Who Was Born Too Late." Negro Digest, 9 (June, 1951), 64-66.

3367. "Plans For Louis-Schmeling and Schmeling-Farr Bouts May Be Dropped in Favor of NYC Louis-Farr." New York Times, (July 1, 1937), p. 14.

3368. "Plans Stalled By Proposal To Move Bout From Soldier Field To Comiskey Park." New York Times, (February 6, 1937), p. 21.

3369. "Price For Braddock-Louis Fight Set." New York Times, (February 25, 1937), 27; (February 27, 1937), p. 13.

3370. "Promoter Louis." Newsweek, 33 (March 14, 1949), 75-6.

3371. "Psychiatrists Treat Joe Louis." The Afro American, (May 9, 1970).

3372. Pye, B. "Joe Louis and Wife Score K.O. As Promoters." Sepia, 11 (July 1962), 39-41.

3373. "Real Champion: Joe Louis." Opportunity, (October 1939), 290-91.

3374. "Released From Hospital; Was There Since May, Because of Emotional Disorder." New York Times, (October 16, 1970), p. 32.

3375. "Rev. M.C. Faulkner Drops Alienation of Affection Suit After Settlement." New York Times, (June 28, 1950), p. 15.

3376. Reynolds, Quentin. "Dark Dynamite." Collier, 95 (June 22, 1935), 64-6+.

3377. Robinson, Louie. "Joe Louis At Sixty." Ebony, 28 (October 1973), 64-6+.

3378. Roxborough, J.W. "How I Discovered Joe Louis." Ebony, 9 (October 1954), 64-70+.

3379. "Russ Cowans Talk About Joe Louis." Michigan Chronicle, (August 22, 1970).

3380. "Salute To Champ A Success." Pittsburgh Courier, (August 15, 1970).

3381. Santos, Frank. "Brown Bomber Was Indeed The Greatest." Pittsburgh Courier, (August 16, 1970).

3382. "Say It Ain't So, Joe." Look, 20 (June 12, 1956), 62-3+.

3383. "Seeks Bout To Pay Tax Arrears." New York Times, (July 25, 1950), p. 34; (July 29, 1950), p. 8.

3384. "Seeks Compromis On Income Tax Arrears." New York Times, (October 3, 1950), p. 38.

3385. "Sinatra's Fete For Joe Louis Raise Over 1/2 Million." Jet, 55 (November 30, 1978), 8-9+.

3386. "Sports: Pageant Salutes Joe Louis, A Great Guy, An Epic Fighter, An American Legend." Negro History Bulletin, 16 (June 1953), 16.

3387. "Sports Writers Chose Louis by Knockout." New York Times, (September 15, 1935), p. 5.

3388. Stephens, Louise. "Refuse Joe Louis As Candidate For Who's Who." Chicago Defender, (September 21, 1946), p. 1.

3389. Talese, Gay. "Joe Louis: The King As A Middle-Aged Man." Esquire, 57 (June 1962), 92-98.

3390. "Ten Biggest Lies About Joe Louis." Ebony, 8 (August 1953), 52-58+.

3391. "20th Century Sporting Club To Relinquish Rights To Madison Square Garden: New Corp. To Be Associated With International Boxing Club Headed By Joe Louis." New York Times, (May 6, 1949), 33.

3392. Tyler, T. "Tribute To Joe Louis." Sport, 68 (May 1979), 90-93+.

3393. "Vancouver Bans Joe Louis Exibitions." New York Times, (December 20, 1949), p. 40.

3394. Vidmer, R. "In This Corner: Facts About the Champion." Current History, 51 (March, 1940), 49-50.

3395. "We Let Joe Know We Still Love Him." Michigan Chronicle, (August 22, 1970).

3396. "Winner of Louis-Schmeling Bout Will Be Contender For Title Of J.J. Braddock." New York Times, (May 20, 1936), p. 31.

3397. "World Boxing Commission Orders Louis To Meet Schmeling Or Lose Title." New York Times, (April 23, 1930), p. 12.

3398. "Writers Grant Louis the Title Braddock Still Holds." Newsweek, 6 (October 5, 1935), 24-5.

3399. "X's Mark Sport Where Louis Scored Another Knockout." Newsweek, 6 (December 21, 1935), 40.

3400. Young, Andrew S. "Joe Louis Marries Again." Sepia, 7 (June 1959), 8-12.

TOM MOLINEAUX

3401. Magriel, Paul. "Tom Molineaux." Phylon, 12 (December 1951), 329-36.

ARCHIE MOORE

3402. "A. Moore Light Heavyweight, Suspended By Dist. of Columbia Comm. For Failing to Appear for Bout." New York Times, (January 22, 1946), 23.

3403. "Archie Moore." Ebony, 8 (April 1953), 52-56.

3404. "Archie Moore: Boxing's New Cinderella Man Is 37 Year-Old Puncher Who Waited 18 Years For World Title." Ebony, 8 (April 1953), 52-56.

3405. Bowen, E., and M. Kane. "Conversation Piece: Archie Moore." Sports Illustrated, 3 (September 19, 1955), 18-21.

3406. Heinz, W.C. "Mystery Of Archie Moore." Saturday Evening Post, 228 (September 17, 1955), 26-27.

3407. Kane, M. "Breathing Easy: Archie Moore - Besmanoff Fight." Sports Illustrated, (June 6, 1960), 58.

3408. Kane, M. "Last Chance For Old Arch." Sports Illustrated, 15 (November 26, 1956), 34-36.

3409. Kane, M. "The Man The System Could Not Beat." Sports Illustrated, 5 (November 26, 1956), 34-36.

3410. Kane, M. "Overmatched, the NBA Concedes to Archie Moore." Sports Illustrated, 12 (March 14, 1960), 47-48.

3411. Lardner, John. "An He Can't Play a Comb." Newsweek, 44 (August 23, 1954), 73.

3412. Lardner, John. "King of The Sharecroppers: Archie Moore." Newsweek, (August 8, 1955), 75.

3413. Lardner, John. "Old Man's Price: Archie Moore." Newsweek, 50 (July 1, 1957), 73.

3414. Liebling, A.J. "Reporter At Large: Moore-Johnson Fight." New Yorker, 30 (September 4, 1956), 44.

3415. Lyon, P. "Archie Moore, the Oldest Youth." Holiday, 26 (December 1959), 133-135.

3416. Millstein, G. "In This Corner, at Long Last, Archie Moore!" New York Times Magazine, (September 11, 1955), 26.

3417. Moore, G. "Boxing Killed My Husband." Ebony, 18 (July 1963), 31-32.

3418. Murphy, J. "Profiles: Archie Moore." New Yorker, 37 (November 11, 1961), 61-62.

3419. "One of the Great Ones: Archie Moore." Newsweek, 53 (February 23, 1959), 92.

3420. Stewart-Gordon, J. "Boxing's Old Man River-Archie Moore." Rotarian, 95 (July 1959), 18-19.

3421. "Time Runs Out for Archie Moore." Sports Illustrated, 13 (November 7, 1960), 20.

3422. Young, Andrew S. "Boxing's Elder Statesman, Archie Moore."
Ebony, 13 (January 1958), 63-72.

3423. "Youngest Champ of Heavyweights: Archie Moore." Life, 41
(December 10, 1956), 54-55.

KEN NORTON

3424. Antoine, Roane. "How Larry Holmes Upset Ken Norton." Sepia, 27
(August 1978), 60-67.

3425. Barron, Allan P. "Norton Wuz Robbed." Black Sports, 9 (December
1976), 4.

3426. "Hypnotist Holds Key To Ken Norton's Win." Jet, 44 (April 19,
1973), 45.

3427. "Ken Norton: Best Bet To Succeed Ali." Jet, 53 (December 15,
1977), 54-56.

3428. Norman, Shirley. "Will Norton End The Muhammad Ali Reign In
Boxing." Sepia, 25 (September 1976), 26-30+.

3429. "Norton Dedicated Fight To Minnie Riperton; It May Have Been His
Last." Jet, 56 (September 6, 1979), 52.

3430. "Norton No 'Boy' Stomps Out of N.Y. Restaurant." Jet, 57 (June
9, 1977), 48.

3431. "Norton Wins Split Decision In California." Washington Post,
(April 1, 1973), p. 1, sec. D.

3432. "Rap With Ken Norton, Movie Star: Interview." Black Sports, 4
(February 1975), 14-15+.

3433. Simms, Gregory. "Norton Says He Must Stop Bobick, The Great
White Hope." Jet, 52 (April 28, 1977), 48-49.

3434. Simpson, Coreen. "Two Women Look At Ali-Norton, Before and
After." Black Sports, 6 (January 1977), 27-30+.

FLOYD PATTERSON

3435. "Ali Shuts Patterson's Eye To Gain TKO." Jet, 43 (October 5,
1972), 54.

3436. "Boxing's Biggest Bout." Ebony, 18 (Nobember 1962), 36-38.

3437. "Boxing's Rookie Of The Year: Floyd Patterson." Ebony, 60
(March 1954), 38-43.

3438. Brown, George F. "One Thing Floyd Patterson Never Forgot."
Sepia, 11 (May 1962), 32-34.

3439. Gottehrer, B. "Reluctant Dragon: Floyd Patterson." Newsweek, 58
(December 18, 1961), 71.

3440. Gross, M. "Floyd Patterson: I Want To Destory Clay." Sports Illustrated, 21 (October 19, 1964), 42-44.

3441. Hamill, Pete. "Floyd's Fight To Save Hs Pride." Saturday Evening Post, 237 (June 27, 1964), 76-78.

3442. Hoban, R. "An Artist Looks At His Subject: Floyd Patterson." Sports Illustrated, 6 (March 18, 1957), 34.

3443. Kane, M. "And the Veep Sat Down." Sports Illustrated, 7 (September 2, 1957), 15-16.

3444. Kane, M. "Beyond Endurance" Patterson vs. Jackson." Sports Illustrated, 7 (August 7, 1957), 12-13.

3445. Kane, M. "EE-Yah: Johansson-Patterson Fight." Sports Illustrated, 18 (June 27, 1960), 16-19.

3446. Kane, M. "The Man The System Could Not Beat." Sports Illustrated, 5 (December 10, 1956), 8-14.

3448. Kane, M. "Patterson by TKO." Sports Illustrated, 7 (July 29, 2957), 24-29.

3449. Kane, M. "Why Ingo Will Do It Again: Johannson-Patterson Fight." Sports Illustrated, 12 (June 20, 1960), 16-22.

3450. Lewis, Bill. "I'd Say Bring Back The Mafia." Black Sports, 7 (May 1978), 29-31.

3451. Liebling, A.J. "Sporting Scene: Patterson vs. Liston Return Fight." New Yorker, 39 (August 10, 1963), 62.

3452. MacLeod, R. "Hysterical Calm Grips Toronto: Patterson-McNeeley Fight." Sports Illustrated, 15 (December 4, 1961), 62-63.

3453. Mailer, Norman. "Ten Thousand Words A Minute: Floyd Patterson." Esquire, 59 (February 1963), 109-120.

3454. Martin, H.L. "Floyd Patterson Revisited." Negro Digest, 12 (March 1963), 33-37.

3455. Morrison, Allan. "Boxing's Most Misunderstood Champion: Floyd Patterson." Ebony, 14 (April 1959), 78-81.

3456. "Night Floyd Patterson Wept." Sepia, 14 (April 1965), 52-55.

3457. O'Neil, P. "Meet the Next Heavyweight Champion: Floyd Patterson." Sports Illustrated, 4 (January 30, 1956), 19-21.

3458. "Patterson Strikes Out at Black Muslim Champ." Sepia, 13 (December 1964), 64-65.

3459. Rogin, G. "Drama In Miami: Johansson-Patterson Fight." Sports Illustrated, 14 (March 20, 1960), 16-21.

3460. Rogin, G. "Facts About The Big Fight: Liston-Patterson Fight."
      Sports Illustrated, 17 (October 8, 1962), 20-27.

3461. Rogin, G. "Mild Champion Beats An Inferior Brawler: Patterson-
      McNeeley Fight." Sports Illustrated, 15 (December 11, 1961),
      24-25.

3462. Skeleton, B. "Sparring Partner Looks Them Over." Sports
      Illustrated, 17 (September 24, 1962), 26.

3463. Talese, Gay. "Loser: Floyd Patterson." Esquire, 61 (March 1964),
      65-68.

3464. Talese, Gay. "Portrait of the Ascetic Champ: Floyd Patterson."
      New York Times Magazine, (March 5, 1961), 34.

3465. "Tuning Up For Ingo in Indiana: Patterson-Johansson Fight."
      Sports Illustrated, 10 (May 11, 1959), 34-36.

3466. "Whatever Happened Too--Floyd Patterson." Ebony, 33 (November
      1977), 44-46+.

                        SUGAR RAY ROBINSON

3467. Breslin, J. "Last Days of Sugar Ray." Saturday Evening Post,
      235 (March 17, 1962), 30-31.

3468. "Can Sugar Ray Be A 3 Time Winner?" Our World, 7 (June 1952),
      42-44.

3469. "Did Turpin Make Sugar Quit Boxing?" Our World, 8 (November
      1953), 71-74.

3470. "Final Bell: Ray Robinson." Time, 65 (January 31, 1953), 42.

3471. Goodrich, J. "Fighter Without A Fight." Negro Digest, 8
      (June 1950), 11-14.

3472. "Grace Under Pressure: Ray Robinson." Newsweek, 49 (January
      14, 1957), 54.

3473. Greenfeld, J. "Power of A Postive Left Hook to the Jaw: Sugar
      Ray Robinson." Reporter, 16 (May 30, 1957), 41-42.

3474. Hepburn, D. "It's Sugar's Fight By An Early Kay O." Our World,
      6 (October 1951), 61-63.

3475. Hepburn, D. "Sugar Ray Robinson: Boxing's Santa." Our World, 6
      (January 1951), 44-46+.

3476. Kane, M. "Handicap, My Eye!" Sports Illustrated, 8 (April 7,
      1958), 18-20.

3477. Kane, M. "Young Body Over Old Mind." Sports Illustrated, 7
      (September 30, 1957), 10.

3478. King, L.L. "Sugar: Down But Not Quite Out." Sports Illustrated, 23 (September 6, 1965), 58-66.

3479. Lardner, John. "No Scar, No Mino: Sugar Ray Robinson." Newsweek, 49 (May 13, 1957), 77.

3480. Lardner, J. "Whiz Kid of Boxing and Business." Negro Digest, 9 (July 1951), 45-49.

3481. "Last Prizefighter: Ray Robinson." Newsweek, 50 (September 23, 1957), 106.

3482. "Last Seconds of a Champion: Sugar Ray Robinson." Sports Illustrated, 6 (January 14, 1957), 8-10.

3483. Lawry, R. "For the Middleweight Championship: Blood Wedding in Chicago-Ray Robinson's Fight." American Mercury, 72 (May 1951), 578-92.

3484. Liebling, A.J. "Reporter At Large: Sugar Ray Robinson." New Yorker, 27 (September 29, 1951), 76; 28 (July 12, 1952), 62.

3485. "Man Who Came Back: Sugar Ray Makes Good on Boast: I'm Here To Make History." Ebony, 11 (March 1956), 31-34.

3486. Murray, J. "Put Away the Flowers: Ray Robinson's Comeback." Sports Illustrated, 13 (December 12, 1960), 17-19.

3487. Nipson, Herb. "Sweet Sugar the Great." Ebony, 13 (June 1958), 150-154.

3488. Robinson, E.M. "Sugar Ray Fights Cancer." Our World, (June 1951), 56-57.

3489. "Robinson Voted Best Boxer Ever." Winston-Salem Journal, (May 10, 1978).

3490. Rogin, G. "The Death of A King: Sugar Ray Robinson." Sports Illustrated, 12 (June 20, 1960), 54-55.

3491. Rogin, G. "Sugar's Show Goes On." Sports Illustrated, 12 (February 1, 1960), 31-33.

3492. "Salt From Sugar Ray Robinson." Newsweek, 139 (January 15, 1951), 23.

3493. Schulberge, B. "Sugar Ray: A Will and Five Inspired Seconds." Sports Illustrated, 3 (December 19, 1955), 36-37.

3494. "Sugar Ray Conquers Paris, Loses Title." Ebony, 6 (September 1951), 91-95.

3495. "Sugar Ray Dares the Odds: Basilio-Robionson Fight." Sports Illustrated, 8 (March 24, 1958), 20-24.

3496. "Sugar Ray Robinson's Dream House; Ex-Middle Weight Champion Says New House Is Kind of Home I've Wanted All My Life." _Ebony_, 8 (June 1953), 41-47.

3497. "Sugar Ray's Farewell To Boxing." _Sepia_, 15 (March 1966), 53-55.

3498. "Sugar Ray's New Face." _Our World_, 8 (January 1953), 40-43.

3499. "Sweet Sugar the Great." _Ebony_, 13 (June 1958), 150-154.

3500. "What's Wrong With Sugar Ray?" _Ebony_, 9 (April 1954), 70-74.

3501. "Why I'm the Bad Boy of Boxing." _Ebony_, 6 (November 1950), 72-74+.

3502. "Why Sugar Ray Broke His Promise To God." _Ebony_, 10 (February 1955), 51-53.

3503. Maule, Tex. "No Place To Wear His Crown." _Sports Illustrated_, 22 (March 15, 1965), 28-29.

BOB SATTERFIELD

3504. "Bob Satterfield: Boxer or Bum?" _Ebony_, 9 (November 1953), 136-40.

JOHNNY SAXTON

3505. Kane, M. "A Mighty Peculiar Fight: Johnny Saxton Defeats Basilio." _Sports Illustrated_, 4 (March 26, 1956), 31-32.

3506. Kane, M. "Cleveland Clincher: Basilio-Saxton Fight." _Sports Illustrated_, 6 (March 4, 1957), 26.

3507. Kane, M. "Terror: 342 Seconds With Basilio-Saxton." _Sports Illustrated_, 6 (March 4, 1957), 22-23.

3508. Lardner, John. Plain Guy Wins: Johnny Saxton." _Newsweek_, 48 (September 24, 1956), 72

3509. "Philadelphia Fiasco: Johnny Saxton." _Time_, 44 (November 1, 1954), 57.

3510. Terrell, R. "And Down Went Number One: Johnny Saxon!" _Sports Illustrated_, 15 (November 27, 1961), 22-25.

ERNIE SHAVER

3511. "Holmes Gambles WBC Belt vs. Shavers In Las Vegas." _Jet_, 56 (September 6, 1979), 50.

3512. "Shavers Shapes Up Now That His Wife Is Boss." _Jet_, 56 (June 7, 1979, 53.

LEON SPINKS

3513. "Brothers Hands Were Nice." Black Sports, 9 (November 1976), 39-43.

3514. Cheers, Michael. "Fight Fans Slur Spinks With Cries of Nigger." Jet, 54 (July 27, 1978), 52-53.

3515. Kisner, Ronald E. "Leon Spinks Changes The Heavyweight Pace." Jet, 53 (March 9, 1978), 44-47.

3516. "Leon Spinks Defeats Muhammad Ali For World's Heavyweight Crown." Washington Post, (February 16, 1978), p. 1, sec. D.

3517. "Leon Spinks Is Laughing All The Way To The Bank With His Black Lawyers." Jet, 55 (October 19, 1978), 53.

3518. "Leon Spinks: The Boy Who Did A Man's Job On Muhammad Ali." Ebony, 33 (May 1978), 130-1.

3519. Simms, Gregory. "Butch Lewis and Leon Spinks Knew All Along." Jet, 53 (March 9, 1978), 48, 50.

3520. Simms, Gregory. "Leon and Micheal Spinks: Star Boxing Brothers Give Advice On How To Handle Instant Glory." Jet, 52 (May 19, 1977), 48-49.

3521. Simms, Gregory and Vandell Cobb." Other Side of Leon Spinks." Jet, 54 (June 8, 1978), 26-31.

3522. "Spinks His Own Manager Has Plan To Regain Title." Jet, 57 (December 13, 1979), 48.

JOHN VAUGHN

3524. Hincher, Lee. "Boxer With Talent." Encore, 5 (February 1976), 44.

JOE WALCOTT

3525. Burley, Dan. "Why Walcott Won't Fight." Ebony, 7 (December 1951), 64-66.

3526. "Fiscal Snag Delays Accord On Joe Louis-Joe Walcott Return Bout." New York Times, (February 19, 1948), p. 31.

3527. "Historically Speaking: Joe Walcott." Black Sports, 7 (March 1978), 50+.

3528. "Joe Louis and Joe Walcott Training Plans." New York Times, (May 6, 1948), p. 36.

3529. "Joe Louis and Walcott to Undergo Physical Exams." New York Times, (June 15, 1948), p. 38.

3530. "Joe Walcott Agrees To 20% of Purse." New York Times, (February 7, 1948), p. 11.

3531. "Joe Walcott Drops Manager J. Webster." New York Times, (August 8, 1948), p. 6, sec. 5.

3532. "Joe Walcott Tops In Final '48 Ratings." New York Times, (December 22, 1948), p. 34.

3533. Liebling, A.J. "Reporter At Large: Marciano-Walcott Fight." New Yorker, 28 (October 11, 1952), 81-88.

3534. Liebling, A.J. "Reporter At Larger: Marciano-Walcott Fight." New Yorker, 29 (May 30, 1953), 33-34.

3535. "Louis Favored To Defeat Joe Walcott in Return Bout, Sports Writers Poll." New York Times, (January 6, 1948), p. 20.

3536. "Louis-Walcott Bout-Agreement Reported Near." New York Times, (January 28, 1948), p. 29.

3537. "Louis Walcott Bout Promoters Fail To Agree On Purse Div." New York Times, (January 27, 1948), p. 34.

3538. "Louis-Walcott Bout Radio and Telecast Plans." New York Times, (March 11, 1948), p. 54.

3539. "Louis-Walcott Bout-Louis Wins By Knockout in 11th Round." New York Times, (June 26, 1948), p. 1.

3540. "Louis and Walcott Sign For June 23 Bout." New York Times, (April 15, 1948), p. 32.

3541. "Louis-Walcott Ticket Prices Set." New York Times, (March 28, 1948), p. 33.

3542. "Louis Warns Walcott To Accept Terms or Lose Bout." New York Times, (February 20, 1948), p. 22.

3543. Stevens, Joann. "Jersey Jo Walcott-The Sheriff Never Tires." Black Sports, 6 (July 1976), 51.

3544. "20th Century Sporting Club Confirms Plans for Louis June Bout, NYC; Walcott Likely Opponent Despite Pay Dispute." New York Times, (January 7, 1948), p. 34.

3545. "Walcott Accepts Contract Terms." New York Times, (February 27, 1948), p. 28.

3546. "Walcott Examined." New York Times, (June 18, 1948), p. 28.

3547. "Walcott's Family Comments." New York Times, (June 26, 1948), p. 11.

3548. Young, Andrew S. "What Happened to Jersey Joe's Money?" Ebony, (July 1956), 51-54.

JIMMY YOUNG

3549. Anderson, Dave. "Philadelphia Fighter." Black Sports, 7
      (February 1978), 32-36.

3550. Simms, Gregory. "Young Predicts KO Over Strong Foreman." Jet,
      51 (March 10, 1977), 48+.

3551. Simms, Gregory. "Mrs. Jimmy Young Says Hubby's New Fame Hasn't
      Changed Their Lifestyle." Jet, 52 (April 21, 1977), 50.

FOOTBALL

JIM BROWN

3552. "Acquitted on Charges That He Assaulted Motorist After Minor Traffic Accident." New York Times, (February 6, 1970), p. 28.

3553. "Biggest Man In Pro Football." Ebony, 17 (January 1962), 63-68.

3554. "Brown On Brown." Newsweek, 64 (November 16, 1964), 62-63.

3555. "Brown Power." Newsweek, 71 (January 15, 1968), 75+.

3556. "Elected To Pro Football Hall of Fame." New York Times, (February 5, 1971), p. 14.

3557. "Excerpt of Interview of Ex-Cleveland Browns Fullback." Washington Post, (October 23, 1977), p. 4, sec. D.

3558. Flynn, J. "He's The Greatest Since Jim Thorpe." Life, 55 (October 25, 1963), 47-9.

3559. "Footage Instead of Yardage for Jim Brown: With Report by W. Warga." Life, 62 (May 19, 1967), 103-4+.

3560. "From Pigskin To Redskins." Life, 57 (September 18, 1964), 67-8+.

3561. Gillespie, C. "Jim Brown Comes To Mississippi." Nation, 211 (Septemer 21, 1970), 236-9.

3562. "J. Toback's Memoir of Brown Reviewed." New York Time, (May 16, 1970), p. 44, sec. 7.

3563. "Jim Brown." New York Times, (July 13, 1970), p. 33.

3564. "Jim Brown in "Rio Conchos." Sepia, 13 (December 1964), 22-25.

3565. "Jim Brown Makes It Big In Hollywood." Sepia, 16 (October 1967), 64-68.

3566. "Jimmy Brown's Own Story...Football Bruisers I've Bumped Into;
      Excerpts From Off My Chest." Look, 28 (October 10, 1964),
      104-12+.

3567. "Jimmy Brown's Own Story...My Case Against Paul Brown' Excerpts
      From Off My Chest." Look, 28 (October 6, 1964), 62-4+.

3568. "Jimmy, the Giant Killer." Time, 82 (October 25, 1963), 84.

3569. "Knock For Running." Time, 82 (October 4, 1963), 66+.

3570. Masin, H.L. "Met Mr. Fullback." Senior Scholastic, 81
      (October 31, 1962), 22.

3571. Masin, H.L. "Mr. Fullback and Mr. Halfback." Senior Scholatic,
      98 (September 27, 1968), 40.

3572. Maule, Tex. "Curtain Falls On A Long Run." Sports Illustrated,
      25 (July 25, 1966), 18-20.

3573. Maule, Tex. "Plan That Worked: Cleveland Browns vs. New York
      Giants." Sports Illustrated, 19 (October 21, 1963), 16-19.

3574. Mitchell, F. "Jim Brown Gentle Men Juggernaut." Ebony, 15
      (November 1959), 158+.

3575. "New Day For Black Rock." Time, 88 (July 22, 1966), 48.

3576. "People Are Talking About Jim Brown of the Cleveland Browns."
      Vogue, 142 (December 1963), 122-24.

3577. Poinsett, Alex. "Controversial Jim Brown." Ebony, 20 (December
      1964), 64-6+.

3578. Poinsett, Alex. Pro Football's Mightiest Player." Ebony, 19
      (January 1964), 32-34+.

3579. Sanders, Charles L. "Film Star Jim Brown." Ebony, 24 (December
      1968), 192-194+.

3580. Sanders, Charles L. "Jim Brown: Why I Quit Football." Ebony, 22
      (December 1966), 119-120.

3581. "Syracuse Gets Off The Ground." Life, 41 (October 8, 1956), 147-
      8+.

3582. "Waves For Family Fun." American City, 86 (October 1971),
      101-102.

3583. "Why Women Worry Football's Jim Brown." Sepia, 15 (March 1966),
      28-32.

3584. "Wins TD Club Timmie Award." Washington Post, (January 18, 1976),
      p. 8, sec. C.

ROOSEVELT BROWN

3585. Wallace, W.N.   "Left Tackle: Roosevelt Brown."   New York Times Magazine, (November 8, 1964), 137-41.

KEN BURROUGH

3586. Twersky, Marty.   "The Superstar Nobody Knows."   Black Sports, 7 (November 1977), 55-57.

EARL CAMPBELL

3587. "Black Gridders Urged To Ignore Heisman Trophy."   Jet, 53 (December 29, 1977), 51.

3588. Burgen, Michele.   "Very Proud Mom."   Ebony, 33 (March 1978), 56-58+.

3589. Lincoln, M.L.   "Real Earl Campbell Stands Up."   Sport, 69 (September 1979), 20-1+.

3590. Newman, B.   "Roots of Greatness."   Sports Illustrated, 51 (September 3, 1979), 94-8+.

ANTHONY DAVIS

3591. "Anthony Davis Gets 2nd Grid Pact-And 2nd Rolls-Royce."   Jet, 49 (November 20, 1975), 47.

3592. Trubo, Richard.   "Football or Baseball...Where Will Anthony Davis Make His First $1 Million."   Sepia, 23 (August 1974), 24-38.

ERNIE DAVIS

3593. Davis, Ernie and Bob August.   "I'm Not Unlucky."   Saturday Evening Post, 236 (March 20, 1963), 60-62.

3594. "Ernie Davis: Everybody's All America."   Ebony, 17 (December 1961), 73-74.

3595. "Pro Patient: Ernie Davis."   Newsweek, 60 (October 22, 1962), 76.

3596. Wright, A.   "Ernie Davis: A Man of Courage."   Sports Illustrated, 18 (May 17, 1963), 24-25.

WILLIE DAVIS

3597. "Willie Davis Helps All-Stars Prep For Kansas City Chiefs."   Philadelphia Tribune, (August 1, 1970).

TONY DORSETT

3598. Axelrod, Phil.   "Tony Dorsett's Number Comes Due."   Black Sport, 9 (December 1976), 44+.

3599. Marshall, J. "Tony D. Comes To Big D." Sports Illustrated, 47 (September 19, 1977), 38-43+.

3600. Ribowsky, Mark. "Flash, Smash and That Ole Time Religion." Black Sports, 7 (December 1977), 16-29.

3601. "Rookie Runs For The Super Bowl." Sport, 66 (January 1978), 18-21.

3602. Sanders, Charles L. "Tony Dorsett." Ebony, 33 (August 1978), 132-4+.

3603. Simms, Gregory and Vandell Cobb. "Tony Dorsett Bumps Into Success, and Gets Bruised." Jet, 54 (May 11, 1978), 46-48+.

CHUCK FOREMAN

3604. Holbert, Allan. "Why Vikings Fans Are Cheering, Pay Foreman More." Black Sports, 9 (November 1976), 22+.

JOE GILLIAM

3605. Kisner, Ronald E. "Super Hopes For QB Gilliam." Jet, 49 (February 5, 1976), 48+.

3606. "QB Joe Gilliam Resting After Baltimore Attack." Jet, 56 (September 6, 1979), 48.

3607. Stevens, Joann. "How Joe Gilliam Blew His Biggest Chance." Black Sports, 6 (October 1976), 40-43.

JOE GREENE

3608. "Rap With Pittsburgh Steelers Front Four: Interview." Black Sports, 5 (February 1976), 32-36+.

ARCHIE GRIFFIN

3609. "Griffin's Greatest Gain." Ebony, 31 (February 1976), 96-98+.

FRANCO HARRIS

3610. Fraker, S. and S. Lesher. "Offside In Pittsburgh?" Newsweek, 89 (May 9, 1977), 40.

3611. Roden, Bill. "Franco Harris: I've Been Lucky-But Only When I've Worked Hard." Ebony, (October 1976), 112-114+.

BOB HAYES

3612. Underwood, J. "How Fast Is The Fastest Man Alive?" Sports Illustrated, 20 (May 18, 1964), 26-29.

DAVE JONES

3613. "Deacon Misses Football, Considers Job As Coach." Jet, 56 (August 16, 1979), 48.

ED "TO TALL" JONES

3614. "Jones Quits Cowboys For Ring." Winston-Salem Journal, (June 20, 1979).

GENE LIPSCOMB

3615. "Big Daddy From Baltimore." Life, 47 (October 26, 1959), 141.

3616. "Big Daddy Lipscomb." Ebony, 15 (January 1960), 37-40.

3617. Linn, E. "Sad End of Big Daddy Lipscomb." Saturday Evening Post, 236 (July 27, 1963), 73-74.

3618. Lipscomb, Eugene "Big Daddy: I'm Still Scared." Saturday Evening Post, 233 (November 12, 1965), 80.

FLOYD LITTLE

3619. "Floyd Little On The Run." Ebony, 21 (December 1965), 86-88.

3620. "Ghostly Power of Old 44: Floyd Little." Life, 59 (November 26, 1965), 111-12.

3621. Stevens, Jo Ann. "Floyd Little: Ex-Bronco Running Back Extends Helping Hand To Youth..." Black Sports, 5 (May 1976), 44+.

LAWRENCE McCUTHEON

3622. Green, Ted. "McCutcheon Hasn't Gone Hollywood Yet...And Probably Never Will." Black Sports, 9 (November 1976), 30-31+.

REGGIE MCKENZIE

3623. "An Interview With Reggie McKenzie." Black Sports, 7 (October 1977), 48-54.

Ollie Matson

3624. "Football Coach's Dream Player: Ollie Matson." Ebony, 12 (January 1957), 23-32.

BOBBY MITCHELL

3625. "For 30 Years No Black Player Had Worn The Uniform of the Washington Redskins, In 1962 The Door Was Finally Opened." Black Sports, 7 (January 1978), 57+.

LYDELL MITCHELL

3626. Ribowsky, Mark. "Lydell Does Everything But Sell Hot Dogs."
Black Sports, 9 (November 1976), 28-29+.

LENNY MOORE

3627. "Artful Dodger: Lenny Moore." Time, 76(December 5, 1960),
45.

3628. Schmidt, J.G. "Lenny Moore: Colt's Sputnik." Sepia, 10
(December 1961), 56-59.

WALTER PAYTON

3629. "Bears and Walter Payton To Agree On Huge Contract." Jet, 54
(August 3, 1978), 50.

3630. "Bears' Payton May Be 1st Gridder To Get $1 Million." Jet, 56
(August 16, 1979), 48.

3631. Bonventre, P. and S. Monroe. "Sweetness In A Bear." Newsweek, 90
(December 5, 1977), 63.

3632. Harris, Ron. "Sweetness." Ebony, 35 (December 1979), 102-44.

3633. "Payton Run All Over The Place." Sports Illustrated, 47 (November
28, 1977), 26-7.

3634. "Running Wild." Time, 110 (December 19, 1977), 90.

GALE SAYERS

3635. "Gale Sayers Is Chosen NFL's Best." Winston-Salem Journal,
(December 4, 1969).

3636. "Gale Sayers: Pro Football Rambling Rookie." Ebony, 21 (January
1966), 70-71.

3637. Harris, Frank. "Gayle Sayers' Life After The Pros." Black
Collegian, 8 (September-October 1978), 152-155.

3638. Masin, H.L. "Gale of Hurricane Force." Senior Scholastic, 85
(October 21, 1964), 22.

3639. Maule, Tex. "Extravagant Outing For A Rare Rookie: Gale Sayers."
Sports Illustrated, 23 (December 6, 1965), 97-99.

3640. "Pain In Knees Retires Speedster Sayers." Jet, 43 (September 28
1972), 52-53.

3641. "Sayers Comes All The Way Back." Black Sports, 9 (November 1976),
16+.

3642. "Sayers' Greatest Run." Winston-Salem Journal-Sentinel,
(December 17, 1969).

O.J. SIMPSON

3643. Anderson, D. "O.J. Simpson's Run To Glory." Reader's Digest, 111 (November 1977), 217-18+.

3644. Axthelm, Pete. "Juice Is Loose." Newsweek, 88 (September 27, 1976), 65+.

3645. Axthelm, Pete. "Juice Runs Wild." Newsweek, 86 (October 27, 1975), 70-2.

3646. Axthelm, Pete. "O.J. The Juice Really Flows." Newsweek, 82 (November 26, 1976), 67-70.

3647. Baum, P. "Meet Superstar O.J. Simpson: Home Is Always Where The Heart Is." Parents Magazine, 52 (February 1977), 42-3.

3648. Blount, R. "Movie Talk." Sports Illustrated, 42 (February 3, 1975), 9.

3649. Bock, Hal. "Simpson Top Male Athlete." Winston-Salem Journal, (January 17, 1974).

3650. Bonfante, J. "O.J." Life, 63 (October 27, 1967), 74A-74B.

3651. Collier, Ken. "O.J. Simpson: The Juice Comes Home." Black Colelgian, 8 (November-December 1978), 74-75.

3652. "Countdown To Pasadena." Time, 92 (October 11, 1968), 42+.

3653. Deford, Frank. "Ready If You Are, O.J." Sports Illustrated, 31 (July 14, 1969), 16-19.

3654. Deford, Frank. "What Price Heroes." Sports Illustrated, 30 (June 9, 1969), 32-4+.

3655. Fimrite, R. "Vintage Juice 1864 and 2003." Sports Illustrated, 39 (December 24, 1978), 26-9.

3656. Jenkins, D. "All The Way With O.J." Sports Illustrated, 27 (November 27, 1967), 16-21.

3657. Jenkins, D. "Great One Confronts O.J." Sports Illustrated, 27 (November 29, 1967), 32-34+.

3658. Jenkins, D. "Juice Is Turned On Again." Sports Illustrated, 43 (October 13, 1975), 28-30+.

3659. Jones, R.F. "Caught Up In The Christmas Rush." Sports Illustrated, 45 (December 13, 1976), 65-6+.

3660. Jones, R.F. "$2.5 Million Man." Sports Illustrated, 45 (July 26, 1976), 20-1.

3661. Larner, John. "O.J. Simpson: I'm Coming Back, I Want It Again!" Saturday Evening Post, 241 (October 5, 1968), 59-61.

3662. McVay, I.R. "O.J. Simpson: USC's Jet Speed Powerhouse." Look, 32 (October 15, 1968), 114-17+.

3663. Marshall, J. "Now You See Him, Now You Don't." Sports Illustrated, 39 (October 29, 1973), 30-2.

3664. Marshall, J. "What's Making O.J. Go?" Sports Illustrated, 45 (July 26, 1976), 20-1.

3665. Masin, H.L. "All The Way With O.J.!" Senior Scholastic, 93 (October 18, 1968), 32.

3666. "O.J. Tells How Sex and Success Threaten Career." Jet, 55 (November 16, 1978), 46-48+.

3667. "O.J. To Go." Newsweek, 73 (January 13, 1969), 76.

3668. Rhoden, Bill. "O.J. Simpson." Ebony, 31 (January 1976), 50-2+.

3669. Robinson, Louie. "O.J. Simpson." Ebony, 24 (December 1968), 170+.

3670. Shrake, Edward. "First Tast of O.J. Is OK." Sports Illustrated, 31 (August 25, 1969), 20-3.

3671. Shrake, Edward. "Juice On A Juicy Road." Sports Illustrated, 41 (August 19, 1974), 36-8+.

3672. Shrake, Edward. "Name of the Game is O.J." Sports Illustrated, 35 (September 6, 1971), 18-19.

3673. "Simpson Settles In." Time, 102 (October 8, 1973), 68.

3674. "Simpson's Career May Be Finished." Winston-Salem Journal, (November 2, 1977).

3675. Slater, Jack. "O.J. Simpson: The Problems of A Superstar." Ebony, 32 (November 1976), 162-164+.

3676. "Split." People, 11 (April 2, 1979), 113.

3677. "Sportsman of Year and Two to Remember." Sports Illustrated, 27 (December 25, 1967), 24-5.

3678. Stuller, J. "O.J's 49er Gold Rush." Sport, 67 (November 1978), 16-18+.

3679. "Surf's Up For A Rejuvenated O.J." People, 9 (June 12, 1978), 44-45.

3680. "Three For The Trophy." Newsweek, 70 (November 27, 1967), 94.

3681. "2,003: O.J's Odyssey." Newsweek, 82 (December 31, 1973), 36.

3682. Underwood, J. "Sportsman of the Year Runner-Up." Sports Illustrated, 43 (December 22, 1975), 46-7.

3683. Valerio, Joseph. "Juice Runs Beyond Daylight." Black Sports, 9 (November 1976), 34-37.

3684. Wood, P. "What Makes Simpson Run?" New York Times Magazine, (December 14, 1975), 38-9+.

3685. "Year of the Okey-Doke." Time, 102 (December 24, 1973), 57.

3686. Zimmerman, P. "All Dressed Up Nowhere To Go." Sports Illustrated, 51 (November 26, 1979), 38-40.

LYNN SWANN

3687. Deford, Frank. "Champagne, Roses and Donuts." Sports Illustrated, 51 (December 10, 1979), 98-102+.

3688. Good, P. "Swann's Way." Sport, 66 (January 1978), 38-43.

DUANE THOMAS

3689. "Duane Thomas Fails In NFL Tryout With Packers." Jet, 56 (September 13, 1979), 48.

EMLEN TUNNELL

3690. "First Negro Pro Football Coach: Emlen Tunnell." Sepia, 15 (October 1966), 20-22.

3691. "The Toughest Man In Football: Emlen Tunnell of the New York Giants." Ebony, 13 (November 1957), 99-104.

GENE WASHINGTON

3692. "Which is Which Gene Washington." Raleigh (N.C.) News and Observer, (December 23, 1970).

SAMMY WHITE

3693. Ribowsky, Mark. "I Saved Tarkenton's Career." Black Sports, 7 (October 1977), 26-29.

PAUL "TANK" YOUNGER

3694. "The Roughest Man In Football: Paul 'Tank' Younger of the Los Angeles Rams." Ebony, 9 (December 1953), 55-60.

GOLF

PETE BROWN

3695. "Big Time Golf: Pete Brown Hurls His Challenge." Ebony, 22
(May 1967), 130-132+.

3696. "Pete Brown: A Golf Champion At Last." Sepia, 12 (July 1964),
62-67.

LEE ELDER

3697. "Article on Pro Golfers in Upcoming Masters Tournament Named in
Augusta, Ga. April 10-15." New York Times, (April 6, 1975),
p. 7, sec. 5.

3698. "Association Honors Elder, Sullivan and Cox." New York Times,
(March 9, 1977), 23.

3699. "Black Pro Golfer Lee Elder Says That His Main Goal Is To Become
1st Black Golfer to Play in Masters Tournament." New York Times,
(September 8, 1972), 24.

3700. "Comment on Arrival of Lee Elder at Masters Tournament,
Augusta, GA." New York Times, (April 8, 1975), p. 43.

3701. "Comments On Blacks In Pro Tour." Washington Post, (March 14,
1972), p. 3 sec. D.

3702. "Comments On Exclusion From Masters." Washington Post, (April 6,
1972), p. 2, sec. G.

3703. "Dave Anderson On 1st Round in Masters Tournament of Lee Elder 1st
Black in Tournament." New York Times, (April 11, 1975), p. 29.

3704. "C.C. Proclaims Lee Elder Day." Washington Post, (May 4, 1974),
p. 1, sec. D.

3705. "Drama Builds As Elder Readies For Masters Tournament in Augusta." <u>Jet</u>, 48 (April 17, 1975), 52.

3706. "Editorials On Winning Golf Tournament." <u>Washington Post</u>, (April 23, 1974), p. 14, sec. A.

3707. "Elder First Black In Masters With Big Win." <u>Jet</u>, 46 (May 9, 1974), 48+.

3708. "Elder in Masters." <u>Winston-Salem Journal</u>, (April 22, 1974).

3709. "Elder Loses Out in First Try at Masters." <u>Jet</u>, 48 (May 1, 1975), 48-19.

3710. "Farewell To Peanuts." <u>Newsweek</u>, 72 (August 26, 1968), 76-7.

3711. "Favorite Maxim Quoted." <u>Washington Post</u>, (July 28, 1974), p. 14, sec. Potomac Magazine.

3712. "1st Black To Win Major Golf Tourney." <u>Washington Post</u>, (January 7, 1972), p. 1, sec. D.

3713. "For Elder, the Final Wait Will Be Worth It." <u>Winston-Salem Journal</u>, (April 22, 1974).

3714. "Gary Player Invites Negro Golfer Lee Elder To Participate In South African Pro Golfers Assn." <u>New York Times</u>, (June 24, 1971), 48.

3715. "Golf Cart Dispute." <u>Washington Post</u>, (May 15, 1976), p. 1, sec. C.

3716. "Golf Match With President Ford Noted." <u>Washington Post</u>, (May 7, 1975), p. 5, sec. D.

3717. "Golf Trip To S. Africa Viewed." <u>Washington Post</u>, (March 7, 1972), p. 2, sec. D.

3718. "Golf Writers Assn. of America Votes Awards To PGA Executive Director Mark Cox and Players Des Sulivan and Lee Elder." <u>New York Times</u>, (February 18, 1977), p. 20.

2719. "Golfer Lee Elder Becomes First Black To Win International Tourney." <u>Jet</u>, 41 (January 13, 1972), 46-47.

3720. Green, Bob. "Elder in Masters T. of C. On His Mind Now." <u>Winston-Salem Journal</u>, (April 23, 1974).

3721. "Illustration." <u>New York Times</u>, (August 19, 1971), p. 48.

3722. "In Sutton Golf Classic Lee Elder Wins $22,800; Barely Misses Masters Berth." <u>Jet</u>, 42 (September 7, 1972), 57.

3723. "Interviewed." <u>Washington Post</u>, (January 4, 1976), p. 8, sec. C.

3724. "Lee Elder Article On His Participation in the Masters, 1st
By A Black." New York Times, (April 6, 1975), p. 2, sec. 5.

3725. "Lee Elder, First Black Golfer To Complete In Masters Tournament,
Fails To Qualify April 11 For Final 2 Rounds." New York Times,
(April 12, 1975), p. 19.

3726. "Lee Elder, 1st Black To Qualify For Masters Golf Tournament,
Comments on Qualifying and On His Chances of Winning." New York
Times, (April 9, 1975), p. 31.

3727. "Lee Elder-Interviewed." Washington Post, (January 4, 1976),
p. 1, sec. D.

3728. "Lee Elder-Profiled." Washington Post, (May 4, 1976), p. 1,
sec. D.

3729. "Lee Elder, To Be 1st Black To Play In Masters Golf Tournament."
New York Times, (April 25, 1974), p. 52.

3730. "Lee Elder To Play in Racially-Torn South Africa, Explain His
Reason." Jet, (September 16, 1971), 5.

3731. "Lee Trevino Defeats Lee Elder in Playoff on September 4 to
Win Greater Hartford (Conn.) Open Golf Tournament." New York
Times, (September 5, 1972), p. 51.

3732. "Negro Golf Pro Lee Elder Agrees To Compete in South African
Championship and To Play Exhibtion Match Against Gary Player."
New York Times, (August 19, 1971), p. 48.

3733. "9th Annual Lee Elder Celebrity Pro-Am Golf Tournament Featured."
Washington Post, (September 3, 1979), p. 1, sec. D.

3734. "Over The Bunkers." Newsweek, 78 (December 6, 1971), 44.

3735. "Profiled." Washington Post, (May 4, 1976), p. 1, sec. D.

3736. "Receives Key To City From D.C. Mayor." Washington Post,
(May 4, 1974), p. 1, sec. D.

3737. Robinson, Louie. "Lee Elder, Hottest Sophomore In Pro Golf."
Ebony, 24 (September), 60-64+.

3738. "Successful Lee Elder Still Sees Prejudice For Black Pro Golfers."
Jet, 56 (September 6, 1979), 47.

3739. "Washington, D.C. Mayor Washington Proclaims May 3, Lee Elder Day
In Home of 1st Black Golfer To Qualify For Masters." New York
Times, (May 2, 1974), p. 68.

3740. "Wins Monsanto Open Golf Tourney." Washington Post, (April 22,
1974), p. 1, sec. A.

3741. "Elder Polishes Putts For Masters Milestone." Black Sports, 4
(April 1975), 10-13.

RICHARD PALMER

3742. "Richard, Palmer Cop AA Golf Tourney." Jet, 41 (February 24, 1972), 52-55.

CHARLIE SIFFORD

3743. "Blacks On The Greens." Time, 93 (February 14, 1969), 56.

3744. Bradley, B. "Charles Sifford Plays In Greates Meet In Golfdom." Sepia, 10 (May 1961), 78-83.

3745. "Charlie Sifford, First Black on PGA Tour-Signs 3 Year Contract as Head Pro at Sleepy Hollow Golf Course (Breacksville, Ohio)." New York Times, (January 23, 1975), p. 42.

2746. "Charlie Sifford, Greater Hartford Open." New York Times, (August 21, 1967), p. 44.

3747. "Charlie Sifford: Top Negro Golfer." Ebony, 11 (June 1956), 81-84.

3748. "Charlie Sifford Wins PGA Seniors Golf Championship on February 2, Orland, Fla." New York Times, (February 3, 1975), p. 18.

3749. "Charlie Sifford Wins Satellite Sea Pines Open, Hilton Head Island, S.C." New York Times, (November 28, 1971), p. 11, sec. 5.

3750. "Comments On Blacks On Pro Tour." Washington Post, (March 14, 1972), p. 3, sec. D.

3751. "Golf Pays Debt To A Real Pro." Ebony, 24 (April 1969), 44-6+.

3752. Jenkins, D. "Old Charlie Jolts the New Tour." Sports Illustrated, 30, (January 20, 1969), 16-17.

3753. Johnson, W. "Call Back The Years." Sports Illustrated, 30 (March 31, 1969), 56-8+.

3754. Trinkle, J. "Golden Boy of the Fairways, Sifford Gains New Horizons As Golf Contender." Sepia, 11 (February 1962), 34-37.

BILL WRIGHT

3755. "Rookie Golf Champ: Bill Wright Wins National Public Links Crown." Ebony, 14 (October 1959), 127-30.

TENNIS

ARTHUR ASHE

3756. "Ace." Time, 86 (August 13, 1965), 50.

3757. "American Ace." Time, 86 (November 19, 1965), 78.

3758. "Arthur Ashe." Negro History Bulletin, 31 (November 1968), 6.

3759. "Arthur Ashe Advances To Tennis Semifinals." Winston-Salem Journal, (January 13, 1970).

3760. "Arthur Ashe Column On Sports Boycotts." Washington Post, (October 22, 1978), p. 20, sec. P.

3761. "Arthur Ashe Commentary on the Davis Cup and South African Apartheid." Washington Post, (March 16, 1978), p. 1, sec. G.

3762. "Arthur Ashe: Defeat Doesn't Scare Him." Senior Scholastic, 110 (September 22, 1977), 7.

3763. "Arthur Ashe, Hottest Commodity On Tennis Horizon." The Courier, (July 19, 1975).

3764. "Arthur Ashe Says Of His Heart Attack: Not Fair." Jet, 56 (September 13, 1979), 58-59.

3765. "Arthur Ashe Thing." Sports Illustrated, 24 (February 21, 1966), 8.

3766. "Arthur Ashe Urges Protest of South African Racial Policies." Washington Post, (February 2, 1978), p. 1, sec. D.

3767. "Arthur Ashe Volleys Alone." St. Louis Sentinel, (April 2, 1974).

3768. "Arthur Ashe Yields In Two Pro-Net Tourneys." Carolina Times, (February 26, 1972).

3769. "Ashe Beats Borg, Collect $10,000 in Hawaii." Jet, 50 (April 8, 1976), 53.

3770. "Ashe 40 Segregation-Love." Journal and Guide, (May 31, 1975).

3771. "Ashe Hangs Up Racket Retires From Tennis." Winston-Salem Journal, (April 17, 1980).

3772. "Ashe 1st Black Man to Win Wimbledon." Pittsburgh Courier, (July 12, 1975).

3773. "Ashe Foils Detractors To Win $50Gs Title." Jet, 48 (May 29, 1975), 53.

3774. "Ashe, Franolovic Advance to Finals." Journal & Sentinel, (July 27, 1969).

3775. "Ashe Refused African Visa." Greensboro Daily News, (January 29, 1970).

3776. "Ashe Resting Easy After His Heart's False Alarm." Jet, 57 (December 20, 1979), 53.

3777. "Ashe Seeded Eighth in $60,000 Open Tennis Tournament." Philadelphia Tribune, (January 31, 1970).

3778. "Ashe Thumped by Okker In $50Gs Paris Match." Jet, 49 (November 20, 1975), 48.

3779. "Ashe Vows To Play Tennis Again After Heart Attack." Jet, 56 (August 23, 1979), 49.

3780. "Ashe Wins Net Title 3rd Time." Winston-Salem Journal, (April 6, 1970).

3781. "Ashe Wins $10,000 In Pro Tennis Tournament." Jet, 42 (August 17, 1972), 53.

3782. "Ashe Yields To Rod Laver In 7th Match." Journal & Guide, (February 2, 1971).

3783. "Ashe's Form Is U.S. Davis Cup Concern." Carolina Times, (August 23, 1969).

3784. Barnes, A.J. "Ashe Make Doubles Debut With Black Tennis Partner." Jet, 54 (August 3, 1978), 46-47.

3785. "Becomes 1st Negro To Win US Men's Amateur Tennis Champ." New York Times, (August 26, 1968), p. 51.

3786. "Black Scholar Interviews: Arthur Ashe." Black Scholar, 7 (November 1975), 40-7.

3787. Bookman, R. "Arthur Ashe: Still Classy After All These Years." World Tennis, 28 (August 1980), 26-8+.

3788. Bookman, R. "Thinking About Arthur." World Tennis, 27 (October 1979), 6.

3789. Brossard, C. "Arthur Ashe: Hottest New Tennis Star." Look, 30 (April 19, 1966), 110-14.

3790. "Catching Connors in the Stretch." Sports Illustrated, 43 (July 21, 1975), 20-1.

3791. "Center Court At Wimbleton." Travel and America, 33 (May, 1970), 48-53.

3792. Chapin, K. "Arthur All The Way." Sports Illustrated, 29 (September 16, 1968), 26-9.

3793. Chapin, K. "Bittersweet Dregs in the Cup: U.S. Team Win The Davis Cup." Sports Illustrated, 30, (January 6, 1969), 20-21.

3794. Coleman, William. "Is There Another Ashe On The Horizon." Dawn Magazine, (December 1976).

3795. Darden, Norman. "Arthur Ashe: The New King of The Courts." Encore, 4 (September 8, 1975), 36.

3796. Darden, Norman. "Arthur, The New King of the Courts." Life, 65 (September 20, 1968), 30-35.

3797. Deford, Frank. "Lull Beneath The Jacaranda Tree." Sports Illustrated, 39 (December 10, 1973), 30-2+.

3798. Deford, Frank. "Once and Future Diplomat." Sports Illustrated, 34 (March 1, 1971), 62-6+.

3799. Deford, Frank. "Service, But First A Smile." Sports Illustrated, 25 (August 29 1966), 47-50.

3800. Deford, Frank. "Shout For Those Aussies: Excerpt From Ashe, Portrait In Motion." Sports Illustrated, 42 (March 10, 1975), 38-40+.

3801. Deford, Frank. "An Understudy Takes Charge: Arthur Ashe." Sports Illustrated, 23 (August 9, 1965), 18-19.

3802. Dent, Tom. "Arthur Ashe And The Emergence of Black Tennis." Black Collegian, 7 (November-December 1976), 50.

3803. Dowling, E. "Arthur Ashe: On Politics and Sports: Interview." Senior Scholastic, 110 (September 22, 1977), 4-6+.

3804. Ebert, A. "Arthur Ashe: Changing Courts." Essence, 11 (September 1980), 88-9+.

3805. "Enter Arthur Ashe." Life, 59 (October 15, 1965), 61-62+.

3806. Ferdinand, Val. "When Is A Champion Not A Champion." Black Collegian, 6 (September-October 1975), 35+.

3807. "1st Excerpt From Arthur Ashe." Washington Post, (June 25, 1975), p. 1, sec. E.

3808. "First Negro Davis Cupper: Arthur Ashe." Ebony, 18 (October 1963), 151-52.

3809. Gordon, H. "Pioneer in Short White Pants." New York Times Magazine, (January 2, 1966), 6-7.

3810. "Is Married at UN Chapel, NYC." New York Times, (February 21, 1977), p. 19.

3811. "Interviewed: Arthur Ashe." Washington Post, (August 16, 1974), p. 1, sec. D.

3812. "Interviewed on 1975 Performance." Washington Post, (October 1, 1975), p. 3, sec. E.

3813. "Interview With Arthur Ashe." Black Sports, 9 (December 1976), 14.

3814. "It Couldn't Be A Heart Attack-But It Was." Sports Illustrated, 51 (September 3, 1979), 24-5.

3815. Jares, Joe. "Arthur Was King For A Day." Sports Illustrated, 23 (September 20, 1965), 36-37.

3816. Jares, Joe. "Centre Court Case." Sports Illustrated, 43 (July 14, 1975), 12-15.

3817. Johnson, Dan. "Better Backhand." Black Sports, 6 (September 1976), 37.

3818. Kalyn, W. "Television." World Tennis, 27 (August 1979), 62.

3819. Kessler, J. "For A Recovering Arthur Ashe His Heart Attack May Not Be A Net Loss." People, 12 (September 17, 1979), 86+.

3820. Kisner, Ronald E. "Ashe Breaks Bachelor Service For Love Match With Photographer." Jet, 51 (March 3, 1977), 12-14.

3821. Kisner, Ronald E. "Ashe Clobbers Conners To Cop Wimbledon Title." Jet, 48 (July 24, 1975), 44-50.

3822. Kisner, Ronald E. "Davis Cup Protesters Only Footnote On History: Ashe." Jet, 52 (May 5, 1977), 54-56.

3823. Kisner, Ronald E. "Tennis Millionaire Begins Another Life With His New Bride." Jet, 52 (March 24, 1977), 20-25+.

3824. Lindsay, Beverly. Portrait In Motion. Essence, 7 (June 1976), 37.

3825. Lupica, M. "Ashe Is Back." World Tennis, 26 (April 1979), 44-6+.

3826. McPhee, J. "Profiles." New Yorker, 45 (June 7, 1969), 45-58+.

3827. McPhee, J. "Profiles." New Yorker, 45 (June 14, 1969), 44-48+.

3828. "My Most Unforgettable Character." Readers Digest, 101 (September 1972), 151-5.

3829. "People Are Talking About." Vogue, 152 (November 15, 1968), 132-133.

3830. "Portrait." New York Times, (January 29, 1970), p. 48.

3831. Powlis, LaVerne. "On Court and Off Ashe Plays A Low-Key Game." Black Sports, 5 (August 1975), 24-27.

3832. "Pressure On Kids Remains But Incentives Are Greater." World Tennis, 26 (June, 1978), 73-74.

3833. "Professional Guide To Watching Tennis." New York Times Magazine, (February 22, 1976), 32-33.

3834. "Pros Want Arthur Ashe." Sepia, 17 (December 1968), 64-67.

3835. "Rejuvenated Ashe Knocks Off Clowning Nastase." Winston-Salem Sentinel, (January 1, 1978).

3836. "Rep Drinan Writes Letter To Editor on October 22, 1978: Arthur Ashe Article On Olympics." Washington Post, (November 3, 1978), p. 22, sec. A.

3837. "Right To Be Oneself." Ebony, 30 (May 1975), 132-133.

3838. Robinson, Louie. "Arthur Ashe First Black Male Tennis Star Reaches Zenith in Honors and Cash Rewards." Ebony, 31 (November 1975), 144-146.

3839. Robinson, Louie. "Arthur Ashe: The Man Who Refused To Quit." Ebony, 34 (April 1979), 74-76+.

3840. Robinson, Louie. "Arthur Ashe." Ebony, 31 (November 1975), 144-6+.

3841. Robinson, Louie. "Arthur Ashe: The Man Who Refused To Quit." Ebony, 34, (April 1979), 74-6+.

3842. Robinson, Louie. "Crown For King Arthur." Ebony, 24 (November 1969), 64-6+.

3843. "2nd Excerpt From Biography." Washington Post, (June 26, 1975), p. 1, sec. E.

3844. "2nd In Series On Blacks In Tennis." Washington Post, (June 16, 1975), p. 1, sec. D.

3845. Smilgis, M. "Couples." People, 11 (March 12, 1979), 79-80+.

3846. Smith, Doug. "Arthur Ashe: Businessman." Black Enterprises, 6 (April 1976), 43.

3847. "South African Davis Cup Team Selection of Peter Lamb Discussed." Washington Post, (February 14, 1978), p. 2, sec. D.

3848. "Sports Hero." Harper' Bazaar, 103 (May 1970), 110-113.

3849. "Subject of Kraft Column." Washington Post, (July 20, 1975), p. 7. sec. C.

3850. Swift, E.M. "It Was A Grave Ending For Arthur." Sports Illustrated, 50 (February 5, 1979), 22-24+.

3851. Taubman, P. "Working Out With Arthur Ashe." Esquire, 91 (June 5, 1979), 33-5.

3852. "Ten Bad Years Ahead Says Arthur Ashe." The Philadelphia Tribune, (March 30, 1971).

3853. "Tennis Clinic Held At the Rock Creek Tennis Stadium." Washington Post, (July 27, 1978), p. 2, sec. DC.

3854. "Tennis Star Arthur Ashe Describes His Heart Attack." Washington Post, (August 29, 1979), p. 1, sec. A.

3855. "Tennis Tips: The Wright Theorum In Which The Writer Progresses-Geometrically-To Rival Ashe." Black Sports, 5 (April 1976), 45+.

3856. "To Wed Jean Marie Moutoussamy February 20." New York Times, (February 17, 1977), p. 52.

3857. "Upset At Wimbledon." Time, 106 (July 14, 1975), 42.

3858. Uys, S. "No To Arthur Ashe." New Republic, 162 (February 14, 1970), 17-18.

3859. "Views Wimbledon Win." Washington Post, (July 19, 1975), p. 1, sec. E.

3860. Watson, Jay. "Astounding Arthur Ashe." Black Collegian, 6 (September-October 1975), 34-35.

3861. "What America Means To Me." Readers Digest, 108 (March 1976), 119-120.

3862. Winn, H.W. "Sporting Scene." New Yorker, 44 (September 28, 1968), 136+.

3863. Winn, H.W. "From Wimbledon To Forest Hills- A Summer To Remember. New Yorker, 51 (October 13, 1975), 120-8+.

ALTHEA GIBSON

3864. "Althea Gibson's Big Switch." Sepia, 14 (August 1965), 32-36.

3865. "Althea's Film Debut." Ebony, 14 (July 1959), 73-74.

3866. "Althea Has Finally Arrived: Tennis Player Who Cracked Tournament Race Bars Wins Major Titles In Europe." Ebony, 11 (August 1956), 35-38.

3867. "Althea's Odyssey." Life, 41 (July 2, 1956), 88+.

3868. "I Wanted To Be Somebody." Saturday Evening Post, 23 (August 23, 1958), 7-19+; (August 30, 1958), 30+; (September 6, 1958), 30+.

3869. "New Althea." Sepia, 11 (July 1962), 28-31.

3870. "Where Are They Now?" Newsweek, 74 (September 1, 1969), 8.

3871. "Update on Althea Gibson." Washington Post, (June 5, 1977), p. 1, sec. F.

APPENDIXES

A

Vertical Files, Scrapbooks, Newspaper Clippings, Letters, Documents, and Doctoral Dissertations

---

A SELECTED LIST

JACK JOHNSON

1. Jack Johnson Verticle File Folders
   Schomburg Collection, New York.

2. Jack Johnson Verticle File Folders
   Howard University, Washington, D.C.

3. Jack Johnson "Confessions," in possession of Ring Magazine
   New York.

JOE LOUIS

1. Scrapbooks and newspaper clippings, 1935-1941. University of
   Michigan, Michigan Historical Collection. Ann Arbor, Michigan.
   This collection includes over ninety bound volumes.

2. Newspaper clippings, letters and documents, Alexander Gumby
   Collection on The American Negro. Columbia University,
   New York, New York.

3. Verticle Files, Moorland Spingarn Research Center, Howard
   University, Washington, D.C.

4. Amsterdam News, Clipping Files, New York.

5. Verticle Files, Wake Forest University, Winston-Salem, N.C.

6. Verticle Files, Winston-Salem State University, Winston-Salem,
   N.C.

JACKIE ROBINSON

1. Verticle Files Folders, Moorland-Spingarn Research Center, Howard University, Washington, D.C.

2. Verticle Files Folders, Schomburg Collection, New York.

3. Verticle Files Folders, Winston-Salem State University, Winston-Salem, N.C.

JESSE WINTERS

Winters, Jesse "Nip" and John Holway. "Baseball Reminiscences of Washington's Jesse "Nip" Winters: How I Struck Out Babe Ruth and Beat Lefty Grove." Records of the Columbia Historical Society of Washington, D.C., 1971-1972. Vol. 48, 1973, pp. 752-757.

DOCTORAL DISSERTATIONS

A Selected List

1. Brower, Jonathan Jacob. "The Black Side of Football: The Salience of Race." Unpublished Doctoral Dissertation, University of California, Santa Barbara, 1972. 375 pp.

2. Farmer, Greene Jr. "Social Implication of Black Professional Baseball in the United States." Unpublished Doctoral Dissertation, United States International University, 1975. 168 pp.

3. Harvey, John. "The Role of American Negroes in Organized Baseball," Unpublished Doctoral Dissertation, Columbia University, Teachers College, 1961. 171 pp.

B

Baseball

MOST VALUABLE PLAYERS

Baseball Writer's Association
National League
(*Black Players)

Year	Players
1949	*Jackie Robinson
1950	Jim Konstanty
1951	*Roy Campanella
1952	Hank Sauer
1953	*Roy Campanella
1954	*Willie Mays
1955	*Roy Campanella
1956	*Don Newcombe
1957	*Henry Aaron
1958	*Ernie Banks
1959	*Ernie Banks
1960	Dick Groat
1961	*Frank Robinson
1962	*Maury Wills
1963	Sandy Koufax
1964	Ken Boyer
1965	*Willie Mays
1966	Roberto Clemente
1967	Orlando Cepeda
1968	*Bob Gibson
1969	*Willie McCovey
1970	Johnny Bench
1971	*Joe Torre
1972	Johnny Bench
1973	Pete Rose
1974	Steve Garvey
1975	*Joe Morgan

1976	*Joe Morgan
1977	*George Foster
1978	*Dave Parker
1979	*Willie Stargell, Keith Hernandez (Tie)

American League
(*Black Players)

Year	Players
1963	*Elston Howard
1964	Brooks Robinson
1965	Zoilo Versailes
1966	*Frank Robinson
1967	Carl Yastrzemski
1968	Denny McLain
1969	Harmon Killebrew
1970	John (Boog) Powell
1971	Vida Blue
1972	*Dick Allen
1973	*Reggie Jackson
1974	Jeff Burroughs
1975	Fred Lynn
1976	Thurman Munson
1977	*Rod Carew
1978	*Jim Rice
1979	*Don Baylor

ALL-TIME HOME RUN LEADERS

Players	HR
*Hank Aaron........	755
Babe Ruth.........	714
*Willie Mays.......	660
*Frank Robinson....	586
Harmon Killebrew...	573
Mickey Mantle.....	536
Jimmy Foxx........	534
Ted Williams......	521
*Willie McCovey....	521
Ed Mathews........	512
*Ernie Banks.......	512
Mel Ott...........	511
Lou Ghrig.........	493
Stan Musial.......	475
*Willie Stargell...	472
*Billy Williams....	426
Carl Yastrzemski..	419
*Reggie Jackson....	410
Duke Snider.......	407
Al Kaline........	399

C

Basketball

NBA MOST VALUABLE PLAYERS
(*Black Players)

Year

1958	*Bill Russell
1959	Bob Pettit
1960	*Wilt Chamberlain
1961	*Bill Russell
1962	*Bill Russell
1963	*Bill Russell
1964	*Oscar Robertson
1965	*Bill Russell
1966	*Wilt Chamberlain
1967	*Wilt Chamberlain
1968	*Wilt Chamberlain
1969	*Wes Unseld
1970	*Willis Reed
1971	*Lew Alcindor
1972	*Kareem Abdul-Jabbar
1973	Dave Cowens
1974	*Kareem Abdul-Jabbar
1975	*Bob McAdoo
1976	*Kareem Abdul-Jabbar
1977	*Kareem Abdul-Jabbar
1978	Bill Walton
1979	*Moses Malone
1980	*Kareem Abdul-Jabbar

NBA SCORING LEADERS

Year	Scoring Champion	Pts.	Avg.
1960	*Wilt Chamberlain...........	2,707	37.9
1961	*Wilt Chamberlain...........	3,033	38.4
1962	*Wilt Chamberlain...........	4,029	50.4
1963	*Wilt Chamberlain...........	3,586	44.8
1964	*Wilt Chamberlain...........	2,948	36.5

NBA Scoring Leaders (cont'd)

1965	*Wilt Chamberlain...........	2,534	34.7
1966	*Wilt Chamberlain...........	2,649	33.5
1967	Rick Barry.................	2,775	35.6
1968	*Dave Bing..................	2,142	27.1
1969	*Elvin Hayes...............	2,327	28.4
1970	Jerry West.................	2,309	31.2
1971	*Lew Alcindor..............	2,596	31.7
1972	*Kareem Abdul-Jabbar(Alcindor)	2,822	34.8
1973	*Nate Archibald............	2,719	34.0
1974	*Bob McAdoo................	2,261	30.6
1975	*Bob McAdoo................	2,831	34.5
1976	*Bob McAdoo................	2,427	31.1
1977	Pete Maravich.............	2,273	31.1
1978	*George Gervin.............	2,232	27.2
1979	*George Gervin.............	2,365	29.6
1980	*George Gervin.............	2,585	33.1

D

Black Boxing Champions
All Divisions

HEAVYWEIGHT

Years Held	Name
1908-1915	Jack Johnson
1937-1949	Joe Louis
1949-1951	Ezzard Charles
1951-1952	Jersey Joe Walcott
1956-1959	Floyd Patterson
1960-1962	
1962-1964	Sonny Liston
	Cassius* Clay
1964-1967*	(Muhammad Ali)
1970-1973	Joe Frazier
1973-1974	George Foreman
1974-1978	Muhammad Ali
1978-1979	Leon Spinks, Muhammad Ali
1978	Ken Norton (WBC) Larry Holmes (WBC)**
1979	John Tate (WBA)*
1980	Mike Weaver (WBA)*

LIGHT HEAVYWEIGHT

Years Held	Name
1922-1923	Battling Siki
1935-1939	John Henry Lewis
1952-1961	Archie Moore
1961-1963	Harold Johnson
1961-1963	Jose Torres
1965-1966	Jose Torres
1966-1968	Dick Tiger
1968-1974	Bob Foster

*World Boxing Association
**World Boxing Council

LIGHT HEAVY WEIGHT (cont'd)

1975-1977	John Conten*
1978	Marvin Johnson*
1979	Matthew Saad Muhammad**
1980	Eddi Mustava Muhammad*

MIDDLEWEIGHT

Years Held	Name
1926	Tiger Flowers
1931-1952	Gorilla Jones
1951; 1951-1952	Sugar Ray Robinson
1955-1957; 1957; 1958-1960	
1951	Randy Turpin
1962-1963; 1965-1966	Dick Tiger
1966-1968	Emile Griffith
1980	Marvin Haglar**

WELTERWEIGHT

Years Held	Name
1901-1904; 1904-1906	Joe Walcott
1931	Young Jack Thompson
1938-1940	Henry Armstrong
1946-1951	Sugar Ray Robinson
1951	Johnny Bratton
1951-1954	Kid Gavilan
1954-1955; 1956	Johnny Saxon
1958	Virgil Akins
1960-1961	Benny Kid Paret
1963-1966	Emile Griffith
1966-1969	Curtis Cokes
1979-1981	Sugar Ray Leonard**

LIGHTWEIGHT

Years Held	Name
1901-1908	Joe Gans
1938-1939	Henry Armstrong
1942-1944 (New York)	Beau Jack
1944-1947 (New York)	Bob Montgomery
1945-1947 (NBA)	Ike Williams
1947-1951	
1951-1952	Jimmy Carter
1952-1954;1954-1955	
1955-1956	Wallace Bud Smith
1956-1962	Joe Brown

FEATHERWEIGHT

Years Held	Name
1890-1899	George Dixon
1932-1934	Kid Chocolate
(New York)	
1937-1938	Henry Armstrong
1941-1942	Chalky Wright
1948-1949;1950-1957	Sandy Saddler
1957-1959	Hogan Kid Bassey
1959-1963	Davey Moore

BANTAMWEIGHT

Years Held	Name
1890-1892	George Dixon
1929-1935	Panama Al Brown
1940	George Pace
1947	Harold Dade
1953-1954	Jimmy Carruthers
	(abandoned title)

E

Football Records
Held by Blacks to 1980

JIM BROWN

Most Games 100 yards or more, Career, 58 (1975-1965)
Most Touchdowns Rushing, Career, 106 (1975-1965)

FRANCO HARRIS

Most Rushing Attempts, Game, 41 (October 17, 1976)

WALTER PAYTON

Most Yards Gained, Game, 275 (November 29, 1077)
Most Rushing Attempts, Season, 369 (1979)

O.J. SIMPSON

Most Yards Gained, Season, 2,003 (1973)
Most Games, 100 Yards or more, Season, 11 (1973)
Most Games, 200 Yards or more Career, 6 (1969-1978)

F

Hall of Fame
Black Members

BASEBALL

Jack Robinson	(1962)*
Roy Campanella	(1969)*
Leroy Robert Paige	(1971)**
Joshua Gibson	(1972)**
Walter Leonard	(1972)**
Monford Irvin	(1973)**
James T. Bill	(1974)**
William J. Johnson	(1975)**
Oscar M. Charleston	(1976)**
John H. Lloyd	(1977)**
Martin Dihigo	(1977)**
Ernest Banks	(1977)*
Willie Howard Mays	(1979)*
Andrew Rube Foster	(1981)**
Bob Gibson	(1981)*

BASKETBALL

Elgin Baylor
Wilt Chamberlain
Oscar Robertson
Bill Russell

*Elected By The Baseball Writers
**Appointed By The Hall of Fame Committee on Negro Baseball Leagues

BOXING

Henry Armstrong, Feather, Light, Welter
Ezzard Charles, Heavy
Kid Chocolate, Feather
George Dixon, Bantam, Feather
Tiger Flowers, Middle
Joe Gans, Light
Kid Gavilan, Welter
Beau Jack, Light
Peter Jackson, Heavy
Joe Jeannette, Heavy
Jack Johnson, Heavy
Sam Langford, Middle
Joe Jouis, Heavy
Tom Molineaux, Heavy
Archie Moore, Light
Bill Richmond, Heavy
Ray Robinson, Middle
Sandy Saddler, Feather
Jersey Joe Walcott, Heavy
Joe Walcott, Welter
Harry Wills, Heavy

FOOTBALL

Jim Brown
Roosevelt Brown
Deacon Jones
Dick (Night Train) Lane
Ollie Matson
Lenny Moore
Marion Motley
Gale Sayers
Emlen Tunnell

G

Black Athletes Hall of Fame* Inductees

Henry Aaron	(Baseball)
Muhammad Ali	(Boxing)
Henry Armstrong	(Boxing)
Arthur Ashe	(Tennis)
Elgin Baylor	(Basketball)
Jim Brown	(Football)
Roy Campanella	(Baseball)
Roberto Clemente	(Baseball)
Alice Coachman	(Olympic Winner)
Chuck Cooper	(Basketball)
Harrison Dillard	(Olympic Winner)
Bob Douglass	(Basketball Organizer)
Joe Frazier	(Boxing)
Althea Gibson	(Tennis)
Josh Gibson	(Baseball)
Edwin B. Henderson	(Author)
William DeHart Hubbard	(Olympic Winner)

*Was started in 1974 by Charlie Mays, a former Olympic high jumper.
**White Members

Monte Irvin	(Baseball)
Jack Johnson	(Boxing)
Rafer Johnson	(Olympic Winner)
Morris Levitt	(Author)
John Henry "Pop" Lloyd	(Baseball)
Hank McDonald	(Football)
Willie Mays	(Baseball)
Ralph Metcalfe	(Olympic Winner)
Jesse Owens	(Olympic Winner)
Satchel Paige	(Baseball)
Eulace Peacock	(Pentathlon Champion)
Pele	(Soccer)
Frederick "Fritz" Pollard .	(Football)
**Branch Rickey	(Baseball Executive)
Paul Robeson	(Football)
"Sugar Ray" Robinson	(Boxing)
Wilma Rudolph	(Olympic Winner)
Bill Russell	(Basketball)
**Abe Saperstein	(Basketball Executive)
Gale Sayers	(Football)
Charlie Sifford	(Golf)
Maurice Stokes	(Basketball)
**Jack Twyman	(Basketball
Willye White	(Long Jump Champion)
Joe Yancey	(Track and Field Coach)
Claude "Buddy" Young	(Football)

H

Black Athletes in Films

MOTION PICTURES

MUHAMMAD ALI

"The Greatest"	(1977)

KAREEM ABDUL-JABBAR

"Game of Death"	(1979)
"Airplane"	(1980)

HENRY ARMSTRONG

"Keep Punching"	(1939)
"The Pittsburgh Kid"	(1942)

VIDA BLUE

"Black Gunn"	(1972)

JIM BROWN

"Rio Conchos"	(1964)
"Dirty Dozens"	(1967)
"The Split"	(1968)
"Ice Station"	(1968)
"Zebra"	(1968)
"Dark of the Sun"	(1968)

"100 Rifles"	(1969)
"Riot"	(1969)
"Kenner"	(1969)
"Tick...Tick...Tick..."	(1970)
"El Condor"	(1970)
"The Grasshopper"	(1970)
"Slaughter"	(1972)
"Black Gunn"	(1972)
"Slaughter's Big Ripoff"	(1973)
"I Escaped From Devils Island"	(1973)
"The Slaves"	(1973)
"Three The Hard Way"	(1974)
"Take A Hard Ride"	(1975)

BERNIE CASEY

"The Guns of The Magnificent Seven"	(1969)
"Tick...Tick...Tick..."	(1970)
"Black Chariot"	(1971)
"Hit Man"	(1972)
"Black Gunn"	(1972)
"Boxcar Bertha"	(1972)
"Maurice"	(1973)
"Cleopatra Jones"	(1973)
"Cornbread"	(1975)
"Earl and Me"	(1975)
"Dr. Black Mr. Hyde"	(1977)
"Brothers"	(1977)

CARL ELLER

"Black Six"	(1974)

ALTHEA GIBSON

"Horse Soldiers"   (1959)

JOE GREENE

"Black Six"   (1974)

ROOSEVELT GRIER

"In Cold Blood"   (1968)

"The Liberation of L.B. Jones"   (1970)

"Skjacked"   (1970)

"The Thing With Two Head"   (1972)

"Evil in The Deep"   (1970)

JACK JOHNSON

"As The World Rolls On"   (1921)

"For His Mother's Sake"   (1922)

"Black Thunderbolt"   (1922)

DEACON JONES

"Black Gunn"   (1972)

WILLIE LANIER

"Black Six"   (1974)

SONNY LISTON

"Moonfire"   (1970)

JOE LOUIS

"The Spirit of Youth"   (1938)

"Colored Champions of Sport"   (1939)

"The Fight That Never Ends,"   (1946)

ARCHIE MOORE

"The Adventures of Huckleberry Finn"   (1960)

"The Carpetbaggers"   (1964)

"The Fortune Cookie"   (1966)

"The Outfit"   (1974)

"Hard Times"   (1975)

"Breakheart Pass"   (1976)

MERCURY MORRIS

"Black Six"   (1974)

KEN NORTON

"Mandingo"   (1970)

JACKIE ROBINSON

"Jackson Robinson Story"   (1950)

SUGAR RAY ROBINSON

"Candy"   (1968)

"The Detective"   (1968)

"Paper Lion"   (1968)

"Telethon"   (1977)

O.J. SIMPSON

"Garth in The Klansman"   (1974)

"The Towering Inferno"   (1974)

"Killer Force"   (1976)

"The Cassandra Crossing"   (1977)

WOODY STRODE

"Sundown"   (1941)

"The Lion Hunters"   (1951)

"Caribbean"   (1952)

"Androcles and The Lion"   (1952)

"The City Beneath The Sea"   (1953)

"Demetrius and The Gladiators"   (1954)

"Gambler From Natchez"   (1954)

"The Ten Commandments"   (1956)

"Tarzan's Fight For Life"	(1958)
"The Buccaneer"	(1958)
"Pork Chop Hill"	(1959)
"Sergeant Rutledge"	(1960)
"The Last Voyage"	(1960)
"Spartacus"	(1960)
"The Sins of Rachel Cade"	(1961)
"Two Rode Together"	(1961)
"The Man Who Shot Liberty Valance"	(1962)
"Tarzan's Three Challenges"	(1963)
"Genghis Khan"	(1965)
"Seven Women"	(1966)
"The Professionals"	(1966)
"Shalako"	(1968)
"Che"	(1969)
"Once Upon A Time in The West"	(1969)
"Black Jesus"	(1971)
"Last Rebel"	(1971)
"The Gatling Gun"	(1971)
"The Deserters"	(1971)
"Narrated Black Rodeo"	(1972)
"The Revengers"	(1972)
"Boot Hill"	(1973)
"The Italian Connection"	(1973)
"Winterhawk"	(1976)

OTIS TAYLOR

"Soul Soldier"	(1970)

JERSEY JOE WALCOTT

"Harder They Fall"	(1956)

GENE WASHINGTON

"Black Gunn"	(1972)
"Black Six"	(1974)

KENNY WASHINGTON

"While Thousands Cheer"	(1947)
"The Foxes of Harrow"	(1947)
"Rogues Regiment"	(1948)
"Easy Living"	(1949)
"Rope of Sand"	(1949)
"Pinky"	(1949)
"Jackie Robinson Story"	(1950)
"Weekend of Fear"	(1966)
"Changes"	(1969)

FRED WILLIAMSON

"M*A*S*H"	(1970)
"Tell Me That You Love Me Junie Moon"	(1970)
"Hammer"	(1972)
"The Legend of Nigger Charley"	(1973)
"Black Caesar"	(1973)
"The Soul of Nigger Charley"	(1973)
"That Man Bolt"	(1973)
"Hell Up in Harlem"	(1973)
"Black Eye"	(1974)
"Three Tough Guys"	(1974)
"Crazy Joe"	(1974)
"Three The Hard Way"	(1974)
"Hero's Welcome"	(1975)
"Buck Town"	(1975)

"Take A Hard Ride"   (1975)

"Boss Nigger"   (1975)

"Mean Johnny Barrow"   (1975)

"Adios Amigo"   (1976)

"No Way Back"   (1976)

"Death Journey"   (1976)

"Joshua"   (1977)

DOCUMENTARIES ON BLACK ATHLETES

MUHAMMAD ALI

"Black View On Race"   (1970)

"The Fighters"   (1974)
  Records the March 1971 fight of Muhammad Ali and Joe Frazier

"Float Like A Butterfly, Sting Like A Bee"   (1969)
  Ali's life between February, 1964 and May 1965

"Muhammad Ali-Skill, Brains and Guts"   (1975)

WILLIE DAVIS

"Biography of A Rookie"   (1961)

JACK JOHNSON

"Jack Johnson"   (1970)
  Narrated by Brock Peters

"Jeffries-Johnson 1910"
  A recreation of this championship bout between Jim Jeffries
  and Jack Johnson. Mr. Johnson's victory over Mr. Jeffries made
  him the first Black heavyweight champion of the world.

JOE LOUIS

"Sergeant Joe Louis on Tour"   (1943)

JACKIE ROBINSON

"Jackie Robinson Story"   (1965)

"Black View On Race"   (1970)

"The Impact of Jackie Robinson"

JERSEY JOE WALCOTT

"The Impact of Jersey Joe Walcott/Sheriff Arnold Cream"
Film of Mr. Walcott as heavyweight champion of the world and
as the first Black sheriff of Camden, N.J.

"The Negro In Sports"   (1950)
Narrated by Jesse Owens.   Many Black athletes are featured.

FILM BIOGRAPHIES OF BLACK ATHLETES

A Selected List

JACK JOHNSON

"The Great White Hope"   1970
 Starring James Earl Jones

JOE LOUIS

"The Joe Louis Story"   1953
 Starring James Edwards

ROY CAMPANELLA

"It's Good To Be Alive"
 A Life Story of Roy Campanella
 Starring Ruby Dee and Paul Winfield

Index

Including authors, joint authors, and editors.
Numbers refer to individual entry numbers.

ABOUT THE COMPILERS

LENWOOD G. DAVIS is Assistant Professor of History at Montclair State College. He received both his B.A. and M.A. degrees in history from North Carolina Central University, Durham, North Carolina, and a doctorate in history from Carnegie-Mellon University. Dr. Davis has compiled more than sixty bibliographies. He is the author of seven books, *I Have a Dream: The Life and Times of Martin Luther King, Jr.* (1973), *The Black Woman in American Society: A Selected Annotated Bibliography* (1975), *The Black Family in the United States: A Selected Bibliography of Annotated Books, Articles, and Dissertations on Black Families in America* (1978), *Sickle Cell Anemia: A Selected Annotated Bibliography* (1978), *Black Artists in the United States: An Annotated Bibliography,* coauthored with Janet L. Sims (1980), *Marcus Garvey: An Annotated Bibliography*, coauthored with Janet L. Sims (1980), and *Black Aged in the United States* (1980). Professor Davis is also completing four other bibliographies to be published in 1982 and 1983.

BELINDA S. DANIELS is Reference Librarian at Winston-Salem State University, Winston-Salem, North Carolina. She received her M.A. degree in Library Science from North Carolina Central University, Durham, North Carolina. This is her first major work. Her previous works have appeared in *Freedomways, Journal of Negro History*, and *Journal of Negro Education.* Miss Daniels is completing two other projects that are scheduled for publication in 1982 and 1983.